HUMANS, DOGS, AND OTHER BEINGS

Humans, Dogs, and Other Beings

Myths, Stories, and History in the Land of Genghis Khan

Baasanjav Terbish

https://www.openbookpublishers.com

©2025 Baasanjav Terbish

Information about any revised edition of this work will be provided at https://doi.org/10.11647/OBP.0450

ISBN Paperback: 978-1-80511-515-1

ISBN Hardback: 978-1-80511-516-8

ISBN PDF: 978-1-80511-517-5

ISBN HTML: 978-1-80511-519-9

ISBN EPUB: 978-1-80511-518-2

DOI: 10.11647/OBP.0450

Cover image: Sharav Baldugiin, *A Day in Mongolia: Summer* (between 1905 and 1913). Tempera on cotton 138cm x 177cm, https://commons.wikimedia.org/wiki/File:Marzan_Sharav_001.jpg. Cover design: Jeevanjot Kaur Nagpal.

Contents

Author's Biography

Baasanjav Terbish is a Social Anthropologist with a PhD from the University of Cambridge. He is the author of several books, including *Sex in the Land of Genghis Khan* (2023). His research focuses on the culture, language, and history of Mongol peoples in Mongolia and Russia. He is currently an Assistant Professor at Masaryk University in the Czech Republic and an affiliated scholar at The Mongolia and Inner Asia Studies Unit at the University of Cambridge.

Introduction

Imagine waking up on an early autumn morning in the vast expanse of Mongolia, where the crisp sky stretches endlessly, and the air carries the earthy scent of the steppe. As dawn breaks, the first sounds to greet you are the soft rustling of livestock stirring from their slumber, accompanied by the cheerful barks of camp dogs. As the sun rises and warms the air, the day unfolds as it has for centuries. After a simple but hearty breakfast, the camp's inhabitants—children and elders alike—participate in the well-practiced routine of moving to new pastures. Here, humans and animals move together in an ancient ritual of survival, companionship, and mutual dependence—a rhythm that has echoed through countless generations. In these moments, time seems to slow, offering a chance to appreciate the profound connection between humans, their animals, and the environment.

Growing up in this world, I did not merely observe this relationship—I lived it. Animals were never just creatures to be tended or hunted; they were deeply interwoven into the very fabric of existence, shaping not only the Mongol way of life but also people's sense of identity, their place in the cosmos, and their worldviews. This book explores these connections, focusing on four animals: dogs, marmots, cats, and camels. These animals were chosen not only for their practical and symbolic roles in Mongol culture but also because each reveals unique insights into the broader human experience of living alongside animals.

Mongol culture offers a perspective on human-animal relationships that contrasts sharply with the increasingly fragmented view of modern industrialized societies. Where many contemporary cultures draw rigid boundaries between humans and animals, Mongol traditions blur these lines, ascribing agency and individuality to animals. Through their interactions with humans, each of the four animals discussed in this book provides a window into Mongol life, culture, and beliefs.

While this book centers on human-animal relationships in Mongolia, it is ultimately about the broader human experience. It explores how people find meaning, identity, and survival through their connections with animals, reminding us of our place in a fragile ecosystem shared with other species. Mongolia's nomadic lifestyle serves as a striking example of how humans and animals can coexist in mutual dependence, offering a stark contrast to the increasing detachment from nature in the modern world.

The book is structured into five chapters and an epilogue. The opening chapter introduces the overarching themes of culture and cosmology, laying a foundation for understanding Mongol perspectives on animals. Each subsequent chapter focuses on one of the four animals, examining their roles in cosmology, history, and modern life. Drawing from my personal experiences, research,[1] and oral histories, these chapters weave together mythology, practical knowledge, stories, and cultural memory to present a broader picture of Mongol life that reaches back to the thirteenth century.

This book is not only a semi-scholarly inquiry but also a personal journey. As a writer of Mongol origin, I offer interpretations of human-animal relationships through both the Mongol cultural lens and my own lived experiences. Some of the content regarding practices and beliefs in modern times is drawn directly from my life, and the narrative occasionally blends into personal memoir. This deliberate inclusion aims to illuminate not only my perspectives and worldviews but also the Mongolia I knew during my teenage years and early adulthood. Additionally, the book incorporates the experiences of some members of my extended family, whose stories you will encounter in the pages ahead.

By exploring human-animal relationships in Mongolia, I hope this book will shed light on the shared history and mutual dependence that define our existence. It is an invitation to rethink how we view and treat the animals around us—not as commodities or curiosities, but as co-inhabitants of a shared world. This exploration is not just about understanding the Mongol way of life but about reconnecting with the universal truth that humans are inextricably linked to the natural world we share.

---

1   Previously, I have published journal articles on animals in Mongolia, including the dog, the cat, and the marmot. See Terbish, 'The Mongolian dog as an intimate other'; Terbish, 'The cat as a mirror of Mongolian society: a good, bad, and ugly animal'; Fijn and Terbish, 'The survival of the marmot: hunting, cosmology and the plague in Mongolia'.

1. Culture and Cosmology

A particular species of naked ape occupies an intermediate level on the food chain, either collecting crumbs from the table or serving as dinner to those higher up. In direct confrontation, individual members of this species stand no chance against chimpanzees or bonobos, their closest evolutionary cousins. More formidable predators—bears, tigers, wolves, and others—are simply out of their league. The animal kingdom to which this species belongs is an unforgiving place where survival and reproduction depend on size, speed, and adaptability. Traits like sharp teeth, strong jaws, muscular bodies, superior senses of smell, endurance, and an accompanying bad temper predominantly determine who occupies the top tier of the food chain.

This naked ape is the human—or, more precisely, the forebears of humans—who endured this precarious existence for a significant portion of their evolutionary history. This remained the fate of humans despite our ancestors using lithic, or stone, tools since the dawn of the genus *Homo* some 2.8 to 2.3 million years ago, and despite some of them beginning to harness fire—a tool with potentially transformative power—as far back as one million, or perhaps even 1.5 million, years ago, with daily use of fire for cooking and warmth starting around 400,000 to 300,000 years ago.

But everything changed in the grand feast of nature when humans developed a remarkable ability to amplify their power. Rather than evolving stronger limbs or sharper teeth, we achieved this by collaborating in large numbers, sharing stories, and creating technologies as extensions of our human capabilities. This transformative shift, which led to the emergence of human culture and is often referred to as the Cognitive Revolution, is believed to have occurred between 70,000 and 50,000 years ago. During this period, early humans developed complex language, abstract thought, and advanced tools, laying the foundation

 https://doi.org/10.11647/OBP.0450.01

for art, social organization, and cultural expression as we know them today. Over generations, cumulative cultural advancements gradually transformed humans into apex predators, elevating our species to the top of the food chain. This transformation, while gradual in human terms, was almost instantaneous when viewed on an evolutionary timescale, occurring merely over tens of thousands of years.

This shift to collective strength was crucial. As individuals, humans lack the physical prowess of many other animals—indeed, a lone human would still be easily overpowered by a chimpanzee or bonobo. Yet, our ability to work together, share knowledge, and innovate collectively became our defining strength. Human culture, in this sense, is our species' true superpower, shaping not only how we survived but also how we thrived. Understanding the Cognitive Revolution is essential for appreciating the development of cultures worldwide, including that of Mongols.

This opening chapter introduces key themes that will recur throughout the book. These include an exploration of the definition of culture, including its functions and transformative powers, the distinction between cosmology and religion, and unique stories known as *bolson yavdal*. These topics will serve as essential tools for analyzing the four animals—dogs, marmots, cats, and camels—in the subsequent chapters.

The Primary Function of Culture

In its most straightforward definition, human culture is a product of human imagination, encompassing a range of complex behaviors that arise from these mental constructs.

Our closest evolutionary cousins, chimpanzees, not only have emotions that are clearly similar to ours but also exhibit rudiments of culture, characterized by varying behaviors and traditions among different chimp communities. Some chimp populations have been observed engaged in group hunting while others have not. Certain groups exhibit tool-making skills by modifying sticks or leaves for specific purposes, a trait not universally observed. Like humans, chimps live in social groups (albeit much smaller than those of humans) with a dominance hierarchy, and form fluid social networks and bonds through grooming, playing, and other social interactions. They are adept problem-solvers, and their societies can simultaneously experience conflicts and cooperation.

While there are obvious parallels here with human societies, the spectrum of human cultural activities is unparalleled both in terms of complexity and scale. A chimp or a dog won't be able to comprehend the majority of human behavior merely by observing people's actions. Our cultural practices, which are by definition complex, such as worship, trade, marriage, and more, would appear to a dog, for example, as a sequence of unrelated movements—people following each other, eating, 'barking', exchanging paper, copulating, fighting, departing, defecating, and repeating—without the contextual understanding that humans attribute to these practices. This is because all human behavioral patterns are imbued with imaginary values and carried out within the framework of fictional connections, hierarchies, and goals that members of a given cultural community share collectively in their brains. Consequently, to the naked eye of an animal that cannot share common myths and fictions with humans and thus cannot see the world through human eyes, understanding and following human cultures becomes impossible.

Creating complex cultures is a uniquely human cognitive ability. Even our closest evolutionary relatives, such as chimps, or our longtime animal companions, like dogs, lack the mental capacity to conceive of 'imaginary bananas' or 'fictional communal sausages' that would enable the creation of imaginary chimp or canine cultural norms and ideas of paradise—concepts that could be used to secure cooperation among a potentially unlimited number of their kind. In contrast, imagination comes as naturally to humans as swimming does to fish. Even babies as young as 18 months demonstrate remarkable imaginative abilities, engaging in pretend play such as using a pebble to represent a car or 'eating' imaginary food. This early stage of symbolic play marks the beginning of our imaginative powers. As we grow, this ability expands, and our cultural lens becomes even more powerful and symbolic, shaping how we see and interact with the world. Objects, animals, and ideas become technology, food evolves into cuisine, sex transforms into sexuality, and nature is reimagined as infrastructure governed by gods and laws.

Some chimps have been observed using tools like sticks to measure depth, stones for digging or cracking open hard nuts, leaves as sponges, and even spears for hunting. Let's call these 'primary tools' or 'primary technologies'. Humans also use these primary technologies, often for similar purposes. However, what sets humans apart is our ability to use primary technologies to imaginatively create secondary technologies, which can then be used to create tertiary technologies, and so forth. This capability aligns with our ability to imagine things that do not exist in nature, share stories, and communicate complex ideas.

A prime example of this is mathematics, which can be seen as a type of primary technology. Historically, mathematics has enabled the development of secondary, more advanced technologies, including systems for taxation, trade and commerce, architecture and engineering, astronomy, and beyond. These secondary technologies have, in turn, paved the way for even more advanced, or upper-level, technologies. In fact, humans can utilize almost anything—whether animate or inanimate, or even abstract concepts—as tools or technologies. For example, in Mongol culture, animals are not only sources of food and materials but also tools for thinking about human society, morality, fears, and the meaning of life, as will be explored throughout the book.

If animals like dogs or chimps possessed similar imaginative powers that threatened our dominance, we humans—competitive as we are— would have long been at their throats. Instead, we keep dogs as pets and chimps as entertainment in zoos, reminding us of our unique position in the animal world. This distinction underscores the extraordinary human ability to transform tools into an endless hierarchy of technologies, shaping not just our survival but the way we perceive and engage with the world.

That said, we shouldn't feel too smug about ourselves and our abilities as individuals. In essence, we are not so different from other mammals and share many traits with the rest of the animal kingdom, such as aggression, fear, stress, and predation, along with primal instincts shaped by our long evolution on the savannah—traits like social behavior, parental care, and play. Moreover, as individuals, we are frail beings who would struggle to survive alone in most environments. Our strength comes from our membership in human groups which are held together by cultures.

Since their emergence, human cultures have served as evolving repositories of accumulated knowledge, enabling us to embrace rationality, temper our primal instincts and individualistic tendencies, and create technology, art, and literature. Most importantly, cultures have facilitated the synchronization of *collective* behavior to achieve common goals.

Historical records reveal how the ancestors of the Mongols, as pastoralists and hunters, adapted to their environment and thrived on the harsh Mongolian Plateau. While imagination shaped human culture, it was also deeply influenced by the co-evolution of humans with animals and the environment.[1] Using creative thinking and logic, the Mongols managed livestock such as cattle, yaks, sheep, and goats. They also relied on dogs for herding and hunting, rode horses for mobility, and used camels to carry loads. Observing animal behavior and adapting to their surroundings were vital for survival. These interactions likely played a key role in the cultural and cognitive development of nomadic societies like the Mongols. Stories, rituals, and etiquette further united them, allowing them to function as a cohesive group.

These cognitive abilities and practices are not unique to the Mongols but are inherent to all members of *Homo sapiens* who live in and are shaped by culture. Evolutionarily, human culture enabled our species to occupy the 'cognitive niche',[2] equipping humans with the skills and technologies to outsmart nature. Consequently, today we not only dominate the food chain but have also decoded the genetic map of life, chronicled our species' origins, explored the nature of matter and energy, left our footprints on the moon, and calculated the origin of the universe.

However, it is important to note that the primary function of human culture is not to elevate humanity to cosmic heights or to represent reality accurately. Rather, culture's function is to interpret the world

---

1 Diamond, *Guns, Germs, and Steel*; Frankopan, *The Earth Transformed*.
2 The concept of the 'cognitive niche' refers to the evolutionary strategy by which humans have adapted to their environments primarily through intelligence and social learning, transmission rather than through physical specialization. This idea, developed in evolutionary psychology and anthropology, suggests that humans survive and thrive by using abstract reasoning, tool-making, cooperation, and cumulative knowledge to solve ecological and social challenges. See Pinker, 'The cognitive niche: Coevolution of intelligence, sociality, and language'.

in ways that promote cooperation, knowledge accumulation, and reproduction. While some accurate understanding of the physical world is essential for these purposes, human culture primarily requires knowledge that helps us navigate the world at the scale at which our bodies operate and perceive reality in ways relevant to our survival and reproduction. In this sense, culture is like a user interface, simplifying and interpreting the complex 'reality' we cannot fully comprehend. This cultural knowledge may include practical insights such as understanding animal behavior, recognizing useful plants, or developing tools. It also encompasses concepts like gods and myths that do not exist in objective reality but help humans navigate the world and build societies.

Our modern understanding of genetics, evolution, physics, and astronomy—concepts describing molecules, immense time scales, ultraviolet light, or particles moving at the speed of light—is a sophisticated by-product of human culture. Humanity thrived for most of its existence without this knowledge. We only uncovered these natural laws, describing particles and phenomena invisible to our eyes, undetectable by our senses, or unfathomable to our brains, relatively recently, thanks to advances in science—a recent outcome of cultural evolution.

In this sense, human culture is closely adapted to our sensory systems, which similarly evolved to help us navigate the world, rather than to reveal ultimate truths or objective reality. For instance, when we look at an apple, we perceive its shape, color, and ripeness—traits that are evolutionary significant for survival and reproduction, such as identifying edible and nutritious food. Beyond these physical properties, an apple can also represent various culturally specific ideas. In Christian and Islamic mythologies, for example, it symbolizes the forbidden fruit, while in other cultural contexts, it might signify prosperity. Beyond that, our sensory perception does not reveal deeper realities, such as the apple's molecular structure, gravitational pull, or the complex forces of nature at work. These details are not directly accessible because they are not essential for our immediate survival. Because our sensory systems prioritize practicality over comprehensiveness, the development of modern science was far from inevitable. Science emerged through specific cultural, historical, and intellectual conditions, enabling us to transcend our sensory limitations. By creating theoretical frameworks and powerful tools, science has enhanced our human capabilities, allowing us to explore dimensions of reality that our evolved senses alone could never detect. Thus, we could just as easily have persisted indefinitely in pre-scientific societies, relying solely on the knowledge necessary for survival, cooperation, and reproduction, and still become apex predators and transformers of our environment.

Consider the many tribal societies across the Amazon, Sub-Saharan Africa, and Melanesia, whose communities lived in pre-scientific conditions until the twentieth century when waves of European-led modernity reached them. These societies exemplify the ways in which advanced science is not a prerequisite for human survival and societal development but rather an optional and relatively recent expansion of our cultural capabilities.

In human culture, almost every belief, concept, or activity is rooted in and communicated through stories. Stories serve as the building blocks of culture and do not necessarily need to convey the truth or faithfully represent reality. In fact, most stories we encounter, believe in, create, or pass down—whether they are myths, religious doctrines, political ideologies, national histories, tribal genealogies, autobiographies, conspiracy theories, or rumors—are subjective interpretations or fictions.

Even scientific explanations, despite their grounding in empirical data, fall within the realm of storytelling. Contrary to popular belief, science is not merely a method for objectively conveying cold, hard facts. Instead, it uses stories to interpret data, observations, and experiments, which are inevitably shaped by the subjective perspectives of scientists. This is why the same data or observation can be interpreted one way and celebrated as a scientific breakthrough, only to be revised or reinterpreted by later scientists, who may discard it as incorrect or refine it through a new narrative.[3] This self-correcting mechanism makes scientific stories uniquely superior in the pursuit of truth, especially compared to other types of stories—such as religious doctrines or political ideologies like Marxism-Leninism—that are often presented as infallible or non-revisable.

---

3   Latour, *Science in Action*; Byers, *The Blind Spot*; Cooke, *Bitch*.

Science's narrative nature also explains why today it is often incorporated into older systems like cosmologies and religions. Traditional frameworks integrate new scientific ideas into their explanatory paradigms, blending old and new narratives. This interplay between past and present is a fundamental aspect of cultural evolution. It reflects how human cultures continually adapt, weaving new stories into older systems to create cohesive, evolving worldviews. For example, as we will explore in Chapter 3, modern Mongols integrate traditional shamanic or Buddhist beliefs with scientific concepts in areas like medicine.

To recap, evolution did not shape the human sensory system to perceive reality as it truly is but rather to guide behavior that supports survival and reproduction. Similarly, human culture serves as a repository of both accurate knowledge and mistaken beliefs or myths, perpetuated by institutions like religion, ideology, mass media, and even science. This duality is essential for understanding how societies function and helps explain why humans can demonstrate remarkable intelligence in some areas while being susceptible to illusions or fantasies in others.

These themes are explored throughout this book, particularly through the example of the Mongols, who collectively achieved extraordinary feats in empire-building and the promotion of art and knowledge[4] while adhering to deeply superstitious rituals and following harmful ideologies. Before examining the Mongol case in detail, however, it is helpful to first provide a brief overview of Mongol history.

A Very Short History of Mongolia

Mongols emerged as a regional power in 1206 when they established the Mongol Empire under the leadership of Genghis Khan (Chinggis Khaan in Mongolian). He not only consolidated all the steppe tribes on the Mongolian Plateau but also proceeded to elevate his empire into a global superpower by conquering new lands, a legacy continued by his sons and grandsons. In the second half of the thirteenth century, Mongol territory, now spanning from Central Europe in the west to the Sea of Japan in the east, was divided into four Genghisid states by his grandsons: Grand Khan's central dominion in Mongolia (since 1206)

---

4   Weatherford, *Genghis Khan*; Rossabi, *The Mongols and Global History*.

and China, also known as the Yuan (–1368); the Ilkhanate of Persia (1265–1335); the Golden Horde of Russia (1266–1502); and the Chagatai state of Central Asia (1264–1705).

The central Yuan dynasty was overthrown in China in 1368 by the 'Red Turban' rebels, who established the Ming dynasty. Fleeing to their ancestral land north of the Great Chinese Wall, the Mongols founded a state known as the Northern Yuan. In contrast, Mongols in other Genghisid states chose not to return to Mongolia but instead stayed in their respective territories, assimilating with local dynasties and establishing various states, some illustrious and others less so. The last of these states persisted until the early twentieth century in Central Asia. One of the most consequential offshoot polities was the Mughal Empire in the Indian subcontinent, founded by Babur (1483-1530), whose mother was a direct descendant of Genghis Khan and whose paternal ancestor was Tamerlane. Tamerlane held the title of *küregen* (Imperial Son-in-Law) due to his marriages to Genghisid princesses, and his paternal lineage traced back to the Barlas, a Mongol clan.

Traditionally, Mongols were shamanists. They were first exposed to Tibetan Buddhism in the thirteenth century under Kubilai, the founder of the Yuan dynasty, even though neither Kubilai nor his immediate successors officially adopted Buddhism as the state religion. After the fall of the Yuan dynasty in 1368, many Mongols returned to traditional shamanism, while some continued to practice Buddhism. A mass conversion to Buddhism did not occur until the sixteenth century, and by 1640 Buddhism was officially declared the state religion among the Mongols and the Oirats.

In 1691, the Buddhist Mongols of Mongolia submitted to the Manchu Qing dynasty, a nomadic people of Jurchen origin which had replaced the Ming in China. The Western Mongols, known as the Oirats, followed suit in 1757.

Mongolia remained a backwater region under foreign dominion until 1911 when, with the overbloated Manchu Qing dynasty in its death throes, the Mongols proclaimed their independence, akin to Jonah from the Biblical story emerging from a whale's belly. They enthroned the Javzandamba Hutugtu, revered as a 'living Buddha', as their theocratic king. However, the young Buddhist kingdom's peace and tranquility were short-lived. In 1924, Mongolia underwent a tumultuous transformation into a people's republic, modeled after the Soviet Union, where the governing atheistic regime remained in power for the next seven decades.

During the socialist era, Mongolia prided itself on being the second socialist country in the world after the Soviet Union. In line with this dedication, Mongolia remained steadfast in its socialist stance, seeking to create an earthly paradise for toilers and herders on the steppes, until early 1990. This made it one of the last nations within the socialist bloc to relinquish state socialism before the Soviet Union itself fragmented at the end of 1991 into fifteen post-Soviet states, each going their own way with a newfound sense of independence.

In the chapters that follow, we will return to Mongolia's history and discuss in greater detail how various animals were treated across different historical periods. For now, let's return to the topic of culture.

Mongol Culture and Its Transformation

People often speak of 'Mongol culture' as if it were a singular, fixed entity. However, it is important to recognize that there has never been a homogeneous, unchanging Mongol culture, despite how the term is often understood or propagated by Mongol nationalists. All cultures are dynamic; after all, if they did not evolve, we would still be living in the pre-Stone Age. In addition, the idea of a timeless, unchanging 'Mongol people' is a fiction—a collective mental construct. Try teaching a chimp or a dog to distinguish between 'Mongol people' and 'Chinese people', or any other human groups, and you'll quickly see that no animal could make this distinction or comprehend concepts like nationalism or patriotism.

Historically, the term 'Mongol people' dates to the time of Genghis Khan, who unified all the nomadic tribes on the Mongolian Plateau, many of which had distinct names and sometimes even different languages. Through this political and military unification, all tribes under Genghis Khan's leadership were brought together under the banner of the Mongol people.

Today, the term 'Mongol people' continues to serve as an umbrella encompassing various groups across the region, each with its own unique stories, rituals, values, technologies—and therefore, cultures— that constantly evolve. Even groups with shared ancestry, origin myths, ecological conditions, a nomadic lifestyle, and Buddhist beliefs tend to differentiate themselves. They do so by subtly modifying the performance of similar rituals, narrating familiar myths and stories with unique variations, adhering to distinct norms, developing specific technologies, aligning with slightly different values, and prioritizing certain animals over others. This explains why, for example, diverse groups across Mongolia today exhibit unique variations in rituals, such as those observed during weddings, childbirth, and funerals. These local variations have been meticulously documented by the Mongolian Academy of Sciences in Ulaanbaatar, which has conducted ethnographic expeditions throughout various regions of the country since the socialist period. What holds true today has been the case in the past.

In the realm of culture, centrifugal and centripetal forces work together. While groups may strive to distinguish themselves by fostering local cultural variations, a countervailing force simultaneously works to bind these groups together, uniting them under a dominant group or culture. Yet historically the term 'Mongol culture' has never managed to square the circle, and there has never been a single, homogeneous culture attributable to all Mongol groups. However, this diversity should not be viewed as a flaw but rather as an integral aspect of every human culture.

One could assert, from a bird's-eye view, that what we understand as 'Mongol culture' is anything Mongol groups make of it, and indeed throughout history, Mongol groups are known to have made of it a surprising variety of things. In fact, this holds true for all cultures such as 'Scottish culture', 'Turkish culture', 'Japanese culture', 'American culture', and so on. Given the dynamism of human cultures, what people proudly identify as cultural elements today may not have been perceived in the same light in the past, especially under different political or religious systems.

Chimps, Bonobos, and Human Culture

Broadly speaking, humans are part of the animal kingdom and share not only a common evolutionary ancestry with other animals but also various traits. Just as chimps and bonobos, our closest evolutionary cousins, can reveal much about humans, so too can other animals, as will be explored later in more detail. If we ask the question, 'What exactly can chimps and bonobos teach us about ourselves that the other four species in this book cannot?' the answer is that these two great apes can shed light, among other things, on the evolution of social behavior in humans—a topic relevant to understanding how human culture operates.

While suspicions about the connection between humans and primates have circulated among scientific circles since the publication of Charles Darwin's *On the Origin of Species* (1859), chimps firmly established their reputation as the model for human ancestry in the 1970s. Chimps live in a hierarchical social structure where individuals hold varying ranks in terms of social status. Chimps in higher positions often exert greater influence and strive to maintain their status by recruiting lower-ranked individuals as followers or assistants. Human societies share similarities with chimp groups in this regard. People in all known cultures dedicate their lives to preserving or enhancing their social or symbolic standing, often by actively recruiting support and assistance.

What is particularly interesting from a philosophical point of view is that, as a hierarchical and social species, we rarely reflect on our inclination to seek followers and assistants or to become others' followers and assistants—much like a fish might be the last to ponder why it lives in water. In contrast to chimps, human primates extend these hierarchical relations to other species. This inclination becomes apparent, as will be discussed in the next chapter, in our natural adoption of dogs.

Besides the hierarchical social structure humans share with chimps, we also share a set of psychological traits, which are products of millions of years of evolution as a single species believed to have diverged into two species approximately six to seven million years ago. While many ingrained psychological traits in both chimps and humans need to be understood on their own terms, and comparisons must be made with scientific caution, we should appreciate that many of our deeply ingrained behavioral instincts, over which we have little control, are products of evolution. In his widely acclaimed book, *The Chimp Paradox* (2012), psychiatrist Steve Peters introduced the concept of the 'inner chimp'. This 'inner chimp' represents the emotional and instinctive part of the human brain, which often hijacks rational thinking and provokes behaviors deemed culturally inappropriate. Peters offers strategies for managing our 'inner chimps' by understanding our thought patterns and improving emotional self-control to achieve both personal and professional success. Fundamentally, Peters' advice centers on mastering control over our deep evolutionary instincts, symbolized by the metaphorical 'inner chimp', and aligning our behavior with societal norms and values, particularly those of the modern West. Peters and other psychologists who recognize the chimp as the best available— albeit approximate—model for human ancestry argue that studying chimp behavior provides valuable insights into the deep workings of the human psyche.

But more crucially for cultural analysis, hierarchical chimps not only mirror human societies but also influence prevailing ideas about human male behavior. The chest-beating, male-bonded, and highly aggressive tendencies observed in male chimps have led to the belief that human males are similarly pre-programmed for violent dominance over both females and social inferiors. Consequently, this perspective has contributed to the establishment of a scientific orthodoxy that postulates the supposedly innate nature of patriarchal structures in human cultures.

However, we aren't related to chimps alone; we are equally related to bonobos, sharing about 99 percent of our DNA with both species. Bonobos and chimps are believed to have diverged from each other around one to two million years ago, implying that their common ancestor, which diverged from our human forebears six to seven million years ago, might have displayed a mix of behavioral characteristics that we observe today in both bonobos and chimps. However, despite their common ancestry, bonobos couldn't be more different from patriarchal and aggressive chimps. They are matriarchal and generally less aggressive, challenging the orthodox notion that great apes, including humans, are naturally predisposed to creating societies dominated by aggressive and violent males. In contrast to chimps, bonobo communities consist of unrelated females forming sisterhoods that overpower and keep larger males in check, especially regarding aggression. Cohesion within bonobo communities relies not only on physical intimidation and fights but mainly on frequent mutual grooming and lovemaking, fostering cooperation, and alleviating competitive tensions.[5]

---

5   Cooke, *Bitch*, 182-210.

This behavior bears remarkable similarity to human social dynamics. Dominated they may be by chimp-style patriarchal structures, many human societies also rely on acts of mutual assistance, playfulness, and passion to maintain cohesion and alleviate tensions. This is also relevant when considering Mongol culture, where hierarchical structures of leadership historically relied on not just physical dominance but also strategic alliances, loyalty, passion, and mutual respect.

Moreover, despite perceiving women as symbolically inferior, the Mongol tradition of revering wives and mothers—evidenced in the influential roles of queens and mothers in nomadic governance— parallels some aspects of bonobo societies, where females maintain authority and foster group harmony.[6] The Mongols' ability to integrate near-egalitarian practices, such as communal decision-making during migrations, with the hierarchical demands of war and empire-building reflects the flexibility inherent in human culture. Just as chimps and bonobos offer contrasting conceptual models of social organization, Mongol culture exemplifies the human capacity to reconcile seemingly contradictory traits—dominance and equality, patriarchy and reverence for women—depending on the context.

While humans share genetic and behavioral traits with both chimps and bonobos, *Homo sapiens* is also a vastly different species, largely shaped by human culture. As mentioned previously, human culture is highly flexible, both accommodating and suppressing natural instincts, while imposing various socially constructed behaviors through stories, rituals, rewards, and sanctions. This explains why different groups develop distinct cultures and why the same societies undergo cultural shifts over time, giving rise to a potentially infinite number of cultural variations.

Despite hierarchical and patriarchal structures observed in chimp troops and modern human societies, it's also crucial to consider the possibility that historically, there may have been cultures characterized by matriarchal or truly egalitarian principles because cultures have a curious tendency to develop a life of their own over time and harbor the capacity to arrange their members in various ways, potentially diverging from human instincts. In this sense, humans are not only active creators

---

6   Broadbridge, *Women and the Making of the Mongol Empire*; Bruno de Nicola, *Women in Mongol Iran*.

of cultures but also passive products of cultures. This is a point worth keeping in mind when contemplating cultures. Just think of recent movements such as the Free Love Movement (which rejects patriarchal norms related to marriage and sexuality), polyamorous communities, LGBTQ+ communities, communal living experiments (aimed at creating egalitarian social structures), and the hippie movements of the 1960s-1970s (which rejected many societal norms, including traditional gender roles). It's almost certain that throughout history, there were groups with social structures distinct from the patriarchal system that today dominates human cultures.[7] If we push this argument further, we find that every human culture harbors its unique conception of paradise, whether in an afterlife or here on Earth—a vision sometimes markedly divergent from known societal structures. While it's true that no group has realized the ideal utopia of its collective imagination, the mere existence of these fantasies stands as a testament to the transformative potential of Sapiens culture.

Living Entities: Sacred Places and Spiritual Animals in Mongol Culture

Grigory Potanin was a Russian ethnographer and one of the most significant early modern researchers to contribute to the study of Mongolia in the late nineteenth and early twentieth centuries. He led an expedition into Northern Mongolia in 1876-77. In his observations of local life, Potanin noted that the indigenous people lived in a world where there were no distinctions between human society, nature, and the supernatural. He found indigenous life intertwined with all-encompassing spiritual elements. Every mountain or valley had a spiritual master or guardian (*sabdag*) who bestowed 'gifts' on humans in the form of game or grass for herd animals that sustained humans. Humans, for their part, had to respect the supernatural realm. Although spiritual masters of nature were sometimes imagined as having animal body parts, more often these masters of mountains and valleys were believed to be the mountains and valleys themselves. For local people, every locality—mountains, forests, the steppe, rivers, etc.—was considered a living entity. The folklore

---

7   For further exploration of the topic of egalitarian societies in the past, see Graber and Wengrow, *Dawn of Everything*.

Potanin collected also showed that many animals, integral to the living landscape, were believed to possess magical or spiritual powers.[8]

Potanin's observations reflected ways of life in Mongolia that had changed little in outward appearance for centuries. If one is to compare thirteenth- and fourteenth-century sources on the shamanic Mongols with Potanin's diaries, one will find many similarities. Across generations, nomads lived in the same nomadic tents (*ger*), ate the same food, tended to the same herds, used similar technologies, worshipped the supernatural, and believed in the awareness and magical powers of places, trees, rocks, natural phenomena, and animals.

The Mongols' mass conversion to Buddhism in the sixteenth century placed new Buddhist lenses atop the old shamanic ones, providing new yet familiar perspectives on the surrounding world. One of the principal distinctions between shamanism and Buddhism lies in their perspectives. Shamanism, characterized by a local outlook, places emphasis on the distinctive features of the local supernatural order, including low deities and spirits with 'dark sides' believed to be able to address the immediate daily problems and pleas of local people. In contrast, Buddhism adopts a universal outlook, venerating high gods and beings whose powers are believed to encompass the entire world and the entirety of humanity. Buddhism also fundamentally revolves around the teachings of Siddhartha Gautama, or the Buddha Shakyamuni, guiding individuals to liberate their minds and attain *nirvana* or eternal bliss as their ultimate goal. In Mongolia, the incorporation of local animistic worldviews into the new Buddhist belief system facilitated a relatively smooth transition from a shamanic society to a Buddhist-dominated one without significantly distorting the previous supernatural order. In this symbiotic relationship, Buddhism piggybacked on the shoulders of shamanism, with the latter shouldering the burden of addressing local spirits and attending to the daily concerns of nomads, while the former claimed credit as the official state religion of the realm. The form of Buddhism practiced among the Mongols was thus a syncretic religion, making it both universal in its goal to save humanity and distinctly local by appeasing—with the help of shamanic-turned-Buddhist concepts,

---

8   Potanin, *Ocherki Severo-Zapadnoi Mongolii.*

deities, and rituals—the unique spiritual pantheons of specific locations across Mongolia.

Broadly speaking, the Buddhification of Mongolia resulted in the substitution of many, if not most, shamanic nature spirits with Buddhist deities. Consequently, many mountains, hills, and valleys are today considered to be under the protection of Buddhist deities. Exceptions are the so-called 'wrathful places' (*doshgin gazar*) or unpacified patches of land scattered across Mongolia where the *sabdag* protectors are believed to have remained shamanic or non-Buddhist. Wild animals inhabiting these 'wrathful places' and areas protected by exceptionally powerful and ill-tempered Buddhist deities are generally not hunted, as doing so may incur the wrath of these deities. I will return to this point concerning the connection between places and animals later.

What is amazing is the fact that despite the 150 or so years that have passed since Potanin's observations, marked by the encroachment of modernity into nomadic life and the socialist experience of Mongolia (1924-90), little has changed in the country regarding how people, especially nomads, see the world around them. Compared with pre-socialist times, even if every location is not currently believed to be protected by a *sabdag* and not every animal is imagined to have spiritual powers (a legacy of Mongolia's recent socialist past), many places are still endowed with supernatural ownership, and many animals are thought to have a magical essence (which is activated when they are under the protection of *sabdags*) that humans must take into account when interacting with them.

The Cultural Foundation: Cosmology and Religion

In its broadest definition, culture encompasses the entire way of life of a specific group including their worldviews, symbols, language, customs, artistic expressions, technologies, economy, and social institutions. This book adopts this expansive definition of culture. In contrast, cosmology constitutes only one part of culture, referring specifically to the metaphysical aspects of the universe as understood in the indigenous worldview.

To illustrate this distinction, we can use an architectural metaphor. Envision culture as a vast, all-encompassing dome, with cosmology serving as its foundation. Structurally speaking, despite being a subsurface element, cosmology—much like a building's foundation—exerts a unifying force that holds a cultural community together. It does so by providing metaphysical or superhuman legitimacy to a shared foundational worldview, which is woven from myths about ancestors, gods, spirits, a nation's destiny, and the like.

If we examine the building blocks of this cultural dome more closely, we see that its cosmological foundation supports subsequent layers, including religion. However, unlike in a real building made of bricks and mortar, this conceptual cultural dome lacks a clear demarcation between its foundation (cosmology) and its ground floor (religion). This is because cosmology and religion often share the same stories and myths about the origins and workings of the universe, frequently involving superhuman or metaphysical entities. In this sense, religion integrates cosmological elements, and, reciprocally, cosmology may be a part of religion.

Put another way, religion is typically defined as a system of beliefs and practices legitimized by sacred texts, prophets, and revelations, whereas cosmology often relies on oral tradition and is accepted based on societal consensus. The philosophical implication of this suggests that even in an ultra-secular society without religion—such as some Scandinavian countries today that are close to this benchmark—there will always be a cosmology consisting of myths and fictions used to unite the cultural community. These myths and fictions may not involve ancient spirits or supernatural elements, but they will still pertain to things that do not exist in nature but rather only in the fertile human imagination. Examples include myths and fictions about inalienable human rights, liberal democratic values, nationalism—cosmological ideas that were not only alien to our ancestors but are also alien to the animal kingdom.

For example, in nature, chimps don't operate under the concept of inalienable rights as humans do today. They don't have a right to life (which would guarantee that no chimp is mauled to death by another chimp), a right to liberty (which would ensure the freedom to make decisions about their own lives), or a right to equality (guaranteeing equal treatment and protection by the alpha chimp). Nor do chimps follow a 'Rule of Law' ensuring all chimps are equal before the law or possess 'Individual Rights' guaranteeing privacy, freedom of mating, or freedom of assembly. Furthermore, there is no 'Protection of Minority Rights' ensuring that smaller packs of chimps are not attacked by larger, more ferocious ones in the jungle. Instead, chimps, like many social animals, follow instinctual behaviors that maintain order and cohesion within their packs. These behaviors are shaped by evolutionary pressures, not abstract principles. Chimps also don't divide themselves into national groups based on physical appearance or origin myths, nor do they seek self-governance or political autonomy.

All these cosmological ideas—rights, laws, equality, and national identity—are products of human imagination, created to unite people and organize societies. Many were formalized relatively recently with the rise of modern nation-states, especially following the establishment of the French Republic in 1792, which marked a shift away from regimes governed by monarchs and religious authorities claiming divine right.[9] As new ideas like nationalism, liberal democracy, and human rights became entrenched in European societies, they were exported globally, often through colonialism, diplomacy, and cultural exchange.

If we resume the discussion of culture using an architectural analogy, in the 'real' world the building remains fixed once its foundation is laid and its walls are built, bound together by mortar. However, in the imaginary cultural dome, both the overall cultural framework and its components—including the foundation (cosmology) and the ground floor (religion)—constantly evolve and influence one another. For instance, the establishment of Buddhism in 1640 as the state religion among the Mongols illustrates this interplay. Buddhism incorporated elements of foundational shamanic cosmology, while shamanic cosmology itself adapted under Buddhism's influence. These organic shifts in foundational myths and fictions embedded in religion and cosmology resonated throughout the entire national culture, shaping the national economy, political systems, art, education, and even healthcare.

The flexibility and resilience of human culture are evident in the Mongol experience. Over time, Mongol society endured historical upheavals, such as transitions from one religion to another, from nomadic lifestyles to socialism, and from one political regime to the next.

---

9   Macfarlane, *The Invention of the Modern World*; Armitage and Subrahmanyam, *The Age of Revolutions in Global Context*.

Despite these changes, Mongol culture absorbed external influences while preserving core elements, such as belief in the supernatural, oral traditions, and enduring cosmological frameworks. As this book will explore, under state socialism, Mongols maintained these cultural pillars even while adapting to modernity.

To understand culture's dynamic nature, it is helpful to move beyond rigid textbook definitions or nationalist portrayals. Instead, imagine Salvador Dali's *The Persistence of Memory*, where melting clocks create a surreal impression of time bending and flowing. Replace the clocks with representations of culture, and you'll have a vivid image of how culture operates: a social construct that is inherently flexible and constantly evolving. Like Dali's clocks, culture bends and shifts while retaining its contours, reflecting the collective beliefs, values, traditions, and behaviors of a society over time. This dynamic balance between continuity and change is what makes culture both resilient and adaptable.

In its broadest definition, cosmology, as we have discussed, not only encompasses ancient metaphysical knowledge but may also include any system of metaphysical knowledge through which members of a given society seek to comprehend the world they inhabit. This extends to modern ideas and stories, captured in unique narratives known in Mongolian as *bolson yavdal*, which can be translated as 'it really happened stories'. Since they shed light on the hidden connections between humans, animals, and the spiritual realm, *bolson yavdal* stories will be extensively used throughout this book. It is therefore important to clarify what these stories are and how they contribute to understanding Mongol culture and beliefs.

Bolson Yavdal Stories

Bolson yavdal stories recount unusual or mysterious events believed to have happened in the recent past; therefore, it is assumed that they have living witnesses. Contrary to the views of skeptics, these stories are not merely strange or amusing anecdotes nor are they horror tales akin to Western urban legends. Instead, they carry significant meaning for many Mongols. These stories serve as moral lessons, reinforcing family ties and reflecting broader social structures, including patriarchal values. They also provide frameworks for understanding causality, morality, and social norms in ways that reflect Mongol cosmology's adaptability to changing contexts, such as urbanization, globalization, regime change, and climate change.

Unlike urban legends, which are often detached from cultural or moral foundations, *bolson yavdal* stories are deeply rooted in Mongol cosmology and carry a sense of believability that reinforces their educational and explanatory purposes. For example, they often explore causality by connecting mysterious events or experiences to moral or cosmological principles, offering a way to make sense of the world and its changes.

These traits—depicting recent events, being highly believable, serving a moral or educational purpose, and explaining causality—set *bolson yavdal* stories apart from other narrative forms such as folk tales, legends, anecdotes, gossip, and myths.

Bolson yavdal stories often revolve around sacred stones, holy springs, spiritual animals, and spiritually-protected locales. In these stories, human protagonists find themselves in trouble due to transgressions of taboos, ignoring omens, removing sacred objects, or mistreating animals in spiritual locales. For example, in many *bolson yavdal* stories, removing sacred stones from *ovoo* cairns leads to individuals suffering or even dying due to supernatural causes. *Ovoo* cairns, dedicated to the spiritual masters of specific areas and serving to consolidate patrilineages by connecting them with the realm of spirits and ancestors, are scattered across Mongolia. This makes such incidents a popular topic, with witnesses found in almost every location—often a friend of a friend or someone else vaguely familiar—adding an element of believability to the story. While some *bolson yavdal* stories are purely fictional, others may be based on real events or experiences, albeit distorted or misinterpreted in the retelling. In these stories, wrongdoers aren't merely individuals facing consequences; their actions often reverberate across their entire families. This narrative choice reflects the core of Mongol social structure, emphasizing the significance of families embedded in patrilineages rather than autonomous individuals. By illustrating the collective repercussions of individual transgressions, *bolson yavdal* stories reinforce family ties, fostering a shared sense of moral responsibility within the community.

Besides oral transmission, *bolson yavdal* stories are now also shared in newspapers, internet forums, or compiled into anthologies alongside accounts of encounters with ghosts. These newspaper articles, online discussions, and books are often presented as testimonies, either collected by the writers or transcribed from the words of witnesses. In other words, these aren't first-hand accounts, but curated stories, making them difficult to verify, which serves such mystical stories well.

The following chapters focus on four animals—the dog, the marmot, the cat, and the camel—exploring them as cosmological beings with spiritual powers recounted in *bolson yavdal* stories as well as flesh-and-blood creatures embedded in Mongol history.

2. The Dog

After the death of her husband, an attractive widow named Alan Goa, or 'Alan the Beautiful', gives birth to three more sons. To explain the circumstances surrounding her seemingly illegitimate pregnancies—particularly with a virile Bayad slave serving in her camp, which raised suspicions among everyone—she offers an astonishing story. She claims that each night, under the cover of darkness, a glowing ray of light penetrated through the roof opening of her nomadic *ger*. By morning, the light would depart, taking on the form of a golden-hued dog, leaving her satisfied and pregnant.[1] Among her three celestial children, Bodonchar stood out, as he was destined to become the forefather of none other than Genghis Khan.

This myth is recounted in *The Secret History of the Mongols*, the earliest Mongol chronicle written in the thirteenth century, which provides a detailed account of the ancestry and life of Genghis Khan (1162–1227) and the early history of the Mongol Empire. This mythological story not only paints a picture of a shamanic era when the lines between the divine, human, and animal realms were fluid, but also contains the first mention of the dog among the Mongols.

Much water has flowed under the bridge since those mythological times, and Mongolia is today a predominantly Buddhist nation with a recent—and, many would argue, traumatic—experience of socialism (1924-90) that has affected every aspect of daily life. However, despite these transformations, dogs continue to hold a special place in Mongol culture as one of the most cherished of companions, offering unwavering loyalty and affection, while contributing to the economic prosperity of their owners by safeguarding livestock and other valuables. As guardians of households, dogs also serve as conduits for expressing family-oriented

---

1   *The Secret History of the Mongols* §21.

   https://doi.org/10.11647/OBP.0450.02

values, fears, and hopes within Mongol society. Consequently, harming or unjustly taking the life of a dog is considered a sinful act. A dog's feeding bowl signifies more than just a vessel; it represents a 'circle of abundance' (*hishgiin hüree*), and it is taboo to step over it.

However, if a foreigner were to spend time in Mongolia, they would quickly notice that the country is not exactly a canine paradise. As much as they are perceived as lovable and essential animals, dogs are often treated with disdain and contempt. The foreigner might be shocked to see that dogs are deliberately kept outside the *ger*, viewed as sources of pollution and danger, and their feeding bowls are reserved for leftovers.

This chapter examines the contradictory treatment of dogs in Mongolia, using it as a lens to explore Mongol culture specifically and human culture more broadly. The chapter is organized into three parts. The first part discusses the place of the dog in Mongol cosmology, which provides valuable insight into understanding the complex, often contradictory views of dogs as imagined animals imbued with both positive and negative traits. The second part delves into the historical treatment of dogs as flesh-and-blood creatures in Mongolia under various political and religious regimes. In the conclusion, I offer reflections on the broader human treatment of dogs, using Mongol society as a case study, and explore what zoophilia and sexuality reveal about Mongol culture from a different perspective.

Before diving into these sections, let's first take a brief look at the role of dogs in nomadic camps, which will help set the stage for the discussions to follow.

The Dog's Role in the Nomadic Camp

Mongol nomads have traditionally kept working dogs for two main purposes: (1) *hotoch nohoi*, dogs responsible for guarding the nomadic camp, and (2) *anch nohoi*, hunting dogs for those who enjoy outdoor adventures. Guarding dogs are typically mongrels or belong to the *banhar* breed of Mongol dogs, known for their large, muscular build and thick double coat. In contrast, hunting dogs are characterized by their long legs, slender bellies, short coats, long straight tails, and speed.

Despite the distinct names and breeds of dogs involved, these two roles are often as intertwined as a dog chasing its own tail. Some camp dogs serve additional functions as herding aids and hunting partners, while hunting dogs are also expected to stand guard at the camp. Consequently, an average nomadic household often ends up with a couple of dogs, but some families boast a dozen or more, reflecting the diverse and essential roles these canine companions play in nomadic life.

Herders who want a good dog go to special dog breeders carrying a *hadag*, a traditional scarf used in various ceremonial and religious occasions. As with many pastoral activities, asking someone for a puppy is a ritualized affair, a bit like a courtship ritual. Referred to as 'taking milk to the mother dog', the ritual is performed as follows. The hopeful puppy seeker offers the breeder the *hadag* and delivers a formal line, 'Could you please bestow a puppy on me?' The breeder takes the scarf, offers the guest a meal and tea, and then engages in a lengthy chat about everything except the puppy. Just as the guest's patience wears thin and he is about to leave, the breeder casually mentions to return some other day to pick up what the guest had come for. When that day finally arrives, the guest brings along milk and treats for the mother dog. Using milk, typically reserved for humans or deities, implies that the puppy and its mother aren't just animals; they are considered top-tier beings, close to humans. In the Western context, offering milk would be somewhat akin to offering bread and wine to a dog—items that are considered sacred and reserved for human consumption in religious rituals such as Communion.

Once the puppy is settled in its new camp and the owners have built it a small shelter—akin to a crib layered with sheepskin or felt to protect it from the elements—the real training begins. If the puppy is destined to become a herding dog, the owners take it to the pasture to familiarize it with the surroundings and the herds. At other times, the puppy is kept near the animal shelter, close to the *ger* but at arm's length, to ensure it does not become too attached to humans and forget its duty. If the puppy dares to dash back to the *ger*, it is met with a stern scolding: 'Go away! Get back to the herds! Why did you come?!' After a few such high-pitched reprimands, the puppy usually learns its lesson. In the pasture, the puppy is trained to be vigilant and to spot predators like wolves, foxes, bears, and occasionally snow leopards.[2]

---

2   Tangad, 'Nohoi tezheezh baisan ardyn ulamjlalt zanshlaas', 29-32.

It is worth noting that the role of Mongol dogs in herding is quite different from that of, say, English sheepdogs, which are trained to round up livestock. Mongol dogs accompany their owners to the pastureland, where their primary role is to guard against dangers such as predators or thieves. The actual herding of livestock is carried out by humans, who follow the animals either on foot or horseback. In this sense, the role of Mongol dogs is distinct from that of Western sheepdogs.[3]

For those aiming to train a skilled hunter, the puppy's breed is as critical as its diet. It must be fed with high-calorie meals in small portions especially before hunting trips. To enhance its agility and loyalty, nomads castrate the puppy, ensuring that as it matures, it doesn't become distracted by bitches to the detriment of its camp duties and loyalty to its owners. These castrated pups are then trained to hunt marmots, hares, antelopes, foxes, and even wolves without damaging valuable fur. Nomads who frequently hunt often keep several of these castrated dogs. These seasoned hunters not only contribute to hunting expeditions but also pass on their knowledge to younger puppies.

All these dogs, whether guarding the camp or chasing down critters, are expected to demonstrate fierce loyalty to their human masters and to react aggressively to strangers, often trying to bite them.[4] It is no surprise, then, that most nomads grow up wary of other people's dogs. If you're ever visiting a nomadic camp, you'd better halt in your tracks and shout at the top of your lungs, *Nohoi hori!* ('Hold your dog!'), which doubles as a traditional greeting and safety measure.

Part I

The Dog in Cosmology

I would like to open this part with a story I heard from a friend. Many years ago, she went to the countryside to visit her friends who lived as nomadic herders. One morning the camp dog bit a sheep's tail and found itself in the midst of a whipping storm as punishment. From that moment on, the dog pulled off a grand performance. It refused to eat, ignored

---

3   Fijn, 'Dog ears and tails: Different relational ways of being in Aboriginal Australia and Mongolia'.
4   Humphrey, 'Some notes on the role of dogs', 17.

calls, and forgot how to bark. The head of the family, nursing some guilt, stepped out of his nomadic *ger* numerous times, attempting to have heart-to-heart conversations with the dog: 'Are you still angry with me? I know, you're just waiting for a ride, you son of a bitch!' As the sun dipped below the horizon, the man revved up his motorbike and called the dog, just to see it leap back to life, tail wagging. Together, they embarked on a motorbike tour around the *ger*. After the ride, harmony was restored, and the pooch went back to being the cheerful, tail-wagging, barking wonder.

Good Dogs

Let's begin with the positive aspects of traditional beliefs regarding dogs. Dogs hold a unique place in nomadic culture, symbolizing not only faithful companionship but also embodying individuality. This bond between humans and dogs is expressed through several distinctive customs, exemplified by the following three where dogs serve as human substitutes.

Puppy selection tradition: When a man seeks to acquire a puppy, it's customary for him to avoid taking one from his in-laws. This practice stems from the old belief that a man shouldn't marry two sisters from the same family. In this situation, a puppy becomes a symbolic substitute for an individual from the in-law's family.

Bridal ritual: In Western Mongolia, a wedding custom that persisted until recently involved a new bride kneeling before her husband's family dog. This dog, a guardian figure in the household, held a special place in the marital ceremony. The bride respectfully tied a *hadag* scarf around the dog's neck and offered a bowl of milk. During this ritual, as the new bride paid her respects to the dog and got to know it, her mother-in-law blessed the dog by proudly recounting its finer qualities—a scene that could have been seen staged in the romantic comedy *Monster-in-Law* (2011). In this movie, the overbearing mother-in-law, portrayed by Jane Fonda, creates challenging and demeaning situations for her son's fiancée, played by Jennifer Lopez.

Naming tradition: Puppies, especially males, are the only animals given individual names. Names like Basar ('giant'), Bars ('leopard'), Asar ('huge'), Arslan ('lion'), Baatar ('hero'), Baavgai ('bear'), Banhar ('strong and stocky'), Bürged ('eagle'), Malch ('herder'), Honich ('sheepherder'), Hurd ('speed'), and others are chosen for their strength, beauty, loyalty, and the dog's role in the nomadic household. Notably, some of these names, like Baatar, Arslan, Bars, and Baavgai, can also be given to baby boys.

Mongols hold traditional ideals for both humans and dogs, often drawing parallels between the two. They envision an ideal dog as one that refrains from attacking small animals (reflecting compassion), avoids unnecessary barking (equivalent to honesty), stays loyal to the household (akin to human loyalty to parents), loves and protects livestock (reminiscent of nomadic values), demonstrates courage, and abstains from stealing food. However, bearing in mind the inevitable gap between ideals and the reality on the ground, dogs, much like humans, may not confirm to these ideals. Yet the essence lies in the shared attribution of these ideals to both humans and dogs, emphasizing the perceived similarities between the two.

Given such a close bond between humans and dogs, it's no wonder that Mongols have composed poems dedicated to their canine companions. In Mongol oral tradition, a genre known as üge ('speech') featuring short poems composed by masters of the spoken word, are worth mentioning. These poems depict nomadic daily life, often featuring animals endowed with human language to express grievances. Through their lamentations, these animals give voice to the less powerful in human society, including commoners, impoverished nomads, and those in need of assistance—in short, the underdogs. Reminiscent of the Western 'Beast Fable' genre, these üge poems provide allegorical commentary on human nature and societal issues. Passed down orally, they sometimes find their way onto paper. One such üge poem, attributed to Sangdag the Storyteller, who lived in the late nineteenth and early twentieth century, is titled 'Words Uttered By a Dog':

> The man who raised me, kind and gentle,
> In my youth, his care was fundamental.
> As I grew, he gave me his trust,
> His belongings to me, he did entrust.
>
> When strangers come on horses grand,
> I bark and guard our family land.
> But at my master's guiding call,
> I pause, let strangers in, and stall.

When the strangers get back on their horses, I bark in spite,
With all my might, I fear no fight.
When they gallop, swift as the breeze,
I return, my master to please.

When wolves appear in shadows black,
I chase them off, no turning back.
With barks, I guard through endless night,
Against their cunning, I hold tight.

In winter's chill, I stood so bold,
Guarding my camp in bitter cold.
At dawn, in morning's chilly light,
I'd return, weary from the night,
Hungry and tired, seeking rest,
But met with beating, I must confess.
Inside the *ger*, I dared to peek,
Only to be driven and kicked, feeling weak.
No grudge I keep, though hurt and sore,
Offended briefly, then no more.

When my camp moves to pastures new,
On foot, I follow, faithful and true.
They call me glutton, bare bones my share,
What can I do, life's burdens I bear.
In peace I wish to live each day,
With my master, come what may.
Together we're meant, an ancient decree,
A long life for him and me.[5]

While dogs have the duty to attack anyone who approaches their camp, accompany their owners to the pasture, participate in hunting trips, and protect the household during the day, their most critical duty begins at night. A good dog is expected to bark relentlessly through the night, deterring intruders such as wild predators, strangers, thieves, and ghosts—all entities that nomads are typically afraid of—from approaching the nomadic camp.

Let's not forget the dog's role in the household economy. There is a saying that 'a household with a good dog prospers'. The dog's loyalty to the household, gauged by its physical proximity and activities in the

---

5   Tangad, 'Nohoi tezheeh baisan ardyn ulamjlalt zanshlaas', 29-30.

vicinity of the household, takes on additional symbolic significance. If a neighbor's dog visits, it's seen as a sign that good fortune is on the horizon. But the real jackpot is when a dog coughs up food while eating. This is interpreted as a sign that wealth and abundance are on the way. To put it another way, it's like a folkloric equivalent of imagining a dog coughing up money instead of kibble, promising to bring its owners great riches. On the flip side, if someone's dog runs away, it's seen as a sign of bad luck and impoverishment for the family.

However, as pointed out above, Mongolia has never been a canine paradise, and Mongols' relationship with their dogs has been complicated. Let's delve into the negative beliefs.

Bad Dogs

Due to their interactions with unclean substances, their habit of grooming their genitalia, licking other dogs' butts, and uncontrolled sexuality, dogs are considered in a perpetual state of pollution. People avoid kissing, hugging, or patting dogs, and objects are considered polluted if a dog walks over them or urinates on them. In many areas, dogs are not even allowed near valuable dung piles (used for fuel) for fear of causing spiritual chaos, as their urination on the piles might anger the fire spirit—a crucial entity in Mongol households that each family strives to keep happy and untainted. That said, in some areas, dogs are allowed to lie on dung piles, as the piles generate heat, enabling the dogs to stay warm outside in cold weather. In certain regions of Western Mongolia, nomads living on the slopes of sacred mountains abstain from keeping dogs altogether, a practice uncommon in nomadic culture. This decision stems from their fear that these 'impure' animals may provoke the wrath of the spiritual guardians of these sacred mountains. In 'ordinary' places, nomads typically prefer to keep male dogs.

As a consequence, female puppies are often separated from their mothers at a very young age, even before they open their eyes, and are left outside in the cold to perish. As it is deemed inauspicious for the head of the family to take on the responsibility of killing the puppies, this thankless task falls to his wife, who is considered a less symbolically important figure in the household (though this does not diminish her critical managerial role, as Mongol wives have historically been vital to the management and functioning of the encampment). With a heavy heart, the wife places the helplessly whining puppies on the freezing ground, uttering a formulaic sentence to explain that there isn't enough space for them in the household and that the family cannot afford to feed extra mouths. This responsibility is assigned to women partly because, like a puppy, a wife is symbolically seen as a guest in her husband's *ger* within this patriarchal society. Yet, unlike the ill-fated pups, she has found shelter within his household. To draw a parallel in Western terms, it is akin to the lord of a manor asking a guest—one with whom he shares an intimate relationship and entrusts with the running of the household—to remove other unwelcome and less valued guests. However, if the pups are a bit older and have opened their eyes to the world, the situation changes. Nomads, instead of resorting to sending them to the afterlife, make efforts to accommodate them and find suitable owners. Nonetheless, those who manage to survive the initial ordeal of being left outside to brave the freezing cold or those deemed unwanted often become scavengers and strays.

Furthermore, despite their feeding bowl being charmingly called a 'circle of blessing', dogs are rarely blessed with good food, as leftovers constitute their usual diet. Often, camp dogs get so hungry that they follow their owners or guests to the open-air loo to await departing gifts of far less salubrious origin—just for a sniff, and perhaps a quick nibble. Times are good when they get the special treat called 'dog's share' consisting of soup, meat leftovers, intestines, and other goodies, during special holidays like the Lunar New Year. That said, dogs, being dogs, should never indulge—even during national holidays—in the exclusive delights meant for humans, such as livestock testicles, fat from the sheep's tail, shoulder blades, and head meat. Transgressing these taboos carries supernatural repercussions.

During my early teens, I spent a summer with my paternal uncle, a camel herder. One day, he castrated a goat and gave one testicle to his son-in-law, who chewed away with gusto. My uncle offered the other testicle to me, cautioning against giving it to the camp dog. Just before taking a bite, I had a change of heart, realizing that testicles weren't my kind of delicacy. I put it back. The following day, the castrated goat was found dead, presumably killed by an enraged deity who disapproved of dogs chewing on testicles. My uncle and his family held me as the prime suspect in the untimely demise of their prized goat. Since this was the only plausible cosmological explanation my uncle's family could come up with, they concluded that I must have given the testicle to the dog after all. That was the first and last time I held any testicle close to my mouth. The innocent dog was also reprimanded for what it could not have possibly done. Due to this poor treatment, dogs are also described as 'the most miserable creatures of all'.

The low status of dogs in Mongol culture is further illustrated in Mongolian idioms and expressions, where the word *nohoi* ('dog') often carries negative connotations. Phrases like *nohoin zamaar oroh* ('to enter a dog's road', meaning something goes wrong), *nohoin hereg* ('dog's business', referring to complicated or messy affairs), *nohoin horoo* ('dog's den', describing a messy place), *nohoi shinjihgüi yüm* ('a thing even a dog wouldn't sniff', denoting something useless or dirty), and *muu nohoi* ('bad dog', used as a curse) show how dogs are often associated with disorder.

Given that dogs are literally 'given a bad name', concepts associated with canines are also symbolically viewed as inauspicious in certain contexts. For instance, according to the Mongol astrological calendar, it is considered unlucky to schedule significant events, such as weddings, during the Year of the Dog or on a Day of the Dog.

Since dogs are thus viewed as sources of impurity, mess, and inauspiciousness, they are strictly prohibited from entering the *ger*, with violations resulting in punishment, as evident in the above *üge* poem. Given the taboo, no matter what gifts the dog lays at its human master's feet, it won't be admitted into his *ger*. Even if the dog were to present its master with a morning offering of a dozen hunted sables, safeguard the household from a midday band of burglars, round up the entire flock without losing a single lamb in the afternoon, locate the master's missing child in the evening, and fend off wolves throughout the night—come sunshine, that diligent dog still won't receive an invite into the *ger*. Such is the power of the taboo against dogs entering the sacred human abode, which is also indicative of the deeply traditional nature of Mongol society. Not only that, one of the most serious transgressions a lowly dog can commit is leaping onto the roof of the *ger* (i.e., above the heads of humans), an act that would drive even the most serene Mongols crazy and cause them to go berserk on the transgressor.

As we can see, dogs occupy a controversial place in the Mongol imagination, embodying both positive and negative qualities. To gain a deeper understanding of this duality, let's now explore the role of the dog in cosmology.

Cosmology

In Mongol cosmology, which has a strong Buddhist influence, dogs are perceived as beings closely linked to humans in the cycle of reincarnation, serving as intermediaries between the animal and human realms. According to this belief, any living being desiring rebirth as a human must first experience life as a lowly dog. Only after this canine existence can a soul be reborn as a human in its subsequent reincarnation.

This concept of reincarnation transcends mere discourse or casual conversation: it profoundly influences the way Mongols see the world in general and interact with canines in particular. This influence is vividly manifested in a distinct funerary ritual. When a dog dies, in anticipation of its potential rebirth as a human, Mongols follow a practice wherein they place a chunk of fat or ghee butter symbolizing pure sustenance into the dead dog's mouth, despite the otherwise unclean habits of licking genitalia and nibbling feces and other impure substances. Additionally, they sever the dog's tail and place it beneath its head as a cozy makeshift pillow. This ritual symbolizes the dog's transcendence from its canine state, and sends it off on a first-class cosmological flight, complete with fine food and a plush pillow, to Arcadia—a superior world where, upon arrival, the traveler reincarnates into a hairless, bipedal ape, only one step lower than the gods themselves. Just as dogs are promoted to humans in their next reincarnation, some naughty or sinful humans may get demoted into dogs or even lower beings, creating interesting karmic cases. For instance, departed individuals are widely believed to choose reincarnation within their own families, assuming the form of family dogs. Similarly, deceased dogs can also return to their former owners as their children.

One *bolson yavdal* story that exemplifies this idea occurred in the countryside of post-socialist Mongolia. In this story, a man called

Chimed had a dog that began killing sheep and goats in the vicinity, creating a dire situation for the local nomads and their herds. Fearing for their livestock's safety, they strongly urged Chimed to take action, which he reluctantly did by ending the dog's life. However, this decision had unforeseen consequences that turned the man's life upside down. In the wake of the dog's demise, a series of unfortunate events unfolded: divorces, accidents, and illnesses afflicted all members of his family, leading to the tragic loss of three lives within a year. Brought to his knees by despair, the man descended into a three-year bout of alcoholism, aggression, and self-destructive behavior. Eventually, Chimed overcame his 'inner chimp' and cleaned up his life. He also reunited with his (ex) wife, who soon gave birth to a baby boy. But instead of crying like a typical infant, the baby barked and howled. To make matters even more eerie, when Chimed held his baby, he witnessed a startling transformation: the baby's face morphed into that of the deceased dog. Terrified and at a loss, the man sought guidance from an astrologist, hoping for an explanation and a solution to his family's bizarre ordeal. The astrologist offered insight: 'All these misfortunes have befallen you because of the dog you killed. You must go and have some mantras recited'. After the ritual, which cost a small fortune, the man's life returned to normalcy.[6]

Endowed with spiritual powers, the dog can not only punish wrongdoers but can also establish an intimate spiritual connection with living humans during its lifetime. Among Mongols, it is a widely held belief that the soul of a living dog has the capacity to 'seek refuge' within a human body, usually that of a child whose body is already inhabited by its own soul. Such converged souls cannot be separated without endangering the lives of both the child and the dog, as is illustrated in yet another bone-chilling *bolson yavdal* story.

The story unfolds in the bustling Mongolian capital, Ulaanbaatar, where a successful businessman named Dorj embarked on a heartwarming mission. It's his daughter's impending fourth birthday, and he decided to gift her a puppy. With great excitement, he called his daughter on the phone to share the news, but to his amazement, she responded with an astonishing revelation: she had already seen the puppy in her dreams. When the long-awaited puppy finally arrived,

---

6   Terbish, 'The Mongolian dog as an intimate other', 145-46.

a bond swiftly blossomed between the pup and the girl. They became inseparable friends and soulmates. One day the girl's mother took her to a village outside Ulaanbaatar, leaving the puppy in the apartment flat, despite her daughter's pleading. Separated by distance but connected by their extraordinary cosmic bond, both the girl and her puppy fell suddenly ill on the same day. By the following morning, the puppy had succumbed to its ailment. Although the young girl eventually regained her health, she began behaving strangely, playing with an invisible dog. While many children believe in the existence of an imaginary friend invisible to the rest of the world, the family became alarmed and concerned, leading the father to seek counsel from a wise monk, accompanied by a fat fee. What he learned was both breathtaking and mystical—the souls of his daughter and the departed puppy had intertwined. This extraordinary union had bestowed upon the girl a remarkable gift: the ability to beckon back that which had departed the world of the living.[7]

These two *bolson yavdal* stories, like many others that may be based on 'facts', could be explained away in terms of visual and auditory illusions, where people see visions, faces, and hear voices that are not present. The human brain is not a perfect organ and is prone to mental health conditions, neurological problems, or transcendent experiences caused by a range of factors, from stress and drug use to psychiatric disorders to intensive meditation. Our ability to imagine and visualize things is called dreaming when we sleep; it is called imagination when we are awake. In cases involving mental and neurological conditions, it can be hallucination when people see and experience things that are not there as if they were present. However, let's not get carried away by modern scientific thinking for now and instead return to the explanations provided by cosmological thinking, which has been one of the prevailing modes of thought throughout Mongolia's history—and, indeed, that of humanity—and is the focus of this section.

In Mongol cosmology, dogs and children are sometimes seen as connected, as shown in these *bolson yavdal* stories. This connection can be partly explained by the Buddhist idea that dogs are future humans, while children are not yet fully human. Because of this, children are

---

7   Ibid., 147.

thought to share traits with both dogs and adults. As a result, there are many Mongol traditions that treat dogs and children as if they belong to the same category. For example, after the birth of a rainbow baby (a child born after a miscarriage), the infant is placed inside a dog's feeding bowl, where the umbilical cord is tied, and the baby is wrapped in a cloth or animal skin. Today, however, families have modernized this ritual by placing the baby in a cradle shaped like a dog's feeding bowl.

On the first day of the Lunar New Year, it is considered taboo to scold children or punish dogs. When a child loses a tooth, it is wrapped in fat and given to a dog with the phrase 'take my bad tooth and give me one of your good ones', akin to the tooth fairy tradition in Western societies. Prior to dressing a child in a new robe, some families smear ghee butter on the robe's inner side and have it licked by a dog. Following a person's passing, it is customary for the bereaved to feed both dogs and neighborhood children. Puppies and human children are traditionally regarded as two of the 'three most beautiful creatures on earth', with the third being the baby camel (as discussed in Chapter 5).

To gain insights into a household, it is said that one only needs to 'observe the children and dogs' because these two not only mimic the grown-ups but also shape the destiny of the household: well-behaved children will care for their parents, while good dogs will protect their masters and livestock. Such examples comparing children with dogs, which abound across Mongolia, may strike observers from foreign countries as bizarre, but when explained in the context of indigenous cosmology, they become understandable.

Anthropology is a social science that gets its teeth into the peculiarities and idiosyncrasies of human cultures across the globe, aiming to understand the diversity of human beliefs and practices. To achieve this, the discipline employs a variety of sharp theories and concepts, complemented by participant observation, in which anthropologists immerse themselves in the daily lives of the subject populations to gain an insider's perspective. To comprehend the dog's cosmological role in Mongolia, it is illuminating to utilize classical theory and take a closer look at the concept of 'a transitional being', as coined by anthropologist Victor Turner. Using this term in relation to *rites of passage*, Turner points out that rites of passage indicate and constitute transitions between 'states', which are understood as 'a relatively fixed or stable condition' prior to and following the transitional period. Transition, which is what rites of passage are all about, is, according to Turner, a process, a becoming, and a transformation. As the transitional period involves identity decomposition, neutrality, ambiguity,[8] and pollution, those undergoing this process (i.e. 'transitional beings') have characteristics of both states. In its broadest sense, a rite of passage refers to a ceremonial event marking the transition from one social or religious status to another. Found in all societies, examples include birth rituals, marriage ceremonies, coronations, initiation rites, funerals, and many others.

The Mongol dog fits Turner's concept of 'a transitional being' in that it doesn't quite fit into the category of a full-fledged beast nor a real human but rather embodies qualities of both. While Turner initially coined this term in the context of human societies, one can apply it to analyze the cosmological transformation from beast through dog to its eventual status as human without necessitating ritual implications. In the case of the dog, the two states, separated by the transitional period (i.e., the dog's status as a liminal, polluted animal), can be identified as the state of being a 'true' beast and that of being a human. During their transitional existence, dogs may oscillate towards either end of the spectrum/state, as observed in instances like (1) stray dogs mating with wolves and attacking people and livestock, and (2) domestic dogs connecting their soul with that of a child. When a dog reaches the end of its life (completing the transitional period/rite of passage and ceasing to be a dog in the cosmological sense), Mongols, as previously mentioned, place goodies in its mouth and chop off its tail to prepare its soul for its subsequent reincarnation into human form.

As transitional beings, dogs are believed to freely traverse the boundaries between the material and spiritual realms, endowed with the supernatural ability to perceive things that often slip past human senses. This is particularly evident in the case of the so-called 'dogs with four eyes' (dörvön nüdtei nohoi), distinguished by two small spots above each eye, resembling mystical eyeglasses for the ethereal. These dogs are renowned for their exceptional ability to detect the unseen, whether it be ghosts, impending natural disasters, or other mysterious phenomena. Tales of dogs alerting their owners by barking at ghosts,

---

8   Turner, 'Betwixt and between', 237.

rescuing individuals before earthquakes and floods, or guiding their human masters away from danger are abundant in *bolson yavdal* stories.

Turning to a broader perspective, the cosmology that shapes the lives of Mongols today, including their treatment of dogs, is not only flexible but also responsive to the forces of cultural evolution. Since all rules are products of human imagination, they naturally allow for exceptions, reflecting the inherent adaptability and dynamism of human cultures. This flexibility also implies that what is considered a norm or a cosmological given today may not have been so in the past. To further explore these ideas, let's now revisit the specific example of the ban on dogs entering human dwellings.

The Ban on Dogs Entering Human Dwellings and Its Origins

As previously discussed, Mongols keep their working dogs out of their *gers*, a ban observed across the country. However, like all human-made rules, there are exceptions to this ban, which are as follows:

1. When a young puppy is introduced to a household, it is offered a lick of milk inside the *ger*. This ritual symbolizes the acceptance of the puppy as a new, albeit inferior, member of the household. To use a historical analogy from the West, it isn't dissimilar to a young servant boy being admitted to the private chambers of the lord of the manor to be welcomed into service and instructed on his duties.

2. In situations where the children of the household bring the camp puppy into the *ger* to engage in play, or when a puppy is in need for a warm place to recuperate by the fireside, many nomadic households allow the puppy to enter.

3. Historically, in caravan camps, female dogs with young puppies were allowed to take shelter in the same tent as caravan drivers.[9] This exception was based on ethical and practical grounds influenced by environmental factors. Caravans depended on dogs for protection and security, and they were constantly on the move. Constructing an external shelter for puppies and their mother at each camp, under varying environmental conditions (especially harsh winters and rainy weather) and in different

---

9   Lattimore, *The Desert Road to Turkestan*, 70.

geographical locations, was impractical. Allowing dogs and their pups into the tent was a practical adaptation to environmental conditions. Additionally, from a cosmological perspective, the caravan tent served as temporary shelter, making it less susceptible to permanent 'spiritual pollution'.

4. Leniency is extended to puppies and their mothers when they are in each other's company in specific situations. In contrast, adult male dogs are generally not granted any exceptions and are expected to bravely face any climatic conditions. While Mongol dogs were subject to stringent regulations regarding their entry into human habitats, one particular foreign breed enjoyed certain privileges: the Pekingese, known in Mongolian as *Beijin hav*. This exception arose when Mongolia became part of the Manchu Qing Empire in 1691, leading to cultural adaptations influenced by new political norms and practices. The Pekingese, a toy breed resembling puppies, held historical significance in the Chinese imperial court and was later embraced by the Manchu Emperor. It made its way to the Mongolian steppes through Mongol nobles traveling to Beijing, with further introduction facilitated by Chinese merchants during the Manchu Qing era. As elements of 'high Mongol culture' were influenced by foreign practices, foods, and animals, the trend of keeping Pekingese dogs gradually spread to ordinary Mongol households, particularly in settlements like Urga (modern-day Ulaanbaatar). Although local breeds were regarded as *working* dogs and typically kept outdoors, the enthusiasm for Pekingese dogs, considered *entertainment* dogs, persisted among Mongols for centuries.

5. In every society, there have always been families that deviate from social norms and codes of conduct. Though uncommon, certain households in Mongolia permit their adult dogs to enter the *ger*—a practice frowned upon by others.

Now, let's take a moment to explore the origins of this ban, which are grounded in several arguments rooted in Buddhist concepts of purity and pollution. These beliefs include: (1) dogs frequently groom their genitalia and display uncontrolled sexuality, (2) dogs carry fleas and are considered physically unclean, and (3) dogs may introduce spiritual pollution from the realm of spirits. Each of these points will now be addressed, incorporating a historical perspective:

(1) In the early thirteenth century, the Mongols emerged on the world stage as practitioners of shamanism. In their shamanic tradition, dogs held a special place of reverence, being viewed both as heavenly creatures connecting the human world and the spirit realm and as loyal companions to humans. As creatures that belonged to a different category of beings, dogs—as far as one can judge based on historical documents—were not held to the same moral benchmarks applied to humans during this period.

Shamanism, as practiced among the Mongols, also had a distinctive perspective on human sexuality, differing significantly from the later-adopted Buddhism. While the latter views sex or sexual craving as one of the Three Poisons (the other two being 'hatred' and 'ignorance') that brings about mental and moral impurity and attaches humans to suffering, the former maintains an indifference to human sexuality. In the eyes of shamanic gods, all forms of carnal pleasure, be it pre-marital intercourse or same-sex relationships or multiple partners, were permissible and devoid of moral condemnation. Therefore, what might be considered under Buddhism as 'lax sexuality' was not a moral concern under shamanism.[10] People, as well as animals such as dogs, were not censured for indulging in carnal pleasure unless the indulgence posed a threat to the established patriarchal order rooted in inheritance (in the case of shamanic dogs, this was impossible to undermine for the simple reason that Mongols never included dogs in their wills). I'll return to sexuality, but for now, let's take a look at the notion of sanitation.

(2) Historical accounts from the Middle Ages, primarily written by Christian envoys and various Mongol vassals, depicted the shamanic Mongols as having different hygiene practices compared to other cultures of their time[11] and even more so compared to our contemporary standards. The nomadic lifestyle of the Mongols, characterized by living in mobile *gers* and limited access to bathing facilities due to constant movement and water scarcity in their arid regions, greatly influenced their bathing habits. Mongols were noted for abstaining from washing for extended periods and rarely changing their clothes. Yet, as was the

---

10 Terbish, *Sex in the Land of Genghis Khan.*
11 Dawson, *The Mongol Mission.*

case until the beginning of the twentieth century, Mongols didn't mind this and were accustomed to the feel and scent of a long-unlaundered garments. Much like people today who aren't repulsed by the fact that our pet dogs don't shower every day, Mongols in medieval times never considered dogs unclean nor perceived themselves as filthy.

Far from being considered 'polluting' animals, shamanic dogs enjoyed close physical proximity with nomads. Although it cannot be definitively verified whether Mongols in the thirteenth century or earlier permitted their dogs to share *gers*, both archaeological findings from the pre-Mongol period and historical sources from the Yuan period (1279-1368) shed light on this matter.

The Xiongnu (Hun), a pioneering confederation of nomadic tribes in Central Asia encompassing the ancestors of Mongols, thrived from the third century BCE to the late first century CE. They wielded significant political and military influence, shaping not only the region's history but also impacting the cultures of subsequent nomadic states. What is particularly relevant to our discussion is that burials from the Xiongnu period are notable for the inclusion of dogs alongside humans, a practice that persisted for centuries among later peoples until the rise of the Mongols in the thirteenth century under Genghis Khan.[12]

In contrast, only a few Mongol-era burials have been found to contain dog remains, and only one Yuan-period Mongol burial has been located which featured a clay figurine of a dog among other objects. This suggests that the practice of burying real dogs with humans became rare, with figurines possibly replacing live animals in these sites. If the shamanic Mongols and their ancestors had viewed dogs as impure or unworthy of sharing human habitat in life, it is unlikely they would have included dogs or their representations in human burials, intended to accompany their masters for eternity.

Another distinguishing feature of the Yuan dynasty, established by Genghis Khan's grandson Kubilai, is that it was during this time that Mongols began residing en masse in palaces and permanent buildings, emulating their Chinese subjects. Numerous poems and paintings from that era depict Mongols, especially the aristocracy, sharing their palaces and houses with their dogs,[13] once again indicating that Mongols didn't

---

12 Gonchigiin, *Nüüdelchdiin Nohoi, I Devter.*
13 Gonchigiin, *Nüüdelchdiin Nohoi, II Devter.*

view dogs as impure animals. Dogs came to be seen as impure following the Mongols' conversion to Buddhism.

(3) The transition of Mongol society from shamanism to Buddhism en masse in the sixteenth century was a watershed moment and had a profound impact on how nomads came to view both themselves and their dogs. Under shamanism, humans and animals enjoyed a harmonious coexistence and spiritual interconnectedness, with no inherent superiority of humans over animals. Dogs were revered as heavenly animals, serving as bridges between the spirit realm and humans.

However, when Buddhism elevated humans to a semi-divine status—just below bodhisattvas and Buddhas—the animal kingdom was correspondingly downgraded. In this transformation, dogs found themselves caught in the revolving wheels of Buddhist cosmology, recognized as the animals closest to humans in the endless cycle of reincarnation. According to these new beliefs, a living being must first be reborn as a dog before being reincarnated as a human. To borrow a metaphor from the movie industry, it would be akin to transitioning from an A-list celebrity to an extra in a B-grade, Groundhog Day-style film. This left dogs in an ambiguous position: viewed as superior to other animals, yet still inferior to humans.

As dogs came to be seen as possessing human-like qualities yet not being equal to humans, the term *nohoi* ('dog') began to be used as an insult, associated with mess, pollution, and inauspiciousness, as previously noted. Not only did Mongols stop burying dogs alongside humans, but calling someone a 'dog' or suggesting they possessed inferior canine traits implied that the individual was not considered fully human.

Imagine a Mongol market scene where a vendor, upon realizing that a customer is trying to haggle extensively, exclaims, 'Stop being such a dog about the price!' to which the customer quips, 'You also stop bitching about it!' Offended and angry, the vendor retaliates, 'Go away and get yourself shagged by a dog!' Little would the two realize that they're inadvertently perpetuating beliefs associating dogs with undesirable qualities. 'Getting oneself shagged by a dog!' (*nohoi chamaig gör döö*) is the Mongolian equivalent of the English 'Fuck off!' and is a frequently heard phrase in Southern Mongolia, especially from the foul mouths of middle-aged and older people. Just like any profanity, this phrase could be delivered in various ways. My paternal uncle, who once accused me of killing his goat by giving its castrated testicle to a camp dog, was excellent at its delivery. Much like Al Pacino's character Tony Montana from the movie *Scarface* (1983), who delivered his profanity-laden dialogue with diverse intonations and tones, my uncle, during his moments of frustration, anger, or boredom, would often utter 'Get yourself shagged by a dog!' to both himself and others with varying intonations and tones, emphasizing nuances in his mood. This phenomenon, where the canine is used as a derogatory term, however, is not unique to Mongolia but is widespread in many societies where dogs are perceived to have human-like qualities.

Unlike shamanism, Buddhism, as pointed out previously, is a fundamentally anti-sex religion due to its belief that carnal pleasure chains humans to the cycle of rebirth (*samsara*), leading to worldly misery and an unenlightened existence. Given a dog's unrestrained sex life, which began to be viewed negatively, canines also came to be seen as impure or polluting. As beings straddling the realms of humans and the supernatural, dogs were also considered dangerous, potentially bringing spiritual pollution from the realm of hungry spirits.

To distill the three points—related to 'uncontrolled sexuality', 'dirt', and 'spiritual pollution'—that contribute to the exclusion of dogs from *gers*, it becomes apparent that the accusations leveled against dogs today, often presumed to have ancient origins, can be traced back to Buddhism, a relatively recent religion among the Mongols. One can infer that dogs were expelled from human habitats not because they behaved wrongly or in polluting ways, but because humans began to see dogs—as well as themselves—in a new light through the lens of Buddhism, which, in the case of dogs, was not very flattering. If a Mongol from the Yuan period were to appear today, he would be greatly surprised witnessing dogs being disparaged as impure creatures and kicked out of human dwellings by his descendants.

Once it became an established dogma that dogs are 'impure animals' and a hazard to keep within human dwellings, it was only a small step to impose further restrictions on them. Mongol groups implemented such restrictions in different ways. As mentioned earlier, in Western Mongolia, for example in Mönh-Hairhan *sum* (village) in Hovd

Province, a tradition exists that forbids dogs from living in proximity to Mönh-Hairhan Mount. This prohibition stems from a concern about displeasing the jealous *sabdag* ('spiritual guardian') of this sacred mount. Allegedly, this *sabdag* disapproves of impure animals running around and marking their territory. Consequently, nomadic households dwelling on the slopes of Mönh-Hairhan Mount abstain from keeping dogs altogether. In contrast, herders from Bulgan *sum* in Bayan-Ölgii Province, residing on the other side of the same mount, do keep dogs and do not buy into the belief in the *sabdag*'s aversion to dogs, despite worshipping and communicating with this deity as fervently as their counterparts from Mönh-Hairhan *sum*. This is one example of how cosmological elements change over time and how related groups differentiate among themselves by slightly modifying shared stories and practices.

Generally speaking, throughout history and across diverse societies, the concepts of purity and pollution have played pivotal roles in the subordination and exclusion of not only animals but entire human groups from places, positions, rituals, and activities deemed 'pure' or of 'high social status'. Thus, in the context of a patriarchal Mongol society, women found themselves relegated to an inferior status in comparison to men, primarily fueled by the notion that women are impure beings. Menstruating women, in particular, have been prohibited from engaging in various activities due to the fear that they might not only pollute those around but also incur the wrath of the gods. Even when not menstruating, women have been prohibited from ascending sacred mountains, participating in certain high-value rituals, or behaving in ways that could potentially belittle their husbands or elders. This systematic subordination of women illustrates a broader pattern: convincing society that certain groups of people or animals are sources of *pollution* becomes a powerful technology to maintain the subordination and exclusion of these groups. Given our natural inclination to avoid polluting substances, often accompanied by feelings of revulsion towards them, this method has been effectively employed throughout history to organize social hierarchies in nearly all societies.

Part II

The History of Human-Dog Relations

Before delving into the heart of the matter, I'd like to recount a true recent story, not a cosmological *bolson yavdal* one. This story involves two dogs—a young one and a middle-aged one—that developed a habit of attacking sheep.

A nomadic household adopted a young puppy that initially barked at the family's herd animals. However, this barking escalated into chasing, ultimately culminating in the young puppy taking the life of its first lamb victim. Despite the family's attempts to dissuade the destructive behavior through kicks and punishment, the puppy persisted. Filled with both guilt and frustration, the father of the family made the difficult decision to put the puppy down. However due to a belief that deems it inauspicious to kill a dog—a belief that extends to the rifle used for such purposes, as it is thought to become faulty during hunting— the father chose not to use his own rifle. Instead, he enlisted the help of an unconventional neighbor who paid no heed to such omens and promptly shot the culprit dead.

Several years later, the same family's middle-aged dog, previously loyal and protective of livestock, also began attacking the herd animals. Feeling betrayed and heartbroken, the family decided to sever their relations with the dog and get rid of it.

Reciprocity, a fundamental social principle among social species like humans, sustains friendships and relationships through a mutual exchange of support, favors, and kindness. Reciprocating positive actions reinforces trust and cultivates a resilient bond through a sense of obligation. The cessation of reciprocity severs this special bond. The reciprocity between dogs and nomads in Mongolia mirrors the reciprocity humans have with one another. Dogs support the nomads by guarding their camp and livestock and showing loyalty. In return, nomads support dogs with food, shelter, and affection, reinforcing the relationship over time. However, if a dog betrays the nomad's trust by attacking livestock, humans withdraw their support, favors, and love for the dog. In human relationships, such severance can be resolved by avoidance, but the nomad-dog bond presents a dilemma because a nomad cannot simply ask the dog to leave the camp. The most commonly adopted solution nowadays is to physically sever the bond by killing the dog.

A Short Overview of the Dog in History

Let's ponder the time and manner in which humans and dogs might have first bonded. One of the oldest dog burials in Eurasia dates back to the late Pleistocene, an epoch that ended about 12,000 years ago.[14] However, dogs might have joined the human pack thousands of years earlier. Over millennia of cohabitation and interaction, humans and dogs co-evolved to communicate with each other so effectively that they not only shared the same camp in life but were also sometimes buried together for eternity in death, as will be discussed later.

Besides sharing eternal resting places with humans, dogs in their earthly existence served as loyal companions during hunting expeditions from early times on. Mongolia boasts an array of petroglyphs sites which were created through carving and painting with ocher. These petroglyphs reached their zenith during the Bronze and early Iron Ages, spanning from approximately 1500 to 500 BCE. Among these ancient artworks, Bichigtiin Am in Bayan-Hongor Province stands out as one of the most abundant and visually striking sites. These petroglyphs predominantly portray scenes of men using bows and arrows to hunt ibex and elk, often assisted by dogs.[15]

As stated at the beginning of this chapter, dogs feature in the earliest Mongol source, *The Secret History of the Mongols*, a thirteenth-century chronicle in which a heavenly dog plays an intimate role in the story of Alan Goa's pregnancy. It also notes that the baby Temüjin, the future world-conqueror Genghis Khan, was afraid of (other people's) dogs—a fear still common among Mongol children and grown-ups today, as dogs have been trained by their masters to attack strangers. The imperial annals suggest that dogs had the power to prophesy bad omens by barking 'in evil ways'.[16] In addition to their divinity, virility, and ferocity, dogs are extoled in *The Secret History of the Mongols* for their unwavering

---

14   Losey, 'Canids as persons'.
15   Atwood, *Encyclopedia of Mongolia*, 436.
16   *The Secret History of the Mongols* §66, §189.

loyalty. This loyalty is exemplified when Genghis Khan's four most devoted and formidable generals—Jebe, Kubilai Noyan,[17] Jelme, and Sübedei—are referred to as his 'four dogs'. Described as 'raised on human flesh' and 'shackled in chains',[18] they were likened to voracious predators, ceaselessly attacking their master's foes.

Dogs also played a practical role in Mongol society, guarding nomadic encampments, participating in hunting, and even courageously marching—as historical sources from the Yuan and Ilkhanate periods attest[19]—into military campaigns. During the era of empire-building, the Mongols were not only known for organizing grand hunting events with large numbers of dogs but also for demanding tributes from their vanquished peoples across Eurasia and beyond. Among these tributes, the most burdensome were *tangsugs*, or 'delicacies', which included hunting dogs, fine horses, falcons, and gold cloth, highlighting the Mongols' appreciation for both canines and luxury items.[20] Plano Carpini, who traveled to Mongol lands between 1245 and 1247, reported seeing 'ten greyhounds' at the Mongol court, brought by the envoys of a Sultan of India. He noted that these greyhounds were 'trained to sit on the back of a horse like leopards'.[21]

Marco Polo, another European who spent an extended period at the Mongol Yuan court, provides detailed insights into the role of dogs in hunting. He uses the example of Kubilai (1215-94), who indulged in elaborate hunting expeditions. According to Marco Polo, the Great Khan employed two 'masters of the hunt', brothers Bayan and Myangan, who were entrusted with organizing these imperial hunting endeavors and overseeing the imperial dog keepers:

> Each of these two brothers has ten thousand men under them controlling the dogs... And among these ten thousand there are two thousand of them who each has a great mastiff dog or two or more, so that they are very great multitudes.[22]

17   This is not Genghis Khan's grandson Kubilai, but Kubilai Noyan, who was a captain of a thousand (myangan).
18   *The Secret History of the Mongols* §195.
19   Gonchigiin, *Nüüdelchdiin Nohoi, II Devter*, 77, 78.
20   Atwood, *Encyclopedia of Mongolia*, 196.
21   Dawson, *The Mongol Mission*, 202.
22   Polo, *The Description of the World*, 228.

Following the establishment of the Mongol Empire, Mongols implemented a horse relay system known as *yam* that connected all corners of the expanding empire. The official organization of this system occurred during the reign of the second Grand Khan, Ögedei (1229-41), Genghis Khan's third son. The system comprised relay horse stations with attached households established every 28 miles. While horses were the primary animals used in these relays, in certain remote areas of Manchuria and Siberia, dog sled relays were employed.[23] It is likely that the Mongols adopted this practice from the indigenous populations. In the eyes of the Mongols, dogs thus held significance as both totemic animals and valuable working beasts, whether in guarding camps, hunting, or pulling sledges.

In many traditional societies, totemic or sacred animals are not only revered but are also sometimes used as sacrificial animals to gods or slain for utilitarian purposes, as in the Mongol case where dog's fur was used to make winter gowns, especially by the poor.[24] One shamanic rite involving dogs was recorded as having been performed during the Yuan dynasty. Carried out at the end of the year, the ritual consisted of shooting arrows at straw and grass models of people (symbolizing enemies) and dogs (their loyal companions), followed by chants of shamans.

But as history marched on, times changed. Following the fall of the Yuan dynasty in 1368, the Mongols returned to their ancestral land.[25] However, it did not take long for them to fragment among themselves and engage in bloody civil war. There is a saying that when the going gets tough, the tough get ritualistic. In ancient Mongol traditions, a unique oath-ritual was performed among warriors before battle, designed to strengthen their bond. This ritual involved sacrificial animals, including

---

23   For example, during the Mongol Yuan dynasty, around 1330, the Mongol dynasty maintained 1400 relay stations, of which 15 in Manchuria were dogsled relays equipped with 218 dogs. These dogsled post stations were used by tribute collectors. In the Golden Horde, another Mongol state established by Genghis Khan's grandson Batu, similar dogsled stations operated in Siberia. Atwood, *Encyclopedia of Mongolia*, 259, 342, 503.

24   Rubruck, *William of Rubruck's Account of the Mongols*.

25   According to *Erdeni-yin Tobchi* (*The Bejewelled Summary*, 1662) by Sagan Setsen, of 400,000 Mongols in the Yuan, 60,000 followed the last Yuan Emperor Togon Temür to Mongolia, and the remaining 340,000 remained in China. Krueger, *The Bejewelled Summary*, 86.

a male dog (symbolizing loyalty and divinity), a stallion (symbolizing divinity, speed, and endurance), and a bull (symbolizing strength), which were slain to demonstrate to the shamanic gods that if the oath-makers failed to keep their pledge of unconditional loyalty to one another, the gods should punish them, just as the warriors killed the sacrificial animals.[26] Symbolically, these animals represented the oath-takers themselves, but in a parallel dimension where they had failed to remain true to their oath. As the Mongols in the post-Yuan period found themselves embroiled in incessant civil war, bloody rituals like these, aimed at securing the favor of the gods, became increasingly prevalent. Just imagine the sight of cavalrymen arriving at the battlefield with a sacrificial dog, stallion, and bull—a spectacle that would have undoubtedly struck fear into the hearts of their adversaries!

In 1640, the temporarily-reunited Mongol groups proclaimed Buddhism as the state religion, at the expense of traditional shamanism, and introduced a new code of laws, the *Mongol-Oirat Regulations* which, among other things, forbade killing certain animals including nomads' furry companions that had been used in shamanic rituals.[27] The spirit of the *Mongol-Oirat Regulations*, including its dog-friendly rulings prohibiting the killing of canines, was reiterated in the *Halha Jirum* code of laws of the eighteenth century.[28]

But whatever the reason behind prohibiting the killing of canines in these two early Mongol codes (*Mongol-Oirat Regulations* and *Halha Jirum*), the real beneficiary was the dog, despite losing its elevated shamanic position. Not only was the dog's life protected by the law, but it also assimilated new Buddhist virtues alongside its ancient shamanic powers. It is worth noting that in subsequent legal codes of Mongolia, there is a conspicuous absence of any mention regarding the prohibition of killing dogs. This absence likely arose from the fact that people had abandoned this practice, making it unnecessary to explicitly forbid an act that had faded into obscurity. As previously mentioned, the legal ban on killing dogs became an inherent part of religious mythology and a taboo, which was only lifted in the socialist era.

---

26 Radhid ad-Din, *Sudryn Chuulgan*, 267.
27 Golstunskii, *Mongolo-Oiratskie Zakony 1640 Goda*, 93.
28 Zhamtsarano, *Khalkha Dzhirum*, 34.

Dogs Under the Qing Rule

After centuries of internal squabbles and civil wars in the post-Yuan era, sporadically interrupted by moments of peace and unity, the Mongols found themselves woven into the fabric of the expanding Manchu Qing Empire, centered in Beijing, following the Great Doloonuur Convention of 1691. This pivotal moment in Mongolia's history opened the floodgates to a wave of Chinese male migrants who poured into the country in such staggering numbers that, by 1918, Mongolia hosted 100,000 Chinese men as opposed to the local population of 645,000. Eighty percent of these Chinese belonged to the merchant class, while the remaining cohort comprised a colorful mosaic of laborers, artisans, farmers, officials, and professionals from diverse walks of life.[29]

Owing to the gender restrictions imposed by the Manchu Qing administration, Chinese women were prohibited from setting foot in Mongol territory. Consequently, these colonies of single Chinese men resembled and behaved like temporary guests at a lively party—complete with services rendered by women in the world's oldest profession—always planning to pack their bags and head back home to their families once they had filled their pockets with enough lucre, making room for the next wave of adventurers and fortune seekers.

These enterprising Chinese were the architects of trade, meticulously constructing a sprawling web of commerce that manifested in the form of shops, trading firms, brothels, and dining halls, which sprouted in nearly every settlement. Individual Chinese traders, fueled by unbridled ambition, traversed every nook and cranny of the vast country. Imagine them as the trailblazing pioneers of door-to-door sales, peddling their wares from one *ger* to the next. They did not do this alone. Embedded as integral cogs in the machinery of commerce were dogs that served as four-legged couriers in a world that had not yet discovered the convenience of telegrams.[30]

In the absence of a proper sanitation system, especially in settlements, dogs also played an essential role in maintaining cleanliness by feeding on human excrement, food leftovers, and remains from slaughtered animals. In this context, they functioned as four-legged sanitation

---

29 Maiskii, *Sovremennaya Mongoliya*, 70-72.
30 Lattimore, *The Desert Road to Turkestan*, 72.

workers. Urga, the capital, stands out as a case in point. The presence of roaming dog packs, coupled with the country's dry and cold climate, contributed to keeping the town relatively clean.

However, the responsibilities of Mongol mutts extended far beyond their humble role as messengers and reliable cleanup crew. Some dogs were destined for higher roles. During the imperial period, Mongols demanded hunting dogs as tributes from their vassals, but under the Manchu Qing dynasty, Mongols themselves began to offer hunting dogs as tribute to the Manchu Emperor[31] who adopted many practices from the Mongols.

Serving as guardians for camel caravans was not a new duty for dogs either; in fact, this duty dates all the way back to the thirteenth century when Mongols held sway over a vast portion of the Silk Road, an ancient highway bustling with camel caravan traffic protected by dogs.[32] During the era of the Manchu Qing dynasty, the entire trade operation in the territory of Mongolia, however, fell under the monopoly of Chinese firms who assumed the role of the caravan operators and kept the wheels of commerce turning.[33] Regardless of the period, these canine protectors were indispensable for caravans, defending against the threats of wild beasts and the mysterious shadows of unfamiliar travelers and ghosts.

The Dog's Role in Funerary Rites

The fear of death and responses to it are deeply personal experiences, yet they are profoundly influenced by cultural factors. Different cultures shape individual perspectives on death, leading to varied attitudes, coping mechanisms, and rituals. In Mongol society, particularly since the introduction of Buddhism in the sixteenth century, Buddhist concepts of karma and reincarnation have profoundly influenced views on life and the afterlife. Although Buddhism openly addresses death through religious liturgy, dances, and art displayed in monasteries, discussing or mentioning death in daily life is considered taboo because of a belief that this may hasten one's demise. When death does occur, cultural

---

31 Gonchigiin, *Nüüdelchdiin Nohoi, II Devter*, 81-95.
32 Ibid., 133-44.
33 Lattimore, *The Desert Road to Turkestan*, 69.

norms encourage restrained expressions of mourning, as excessive grief is thought to potentially harm the soul of the deceased.

Mongol funerary rites serve several purposes, including marking the individual's passing, aiding the soul of the deceased transition from the living world, purifying the relatives from spiritual pollution associated with death, and reestablishing the boundary between the realms of the living and the dead, which becomes unsettled upon someone's death. However, these rites evolve as society changes.

Dogs, as the closest companions to humans, have reflected changes in Mongol society, including the evolution of funerary rites. As these rituals have transformed over time, so too has the role of dogs within them. To understand the foundational principles of modern burials and their historical origins, we must look back at the sixteenth century.

During this period, with the spread of Buddhism among the Mongols, the practice of open-air burials gained popularity. In this tradition, the deceased are placed on the steppe, exposed to the elements and wildlife, including stray dogs. The speed at which the body is consumed by scavengers is believed to reflect the virtue of the deceased: a swift consumption indicates a virtuous life, while those deemed less virtuous face a slower rate or may even remain untouched by the scavengers.

Open-air funerals are typically overseen by monks, whose expertise is crucial for conducting the associated rituals. One of the monk's initial duties is to select an appropriate day and time for the funeral. Additionally, he must approve the direction in which the funeral procession should leave the *ger* and the path it should follow when returning after laying the deceased on the steppe. This practice is intended to confuse the soul of the deceased and prevent any malign spirits present during the funeral from following the procession back home. Throughout these stages, the monk recites mantras and performs various rituals to guide the departed soul on its journey to the afterlife. Once the monk's rituals are completed, the rest is left to dogs.

In pre-revolutionary Mongolia, open-air burials were not limited to rural areas; they also took place in bustling urban centers like Urga. These urban areas had designated open-air cemeteries on their outskirts, where residents laid their loved ones to rest. These locations were often inhabited by packs of feral dogs grown accustomed to a diet including human remains. Living in or around Urga, these dogs lacked socialization with humans, perceiving them as either threats or potential meals. British explorer Beatrix Bulstrode made the following observation about the local dogs during her visit to Urga at the beginning of the twentieth century:

A lasting impression of Urga is that of a city strewn with bones, and horrible, ghoulish, and terribly savage dogs prowling among them. You may count these dogs sometimes in hundreds about the refuse heaps that surround Urga. Often they may be seen silently gnawing, gnawing away at something which makes you shudder as you ride quickly past. One never ventures outside one's door unarmed, for in winter the dogs are very fierce with hunger, and in summer there is always danger of meeting a mad brute. Only a few months before we stayed there a young lama from the temple just outside our compound was torn to pieces by these pariah dogs. He was a fine strong young man, but had gone forth alone one winter's day and was without a weapon. A number of dogs attacked him and before anyone could respond to his cries they had dragged him away to a neighboring refuse heap and there torn him limb from limb.[34]

Mongols, however, did not perceive dogs and their cosmological role negatively. Even those critical of traditional ways of life, such as Natsagdorj Dashdorjiin (1906-37), one of the founding fathers of modern socialist Mongolian literature and an advocate for the abandonment of superstition and old practices, approached the connection between dogs and open-air burials with a melancholic contemplation. In his philosophical poem titled 'Eventually We Will All End Up Feeding Dogs' (1935), Natsagdorj penned these lines:

What joy to live as a human being,
On this earth, under the sun, we're seeing.

How splendid to rejoice in gatherings bright,
Growing up in health, a pure delight.

How swiftly time passes, and nature shifts and turns,
It's interesting to observe beauty as she grows old and yearns.

How tragic to yield to illness' cold seize,
Heart-wrenching to end up feeding the feral dogs in Northern Valley's breeze.[35]

---

34 Bulstrode, *A Tour in Mongolia*, 206
35 Dashdorjiin, *Zohioluud*, 143.

The practice of leaving a corpse for dogs and wildlife shares similarities with Tibetan culture, a connection not surprising. The sky burial, known as *jha-tor* in Tibet, is an ancient funerary ritual where the deceased person's body is placed in an open area, often on a mountaintop or high plateau, exposed to the sky, elements, and various scavengers including vultures, dogs, and other carrion eaters.[36] Before the ritual, the body is typically dismembered as an offering to these scavengers. This act symbolizes the belief that the deceased person's remains return to nature, becoming part of the ongoing cycle of life, highlighting the impermanence of life and the interconnectedness of all living beings with the natural world.

While sky burials in Tibet and open-air burials in Mongolia share similarities, these traditions emphasize different scavengers. In Tibetan sky burials, it is the vulture that is revered as a messenger of the gods, whereas in Mongol open-air burials it is the dog that is regarded as an animal closely connected to humans in the cycle of reincarnation.

It is worth noting that while Buddhism popularized open-air burials in Mongolia, it also preserved or introduced various other forms of burial practices. These included stupa burials, where the embalmed remains of monks were placed inside Buddhist stupas, as well as cremation, inhumation, and rock burials.

In pre-Buddhist Mongol society, a variety of burial practices existed. *The Secret History of the Mongols*, a primary historical source from that era, does not mention open-air burials in the steppe. Instead, it provides accounts of other burial methods, such as rock burials (involving placing corpses in elevated locations like rocks), water burials (submerging corpses in water), and inhumation (burying corpses underground). In certain circumstances, such as during military conflicts when transporting a corpse was impractical, decapitation of the deceased was customary. This decapitation allowed for a subsequent funerary rite in which the head symbolically represented the entire body.[37]

Shamanic burials from the imperial period differed from those of the later Buddhist period in another notable respect: the inclusion of dogs in burial sites. As mentioned earlier, a few shamanic burial sites include dogs interred alongside humans. Such burials have been found

---

36   Martin, 'On the cultural ecology of sky burial on the Himalayan Plateau'.
37   Amarmend, *Mongolyn Nuuts Tovchoon Dahi Yos Zanshil Zan Uiliyn Tailbar Toli*, 185-91.

at two inhumation sites in Chandmani Har Uul, Southern Mongolia and at one rock burial site in Har Uul, Western Mongolia. The origin of this tradition can be traced to the Early Bronze Age (4000 to 3000 BCE), when the oldest known burials in Mongolia containing both human and dog remains were discovered. However, the most significant findings of human burials accompanied by dogs are linked to the later Xiongnu period, as previously noted.

Within Mongolia's borders, twenty Xiongnu burials have been found so far showcasing dog remains interred alongside both adult humans and children. Considering the vast territory historically occupied by the Xiongnu, dog burials associated with this culture have also been found beyond the borders of present-day Mongolia, notably in areas such as the Baikal Lake region in Russia's Siberia.

Further excavations conducted between 1985-91 in the Jundu Mountains north of Beijing in China revealed burial sites belonging to pre-Xiongnu nomadic communities. These excavations unveiled 600 burials containing remains of livestock animals and dogs. Remarkably, a staggering 1448 pieces of dog bones were recovered from these sites.[38]

Successive nomadic states following the Xiongnu tradition continued the practice of dog burials. However, by the time the Mongol Empire was established in the thirteenth century, dog burials had become rare and certainly disappeared by the sixteenth.[39]

Dogs Under State Socialism

Up to this point, I have presented an account of the traditional perspective on dogs, closely intertwined with religious institutions and practices facilitated by occult specialists. Now, let's examine the fate of canines during the socialist era, a period marked by the suppression of religion and the dismissal of traditional cosmological beliefs as mere superstition.

Previously, I noted that human cultures are products of human imagination and that their primary function is not to represent reality accurately or seek the truth, but to connect and unite people. This applies to all cultures, whether they are underpinned by powerful religious institutions, nationalist ideologies, or Marxist-Leninist dogma. They are

---

38 Gonchigiin, *Nüüdelchdiin Nohoi, II Devter*, 70-85.
39 Ibid., 103-72.

all based on myths and fiction whose primary goal is to inspire people, unite them, and instill common values and goals. Seen in this light, communism may have suppressed institutionalized religion and its myths as the regime's primary adversary, but it never got rid of myths; it only replaced the old religious myths with new ones about building a paradise on earth populated with perfect humans.

In 1911, Mongolia declared independence from the Manchu Qing Dynasty, but the young Mongol theocracy soon faced invasions. In 1919, Chinese nationalist troops, driven by the myth of China's territorial integrity that encompassed Mongolia, occupied the country. Shortly afterward, the eccentric White Russian General Baron Ungern-Sternberg—also known as the 'Mad Baron' for his erratic behavior, extreme brutality, and mysticism—expelled the Chinese nationalists with the aim of restoring Mongolia's theocracy and using it as a springboard for anti-Bolshevik operations in the region. Ungern's actions were fueled by his fierce anti-Bolshevik stance and a mystical belief in Mongolia as a sacred battleground akin to the legendary Shambhala—a Buddhist kingdom symbolizing a utopian realm of spiritual purity where forces of good gather to resist moral and spiritual decay.[40] The Mad Baron's activities drew the Bolsheviks mad and prompted them to support Mongol revolutionaries in establishing a people's government and army. With substantial Bolshevik backing and pregnant with new revolutionary mythology, Mongol revolutionaries successfully delivered liberation to the country in 1921.

The rise to power of Bolshevik sympathizers in Mongolia led to a series of relentless yet highly effective measures aimed at overturning the existing social order. Shortly before the revolution, Mongolia boasted an astounding 750 monasteries. However, by the onset of 1940, not a single one remained operational. The monastic community had been disbanded, and many of its members found themselves behind bars or in even graver situations. Other religious practitioners, including shamans and astrologers who operated without formalized institutions, were not spared either; they, too, were forced underground by the atheist state.

One of the fundamental aims of communist dogma was ethno-engineering, intended to cultivate new, atheist, ideologically pure citizens

---

40   Palmer, *The Bloody White Baron.*

to populate the communist paradise. However, the regime, pathologically suspicious of ordinary people, never trusted their wisdom or needs. It firmly believed it knew what was best for the people, whether they liked it or not. Despite its idealistic beginnings, the revolution soon began to devour its own children, with rival factions within the Party and government vying for control, and the regime resorted to an orgy of senseless violence, exterminating its own people. This reached its climax during a dark period from late 1937 to mid-1939, during which approximately 36,000 Mongol citizens, half of whom were monks, were executed in cold blood.[41] Concurrent with the Stalinist Great Purges in the Soviet Union, these mass executions were predominantly based on fabricated counter-revolutionary charges, often involving torture. All these measures were taken in a fanatical pursuit of the grand myth that the country could create an earthly paradise by cleansing society of any remnants of the old regime's beliefs and practices. In other words, representatives of the old regime, including monks, aristocracy, merchants, and anyone who did not believe in the communist myth, were cast not only as sources of pollution but also as obstacles to social evolution.

Armed with new myths and knowledge and motivated by anti-Buddhist ideology, the People's Revolutionary Party initiated a broader cultural campaign known as *soyolyn dovtolgoon*. This campaign aimed to eradicate superstition while simultaneously improving sanitation, promoting secular education, and spreading a socialist worldview among the population. Within this context, revolutionaries banned open-air burials and viewed dogs, particularly strays, as potential carriers of zoonotic diseases such as rabies, ringworm, brucellosis, and others. While Buddhist dogma primarily regarded dogs as spiritually impure beings, socialist dogma asserted that dogs were contagious biological species, with mouths teeming with harmful bacteria. Thus, the state embarked on a mission to exterminate dogs in the name of public health. Between 1950 and 1960, a series of dog-killing campaigns were carried out, resulting in a staggering decline in their numbers. In the 1920s, the estimated canine population ranged from 200,000 to 300,000. However, by the end of these decade-long campaigns, these numbers had plummeted to a mere 10,000 to 20,000, according to

---

41 Kaplonski, *The Lama Question*.

some sources.[42] Unlike the mass executions under 'Mongolia's Stalin', Choibalsan, which ceased in the late 1930s with the threat dissipating after the dictator's death in 1952, the dog-hunting operations continued throughout the socialist era, albeit not to the same extent.

While the state's dog-hunting campaigns were framed as a public health measure, they inadvertently intersected with Mongolia's deep-rooted hunting traditions. Unlike these mass exterminations driven by socialist ideology, traditional hunting had long been a respected practice, embedded in Mongolia's cultural fabric. Traditionally, hunting has been a predominantly male pursuit, closely linked to practical endeavors such as procuring food, protecting livestock from predators, and fostering camaraderie among fellow hunters. Beyond these practicalities, hunting was also viewed as a romantic adventure, where a hunter could uplift his spirits, sharpen his manly skills, and sing melancholic songs of a distant beloved. This sentiment is beautifully expressed in the popular 'Hunter's Song', composed by the renowned writer Damdinsüren Tsendiin (1908–86), who drew inspiration from folk motifs. This song can be performed with the techniques of throat singing, where the singer generates two pitches simultaneously—both high and low—mimicking sounds from nature. In this way, the sentimental lyrics become part of the natural world, enveloped by the sounds of wind, water, or birds chirping:

> Many-colored flowers, blooming
> On Northern Mountain slopes,
> Are beautiful;
> My dearest, sweet girl,
> You are more beautiful than they.
>
> Brightly-colored flowers, thriving
> On Southern Mountain slopes,
> Are beautiful;
> My beloved, my girl,
> You are more beautiful than they.
>
> Many antlered deer, wandering
> On Hangai slopes,
> Are beautiful;
> My sweet girl, lovely girl,
> You are more beautiful than they.

---

42   Terbish, 'The Mongolian dog', 152.

Despite this traditional image, the socialist-era dog-hunter was far from the romanticized figure one might expect. It was incomprehensible for many, even those deeply enchanted by state ideology, to imagine hunters serenading love songs while slaughtering stray dogs in the dozens. The populace at large could not perceive the dog-hunters as anything but lowly, albeit necessary, killers. The childhood memories of many people from my generation, or those older than me who grew up in socialist Mongolia, include witnessing periodic dog-killing campaigns. During these campaigns, state-appointed hunters shot dogs dead and callously broke the necks of whining puppies, all before horrified onlookers.

With no religious specialists left to protect and impose knowledge about the disrupted occult order, dogs were stripped of their spiritual significance, especially in urban areas that were closely monitored by the state. As a result, people's apprehension about mistreating them waned. Growing up in an environment marked by atheism and an anti-sex ideology, and influenced by the brutal tactics exhibited by state-funded dog hunters, many teenagers and children engaged in acts of violence against dogs, often targeting stray or mating dogs in particular.

Anthropologists have extensively studied how cultures worldwide are in a perpetual state of change. Every culture harbors inherent contradictions that give rise to transformation, innovation, and exceptions. A general rule of thumb suggests that the more utopian and idealistic a culture or society appears on the surface, the more concealed contradictions it tends to harbor. Contrary to the image it projected, socialist Mongolia never exerted complete control over the population. Despite its professed image, the People's Revolutionary Party never held complete sway over the minds and hearts of the toilers and herders.

Much like certain animals that, when confronted by rivals, inflate themselves to appear larger and more intimidating than they truly are, the Party projected an image of omnipresence, omnipotence, and omniscience. Especially in remote regions where the Party's influence was limited and ideological indoctrination remained partial, many individuals felt little pressure to conform to politically correct behaviors and worldviews. For instance, despite being banned, people in the farthest corners of the countryside continued to practice open-air burials up until the 1960s, in which dogs retained their cosmological role of disposing of human remains. When their dogs passed away, many herders continued to place a piece of fat or ghee butter in the dog's mouth and cut off their tails as part of the old belief.

Previously, I discussed how in traditional societies like Mongolia, the concepts of culture, religion, and cosmology are intertwined, similar to Mexican nesting dolls where smaller figurines fit into larger ones. Each layer reflects elements of Mexican folklore, historical themes, and more. Consequently, removing one element inevitably impacts the others. In the case of socialist Mongolia, the state sought to remove Buddhism from the equation, surgically replacing it with a political ideology imported from the Soviet Union, while also attempting to alter aspects of national culture through a 'cultural campaign'. However, these efforts did not yield the clean results the state had anticipated. Not only did the state fail to eradicate Buddhism, but it also introduced new communist myths that coexisted with the cosmological thinking of the population. As a result, nomads continued to secretly view dogs through the lens of cosmological beliefs.

This coexistence of new and old beliefs and myths allowed a broader pattern where taboos and superstitions continued to be observed on a daily basis by socialist citizens. Here is a shortened list of such taboos: holding ones' arms behind the back, resting one's jaw on the hand, crossing one's arms, lifting legs upwards to the sky, spitting into fire, whistling inside the house or *ger*, washing hair after sunset, leaning against the door, singing or crying in bed, and discarding nails and cut hair on the ground. If Mongol citizens were unwilling to relinquish these and many similar superstitions from their daily lives, there was no real chance for the atheist state to fully control the people.

However, this does not mean that the phenomenon of socialist non-conformism inherently aimed to subvert the regime, nor did those who practiced forbidden rituals or followed taboos in daily life necessarily desire the overthrow of the state. On the contrary, socialist Mongol culture was a testament to the simultaneous existence of popular loyalty and resistance within the system, as was the case in other socialist countries. Socialist citizens displayed a remarkable capacity to adapt to the demands placed upon them for survival.

My father was one of many citizens who embodied this duality. As a loyal member of the People's Revolutionary Party, he diligently studied books on dialectical materialism, worshipped the Founding Fathers of the communist movement, and believed in the Party's myth of building an earthly paradise in Mongolia. Simultaneously, as a devout Buddhist, he conducted Buddhist rituals at home, recited mantras, performed simple Buddhist ceremonies, adhered to many daily taboos, and was a fan of folk medicine.

Sharik the Dog

Before continuing with the topic of the treatment of dogs in socialist Mongolia, I wish to share the story of one particular dog, who serves as an example of my father's belief in folk medicine involving dogs.

During my early teens, I had the misfortune of encountering a heap of white industrial fuel waste that had been dumped alongside the railway, which illustrated the authorities' disregard for the health and safety of the people. I mistook it for a pile of sand and joyously ran into the middle of it, only to realize what it really was, screaming in painful agony. As a result, both of my legs suffered severe burns, and I spent a couple of months unable to walk. My treatment regimen involved visits to a modern socialist hospital for dressing changes, but it was complemented by a folk remedy that my father administered at home. To carry out this alternative treatment, we enlisted the help of a male mongrel that lived outside our apartment block, whom I fed and played with. In fact, I had known the mongrel from its puppyhood—when it was just a few days old, my siblings and I sheltered it, along with other pups from its litter, in our flat during a dog hunting campaign. Due to its yellow fur and ball-like complexion, we named it Sharik, the Russian word for 'ball'. As Sharik grew up, it became a yard dog, treating our apartment block and its vicinity as its territory by marking it through urination, chasing away other dogs, and playing with the local children. When my father decided that I needed a traditional treatment involving dog's blood, Sharik was the obvious choice. Using scissors, my father carefully cut Sharik's ears, collecting the blood in a cup. He then applied this blood to my wounds, reciting Buddhist mantras during the process. After several sessions, the treatment concluded, and I began to recover. Sharik, who played a crucial role in this folk remedy, became a possessor of ears drooping like a mop.

After donating blood for my treatment, Sharik assumed a new role as caretaker for our youngest baby brother. Diligently, it guarded our brother's stroller, standing watchful and protective. Despite its services, our father, a deeply traditional man, never let Sharik inside our flat, though I would sneak the dog in whenever my parents were out. The only other time Sharik was allowed into my father's office was during another round of a dog-killing campaign, when it was wounded in the head and lost its right eye. My father and I nursed Sharik back to health. In order to protect Sharik from future threats, my father made a crucial decision: he sent Sharik to live with his elder sister in the administrative center of Dundgobi Province in Southern Mongolia. In retrospect, it was a wise decision, as all of Sharik's siblings who stayed behind were killed one by one in consecutive dog-killing campaigns, leaving Sharik as the only survivor from its litter. In Dundgobi Province, Sharik endeared itself to my aunt's family, becoming their cherished companion and protector of their *ger* for several years until it was tragically struck by a car on its right side, where the poor dog had lost eyesight. One of my aunt's sons took Sharik to the countryside, where he performed the final ritual owed to Sharik by his family— cutting its tail and placing it beneath the head as a symbolic pillow for its next reincarnation as a human.

Dogs, Ghosts, and Socialism

My father also cut the tails off dead dogs. I witnessed him doing this several times after dog-killing campaigns. After cutting the tail, he would send the carcass to his elder sister in Dundgobi Province, who had adopted Sharik. One of her other sons suffered from a respiratory disease. In Mongol folk medicine, dog meat is believed to be beneficial for respiratory conditions like tuberculosis, bronchitis, and pneumonia. After receiving the meat, my father's sister would prepare food, usually dumplings, in an attempt to cure her son. However, despite consuming numerous dogs, his condition never improved.

From these examples, it should be evident that my father also believed in ghosts, omens, wrathful places, and the afterlife just as strongly as he believed in the communist myths about perfect humans, social evolution culminating in communism, and the power of Lenin's tomb. He was also an avid listener and storyteller of *bolson yavdal* tales, and he saw no contradiction in embracing seemingly opposing worldviews. Similar to many members of his extended family, with whom I was well acquainted, my father possessed the ability to compartmentalize his religiosity from his communist convictions. In social sciences and psychology, this cognitive approach is also referred to as 'cognitive dissonance', where individuals simultaneously accept two or more mutually contradictory beliefs or behaviors as valid. While this might be perceived as a failure of human reasoning, cognitive dissonance should, in reality, be celebrated as one of the most crucial strengths of human cognition. Not only does it help individuals to stay sane, but it also enables us to sustain societies and cultures that are inherently self-contradictory.

Considering the circumstances, it is understandable that many dogs in Mongolia continued to receive traditional treatments from socialist families who believed in ghosts, reincarnation, and the supernatural. These traditional views toward dogs were more pronounced in rural areas, where herders were more committed to traditional values compared to their urban counterparts. This divergence in attitudes and practices not only reflected the urban-rural divide but also underscored generational differences, with the older generation adhering to a more traditional lifestyle and the younger generation embracing new communist ideals.

Factors such as social status, geographical location, and personal aspirations played significant roles in shaping how people perceived and treated animals, even within a supposedly classless, egalitarian society like socialist Mongolia. In this society, there was no official distinction between the rich and the poor, no ideological differentiation between the urban and the rural, and everyone was equal when they pledged their unwavering loyalty to the communist cause. If we were to peel back this façade, in urban areas, including Ulaanbaatar, a majority of citizens resided in traditional *gers* in proletarian neighborhoods. These households, characterized by limited resources, educational opportunities, and patriotic ambitions compared to their better-off counterparts in more upscale apartment blocks, typically kept one dog for purely utilitarian purposes like protection from thieves. In fact, theft was just one item on a long list of things that were not even supposed to exist in a proletarian paradise but nevertheless persisted.

This non-comprehensive list included black markets, prostitution, corruption, rampant alcoholism, income inequality, oppressive bureaucracy, shortages of consumer goods, dissent and opposition, political repression, and economic inefficiencies. Rather than grabbing the bull by the horns, the socialist state often chose to sweep this extensive array of embarrassing issues under the rug, maintaining the façade that they did not exist. As a result, dogs in these downscale *ger* neighborhoods were not pampered pets but rather served as walking alarm systems against thieves and intruders, always on high alert and often just as hungry and angry.

Yet, it is important to highlight that not all urban dogs, whose treatment was heavily influenced by state ideology, endured hardships during this period. The post-World War II era marked a period of rapid urbanization in Mongolia, increased cultural exchange with the Soviet Union, and the arrival of Soviet specialists en masse who brought their pets with them. These developments prompted young, cosmopolitan Mongol families, often educated in the Soviet Union and enjoying more spacious apartments and financial resources, to welcome dogs into their modern, secular households. In doing so, they copied the behaviors of Soviet specialists, who were not only respected for their technical expertise but also seen as cultural trendsetters. Having pets at home became a hallmark of being 'cultured', 'sophisticated', and 'atheistic'. Socialist Mongol culture among these elites in Ulaanbaatar was a Soviet copycat. These lucky dogs now enjoyed lives akin to those of Party officials, without any need to aspire to reincarnate as humans in their subsequent lives. They shared living spaces with humans, dozed off in rooms warmed by centralized heating, dined on cooked meat, bathed in running water, reveled in affectionate kisses from their owners, and even had the privilege of tasting divine ghee butter— activities that would have been utterly unimaginable just a few decades earlier.

State socialism also placed a strong emphasis on the value of collective, productive labor, and loyalty to the Party, demanding that every citizen be dedicated to the communist cause and contribute according to their abilities. This principle extended to a degree to working dogs as well. The practice of employing dogs as working animals was nothing new in Mongolia, as their historical roles as message carriers and caravan alarm systems dated back to the pre-revolutionary era. However, it was during the socialist period that specific breeds, most notably the German Shepherd, gained widespread recognition for their roles in the security and military sectors, including the people's police, national prisons, and armed forces.

To lionize military dogs and showcase their contribution to safeguarding the socialist Motherland, the state organized *Public Dog Shows* starting in 1963, which continued throughout the socialist period. These shows served as a platform to celebrate the vital contributions of these canines and their human handlers to the collective welfare and safety of the nation.[43] Many organizations involved in state security and policing proudly displayed propagandic paintings at their entrances depicting patriotic servicemen alongside their loyal dogs. Among these professions closely tied to security, the most clandestine, indoctrinated, murderous, and feared was that of the secret police. Their roles encompassed suppressing dissent, instilling fear in the population, keeping an eye on the country's moral climate, and counteracting foreign ideology. Under the leadership of 'Mongolia's Stalin', Choibalsan, the secret police became the primary organization responsible for carrying out tortures and mass executions modelled after the Soviet Union's Great Purges. It was no coincidence that, as a group doggedly loyal to the country's leadership and perceived as constantly poking their noses around to make a kill, they were despised and commonly referred to by the populace as 'dogs', a tag that endures to this day.

State of Dogs After State Socialism

Mongolia's sagacious leadership held an unwavering belief throughout the socialist era that the gravest threat to their cherished socialism stemmed from nefarious Western imperialists and their minions. Little did they know that they were barking up the wrong tree. The mortal danger they faced did not emerge from foreign adversaries but from the very beating heart of the communist world—the Kremlin itself.

While initially planned as a quick restructuring of the centralized socialist system, *perestroika*, initiated by the country's leader Mikhail Gorbachev, quickly spiraled out of control, paralyzing the entire system

---

43 Shürhüü, *Mongol Ulsyn Tsagdaagiin Erelch Nohoin Albany Tüüh.*

and hastening its demise in the Soviet Union. This reverberated across the entire socialist bloc, including Mongolia, opening the doors to a resurgence of traditional ideas and practices. In Mongolia, leading this revival were nationalists and religious specialists who had emerged from the underground, closely followed by dogs, whose spiritual significance experienced a renaissance of its own.

Amidst the post-socialist chaos and against the backdrop of a religious revival, in 1998, a documentary film titled *State of Dogs* (*Nohoin Oron*) was screened in cinemas. This groundbreaking creation garnered international recognition, winning two dozen prestigious film awards. However, it was received less favorably in Mongolia, where many patriotic viewers felt the film portrayed the country in a denigrating light.

Set against the haunting backdrop of post-socialist Ulaanbaatar, the film tells the heart-wrenching story of Basar, a dog slain in cold blood by a dog hunter. In the wake of its death, Basar embarks on a roller-coaster journey through the maze of its own memories, seemingly uninterested in progressing to a human life.

As Basar steps through the threshold into the afterworld and embarks on a chaotic journey through the maze of its memories— leaping back and forth between the realms of the dead and the living— the ambiguous conclusion of the dog's soul's odyssey coincides with another event: the birth of a baby. This follows a striking scene in which a female contortionist twists and bends her body into extraordinary positions. This convergence raises three compelling possibilities for viewers to ponder.

Firstly, Basar's soul may have ultimately resolved to reincarnate as a human being (a message the filmmakers described as their goal in interviews). Alternatively, the film's surrealistic narrative might suggest that there is no intrinsic link between Basar's passing and the birth of the baby, with the dog's death symbolizing the end of state socialism and the birth of the child representing the emergence of a new post-socialist society. However, the third interpretation, the most intriguing of all, proposes a departure from convention. In this interpretation, Basar's journey culminates in a decision that defies norms: disinterested in embracing human life, the dog opts not to be reborn as a human.

In the last interpretation of the film's conclusion, Basar's choice not to return to post-socialist Mongolia can be perceived as a poignant commentary on the devaluation of human life during an era when the country grappled with a profound economic, social, and identity crisis, marked by widespread poverty, soaring unemployment, and an escalating issue of alcohol abuse and general violence. This raised a thought-provoking question: Was this human existence truly superior to that of a dog? Many Mongols, myself included, interpreted the film in this pessimistic manner.

To offer a glimpse into life during the early 1990s, let me share a personal experience. During that period, Mongolia grappled with unprecedented food shortages and rationing. One summer, during my teenage years, I visited my paternal aunt and her family in Dundgobi Province—a place I had often frequented, not least because I was always eager to see Sharik the dog. Hosting guests, even relatives, was a significant burden for everyone. My hosts, accustomed to having just one meal a day, left me eagerly anticipating that single daily meal. To bridge the gap between morning tea and a modest dinner, I began visiting the local dining hall every noon, where very few could afford to dine out. I kept my visits a secret, as my hosts playfully teased me, believing I managed well on their meager offerings. That summer, my aunt's family openly increased their dinner portion only when they slaughtered a sheep. They consumed the meat themselves but sold the sheep's intestines to a man named Mr. Muunohoi (meaning 'Bad Dog'), who had a large family of seven or eight young, hungry mouths to feed. With melancholic, mischievous eyes and a big smile infused with angelic charm that lit up his face, Mr. Bad Dog must have been a good-looking man in his youth, somewhat resembling the British actor Hugh Grant. Grant, among his accomplishments, as many would know, made headlines in 1995 when he was arrested in Los Angeles at the height of his fame for engaging in sexual activity with a prostitute in a car in a residential area. In retrospect, when I saw Mr. Bad Dog in the early 1990s, he resembled the Hugh Grant of the 2020s, who, having developed deep facial wrinkles recently, raised many eyebrows by jokingly calling himself 'basically a scrotum' onstage at the 2023 Oscars. Unlike Hugh Grant, Mr. Bad Dog could never afford to purchase lean meat, and local families sold him the less expensive intestines as a gesture of support for his struggling family. While most families lived from hand to mouth, every neighborhood had their own Mr. 'Bad Dog', who were even worse off. So, let me reiterate a question that was in the minds of many: Was it worth it for any dead dog to reincarnate into a human with the possibility of becoming a Mr. Bad Dog or Mrs. Single-Meal-A-Day in its next life? If only a few years ago, most Mongols had proudly believed they were living in an earthly paradise for toilers and herders on the steppes, it was unimaginable that they would now find themselves eking out an existence in the desolate State of Dogs.

The film was produced during a period when Mongolia had overcome some of the most challenging years of its post-socialist transition but was still caught in the space between historical epochs. It was also a time when the country embarked on a mission to revive its pre-revolutionary customs, notably the practice of open-air burials resurrected in certain remote parts of Mongolia, including Western Mongolia. In contrast to pre-revolutionary times, in post-socialist Mongolia, dogs were no longer designated as human corpse scavengers. Many nomadic families who embraced this traditional burial practice laid their loved ones to rest far from human settlements, ensuring that no dogs, whether stray or those living in nomadic camps, could access these burial grounds. The documentary film, while not delving into all the intricacies of these developments, subtly hinted at broader transformations by showcasing people's open acknowledgement of the dog's spirituality.

What made the film truly exceptional, in my view, was its skillful use of allusion. It artfully raised yet another profound question without explicitly stating it: Would the dog killer face supernatural consequences for his actions? This question held significant weight, given the resurgence of *bolson yavdal* stories linking misfortune to dog killings during that era. Remarkably, the film refrained from directly addressing this question, allowing viewers the space to reflect and form their own interpretations.

Resurging Beliefs and Stray Dog Management

The 1990s was a time when the state's ability to consistently fund stray dog-hunting operations was severely limited, leading to a proliferation of the canine population across the country. However, since the mid-2000s, with an improving economy, these operations have resumed uninterrupted. Although many people continue mistreating dogs, a legacy of the socialist past, the resurgence of fear surrounding actual dog killings has the potential to disrupt them. For instance, the municipality of Darhan, a town with a population of around 75,000 people, found itself in a situation where it struggled to find enough local individuals willing to carry out stray dog control measures, even when offered payment. The municipality offered a generous MNT 5000 (USD 4) for each dog killed, while the average monthly salary for civil servants was MNT 300,000 (USD 250). To address this 'pest control' problem, the town had to invite a dog-hunting brigade from Ulaanbaatar, making headlines in 2011. In Ulaanbaatar itself, a city with a population of roughly two million, the municipality employed eleven contracted dog hunters in 2012. These hunters, self-styled as 'dog executioners', claimed to have exterminated a staggering 69,000 stray dogs in the capital in 2012 alone, though this number was likely inflated.

Ulaanbaatar is unique in the region because approximately half of its residents live in nomadic *ger* districts, lacking streetlights and resembling labyrinths, which provide ideal breeding grounds and hiding places for stray dogs. Today, the city municipality receives support from private dog-hunting firms bearing ominous or grandiose names like Bazalt Negdel ('Squeeze Cooperative') and Mönhbuyan Orgil ('Eternal Blessing Summit'). These firms have stepped in, motivated both by financial incentives[44] and a sense of patriotic duty. In the first half of 2023, city authorities reported culling 29,671 stray dogs and cats combined, a more realistic number.

As of 2023, an estimated 160,000 stray dogs roam Ulaanbaatar, a stark contrast to the 48,128 registered home-owned pets. Around 70 percent of these strays inhabit *ger* districts, with 20-25 percent in industrial and commercial areas, and the rest scattered across high-rise districts. This sizable population of stray dogs, surviving on discarded waste and uncollected garbage, highlights the severity of the problem. Despite government-led dog control campaigns, the stray dog population continues to increase, primarily because the general populace is unwilling to resort to killing.

The presence of a large number of strays has strained the relationship between dogs and humans. Every year, hundreds of people fall victim

---

44 In 2013, the fee for each dog culled was raised to MNT 7500; in 2016, it increased to MNT 12,000; and by 2023, it had reached a further MNT 24,000.

to dog attacks. In 2021, Ulaanbaatar alone recorded 1421 dog bites, including 266 cases involving children aged five to nine. Although there have been extensive dog culling efforts nationwide, the number of serious misfortunes linked to dog killings, as recounted in *bolson yavdal* stories, remains relatively low. This disparity can be attributed to the fact that these campaigns are orchestrated by the faceless state with the assistance of a handful of hunters. The main characters in such stories are often dog hunters themselves, drivers involved in accidents with dogs but who didn't undergo the necessary purification rituals, or foreigners unfamiliar with Mongol ancestral wisdom. Acts like beating or kicking stray dogs in self-defense are not perceived as sins or offenses, resulting in a scarcity of stories depicting suffering due to self-defense actions against dogs.

Here is a relevant *bolson yavdal* story that reportedly unfolded in the early 1990s in Töv Province of Central Mongolia. In a certain locale, there lived an abandoned female dog. During a recent operation, the dog hunters, known for their ruthless methods, subjected the bitch to a barrage of gunshots, stabbings, and even skinning. Yet, the cunning canine miraculously survived and thrived, much like the protagonist Sarah Connor in the movie *Terminator*, who escapes the relentless pursuit of a killer machine played by Arnold Schwarzenegger. The bitch's astonishing display of survival endowed her with an aura of supernatural power and invincibility, earning her a place of reverence among the local elders. Whenever they witnessed the bitch's presence, the elders would ritually offer her a libation of milk as if to a deity. The bitch, now considered divine, roamed around freely, occasionally playing with other dogs and even copulating with wolves at will. Given the situation, none of the local residents dared to harm or interfere with this extraordinary canine, except for a newly arrived Chinese man with a peculiar culinary taste. He saw an opportunity to satisfy his appetite by partaking of the exotic, 'undead' dog's meat. The Chinese man was seen walking down the street, quite pleased with himself, much like a cat that had swallowed a canary. However, soon he became uneasy and restless, like a cat on a hot tin roof. Upon his return to Ulaanbaatar, the man was subjected to divine retribution and began exhibiting even more erratic behavior, including barking and growling like a dog. It wasn't long before he found himself in an asylum after returning to his homeland in China. As for the survivor bitch, locals observed her casually sniffing and urinating on the vegetable plot of the Chinese man, mere days after she had apparently been served as a hotdog on his plate.

In this *bolson yavdal*, a remarkable transformation unfolds as an abandoned and mistreated bitch triumphs over adversities, rising to a divine status. Yet, a crucial message of this moral tale is that not only are those who harm dogs punished, but it also sheds light on the shaggy-dog stories that many Mongols are willing to accept at face value. Belief in *bolson yavdal* stories, though seemingly illogical to some, often originates from deeply personal experiences. Growing up in or being exposed to a religious environment lays the foundation for accepting the existence of miraculous beings and supernatural powers. This upbringing provides comfort and explanations, rendering tales of divine canines and extraordinary beings entirely plausible as one matures.

When someone has faith in miracles, divine beings, and supernatural occurrences, it becomes less psychologically challenging for them to accept less peculiar nationalistic myths, such as a nation's divine destiny, spiritual superiority, chosenness, and the purity of nationalist bloodlines. In fact, the stronger one's belief in miracles and cosmic fate, the more likely they are to embrace toxic nationalism. Historically, societies dominated by religious institutions often fostered a sense of exceptionalism, believing in their superiority and the exclusivity of their way of life. Notably, some modern secular societies, such as the Soviet Union and socialist Mongolia, mirrored this mindset due to their adherence to totalitarian ideology (I'll revisit the subjects of Leninism-Stalinism in Chapter 3). In post-socialist Mongolia, where efforts to instill democratic values coexist with the resurgence of religious dogmatism and idealization of its socialist past, a fertile ground has emerged for toxic nationalism to thrive, a topic we delve into next.

Nationalism and Xenophobia in Democracy

In Mongolia, as in many post-socialist states, the collapse of state socialism led to a complex resurgence of nationalism. This phenomenon, though democratic in its resistance against authoritarianism and its myths, was also deeply conservative, aiming to revive pre-socialist customs and myths. This duality created a contradiction: the state, while ostensibly championing democratic principles, simultaneously fostered toxic ethno-nationalism and intolerance toward cultural diversity, falsely attributing these values to pre-socialist Mongolia. This stark contradiction undermined the democratic ideals it claimed to uphold.

One significant challenge that Mongolia's democratic aspirations face is the pervasive xenophobia, particularly Sinophobia—a fear and suspicion of the Chinese that often borders on hatred—which permeates various sectors of society, including nationalists, politicians, academics, and the general populace. This xenophobic sentiment often stems from a myth portraying the Chinese as primordial adversaries aiming to exploit and subjugate Mongolia. However, contemporary Sinophobia, whereby all Chinese are regarded as a monolithic mass plotting to undermine Mongolia, did not emerge from prehistoric origins, as nationalists claim, but has a more recent and nuanced genealogy.

To recount the origins of modern nationalism in a nutshell: the Mongol aristocracy long considered China a part of Greater Mongolia, after losing control of it in 1368. After subsequently submitting to the Manchu Qing in 1691, Mongolia became part of a larger empire that encompassed China, Tibet, and Xinjiang. Within the empire, Mongolia remained a separate administrative region, maintaining relative autonomy in internal affairs, which allowed traditional ways of life to continue uninterrupted. To support this, restrictions on movement across the Mongolia-China border kept the Mongols largely segregated from the rest of China. However, in the early twentieth century, the Qing government reversed this policy, permitting unrestricted Chinese settlement in Mongolia. This alarmed Mongol elites who were concerned about their pastureland and way of life, which were crucial for their power and legitimacy. Despite grievances against rapacious Chinese merchants, Mongols generally did not view ordinary Chinese as inherently malicious, inferior, greedy, or 'stinky'. Notably, unrestricted Chinese settlement never materialized, and the Qing collapsed in 1912.

During the first half of the socialist era, Mongolia actively fostered friendship with its southern neighbor, communist China, promoting proletarian internationalism despite occasional bilateral strains. However, this policy changed during the Sino-Soviet rift in the 1960s. Anxious to tiptoe the official Soviet line, Mongolian authorities vilified China and its people as 'revisionist' and traitors to the true spirit of communism as envisioned by the Communist Party of the Soviet Union.

As a result, Soviet troops were stationed in Mongolia to protect the country from a potential Chinese aggression.

The term Pavlovian conditioning (or classical conditioning) comes from the famous experiments of Russian scientist Ivan Pavlov, who discovered that dogs could be taught to associate a neutral sound, like a bell, with the arrival of food. Before long, the dogs in his lab started salivating at the sound of the bell alone, without any food in sight. Humans aren't all that different. Pavlovian conditioning plays a major role in how we pick up social behaviors and form emotional responses, whether positive or negative. During the Soviet era, Mongols, exposed to a steady stream of Soviet propaganda, began associating the Chinese with negative ideas. Just like Pavlov's dogs responded to bells, Mongols were led through repeated messages to develop negative stereotypes about China and its people.

Although anti-Chinese sentiments and stereotypes simmered beneath the surface like a distant Pavlovian bell during the socialist era, they blared uncontrollably like a fire alarm after the collapse of state socialism. While the new democratic government tried to turn down the volume, attempting to improve economic and political relations with China, the newly liberated nationalist media acted like a deafening loudspeaker, amplifying these negative feelings. China's increasing regional posturing, coupled with Mongolia's growing economic dependence on China, has only intensified Sinophobia, adding fuel to the fire.

The Mongols' apprehension toward China, however, is not merely a product of imagination, or Pavlovian-type conditioning, or false memories implanted by Soviet propaganda, but also has tangible foundations that made Soviet propaganda effective in the first place. In Chinese political thinking and historiography, periods of imperial unity under a single dynasty are typically presented as golden ages of order and unity, while times of political fragmentation are characterized as dark ages of chaos and disunity. This perspective significantly influences Chinese historical interpretation, not only viewing foreign-originated dynasties like the Yuan Mongols (1271-1368) and Manchu Qing (1644-1912) as 'Chinese' but also encouraging efforts to reunify territories after an empire's collapse.

After the collapse of the Yuan, the succeeding Ming dynasty claimed most territories previously under the Yuan, although they primarily tried to keep the Mongol barbarians north of the Great Wall by strengthening it. Dubbed the Ming Great Wall, this part forms the most visible sections of the Great Wall today. In contrast, following the Manchu Qing's demise in 1912 and Mongolia's declaration of independence a year earlier, modern China, which sees itself as the heir to the Qing, regarded Mongolia as part of its territory and attempted to reunify Mongolia with mainland China. Chinese nationalist troops occupied Mongolia in 1919, and it was not until 1949 that China, under Soviet pressure, grudgingly recognized Mongolia's independence. However, this did not stop China from opposing Mongolia's 1955 application to become a member of the United Nations, citing the grounds that China viewed Mongolia as part of its historical territory. Mongolia managed to join the United Nations in 1961 after the Soviet Union intervened by using its formidable political and bargaining firepower.

Many Mongols are aware of this recent history and harbor deep concerns about China's growing ambitions and presumed long-term goals of annexing Mongolia. While the idea of annexing Mongolia has been voiced by Chinese nationalists since 1912, Mongols widely believe that China's plans to annex the country and humiliate the Mongols have been a longstanding 'secret' policy dating back to ancient times.

Sinophobia influences how Mongols in Mongolia perceive other related groups living outside the country. Beyond Mongolia, various Mongol communities are scattered across several countries, including China, Russia, and Kyrgyzstan. China has the largest Mongol population, estimated at six million, followed by over three million in Mongolia, one million in Russia, and a smaller group of around 20,000 in Kyrgyzstan. Mongols in Mongolia often harbor suspicions about the authenticity of Mongols in China, viewing them as less 'genuine' due to the lasting impact of Chinese influence and intermarriage over generations. These sentiments are particularly strong among those Mongols in Mongolia who lack direct interactions with their counterparts across the Mongolia-China border, often leading to deeply ingrained negative perceptions.

Given the situation, it is not difficult to guess that in Mongolia, Sinophobia has placed mixed-race individuals, especially those born to a Chinese father and a Mongol mother, in a precarious situation.

Referred to as *erliiz* in Mongolian, these individuals are perceived as having 'impure' blood, making them prone to stabbing the Mongolian Motherland in the back in service of a foreign nation.

Erliiz people are often juxtaposed against 'real Mongols'. In the nationalist imagination, 'a real Mongol woman' is idealized similarly to the Madonna in Western culture, symbolizing purity, beauty, compassion, loyalty, and submissiveness. In a similar vein, 'a real Mongol man' is hyper-masculinized, imbued with superior mental qualities, a strong body, patriotism, and sexual propriety and virility. However, it is not only *erliiz* who are measured against these idealized images; any Mongol person who does not fit these propaganda standards can also be excluded and have their Mongolness questioned. One method used in this exclusion is the 'No True Mongol' fallacy (modelled after the 'No True Scotsman' fallacy). This fallacy can be illustrated in the following imaginary scenario: *Bazar opens a newspaper and reads about a Kazakh sexual maniac detained by the police in the town of Mörön in Western Mongolia. During the interrogation, it was revealed that the maniac not only raped young women but also engaged in lovemaking with his dog. Shocked, Bazar exclaims, 'What a moron! No Mongol man would do this!' The next morning, while enjoying his tea, Bazar opens a newspaper and reads an even more bizarre story—this time about a Mongol sexual maniac arrested on the other side of the country, in the village of Mörön in Eastern Mongolia. Before the police even could interrogate him, the man admitted not only to brutally raping many elderly women but also sexually terrorizing local ewes, goats, and dogs, making the actions of the Kazakh maniac seem almost saintly by comparison. Bazar exclaims, 'Well, no real Mongol man would do this!'*

It goes without saying that the 'real Mongol man' or 'real Mongol woman' in nationalist myths don't represent flesh-and-blood individuals with diverse interests, backgrounds, moral values, and weaknesses. Rather, both are one-dimensional, mythical figures embodying a set of idealized characteristics, much like the *erliiz* embodies an imaginary figure with vilified traits.

Given the situation, nothing is more revolting and dangerous to Mongol nationalists, as well as many ordinary citizens, than the prospect of sexual relations and marriage between Mongol women and Chinese men. Real or suspected instances of sexual intercourse between these two groups often elicit vehement emotional reactions among many good Mongols, escalating at times into outright physical violence. A particularly prominent ultra-nationalist group, known as *Dayar Mongol* ('Universal Mongolia'), distinguished itself in the 1990s by actively disseminating Sinophobic articles in newspapers and organizing controversial press conferences, issuing stern warning to Mongol women against engaging in romantic relationships with Chinese men. In 2009, the ultra-nationalists unleashed their 'inner chimps' and carried out their long-delayed threat by releasing a YouTube video in which a member of the group is shown forcefully shaving the head of a Mongol woman with an electric shaver, claiming she was a whore who had fornicated with a Chinese man. The group used this act as a form of public naming and shaming. Similar to other groups of its kind, *Dayar Mongol* members are virulently patriarchal and advocate aggressive Sinophobia and the protection of the purity of Mongol blood. Unlike many nationalist movements, the group venerates Adolf Hitler, wears Nazi attire, and gives the Sieg Heil salute to each other. Despite their spine-chilling uniforms and rituals, these Mongol Nazis come across more like a bunch of incessant chatterboxes and undisciplined loiterers. Their 'wonder weapon' arsenal includes nothing more than noisy threats, electric shavers, graffiti sprays, and ultra-nationalist fists. However, given the present circumstances, these Hitler worshippers should exercise maximum caution not to attract the attention of Russia's President Vladimir Putin, nicknamed 'Vladolf Putler', who, having invaded Ukraine since February 2022, might be tempted to invade another post-socialist neighbor in a similar fashion, using the pretext of *Dayar Mongol* to 'denazify' and 'liberate' Mongolia.

The apprehension and skepticism directed towards *erliiz* individuals, understood to have 'impure' blood and being somewhat 'degenerate', not coincidentally, found a parallel in the post-socialist era's treatment of dogs. Consequently, an increasing number of people are now advocating for measures to protect the 'pure' Mongol dogs, mirroring their calls to preserve the 'pure' ethnic blood from perceived contamination.

Dogs in Nationalist Discourse

An episode from the radio series titled *Tengeriin Güür* ('Heavenly Bridge'), broadcast in 1993, provides insight into this nationalist mindset. Dedicated to the preservation of the 'pure' breed of Mongol dogs, the program's host began her broadcast with this assertion:

> There is evidence to suggest that the Mongol dog is the oldest breed. In other words, there is no dog like the Mongol one in the world. The Mongol dog has a deep and strong voice, beefy flesh, a big head and muzzle, hanging ears and round eyes. Its neck is thick, its chest is wide, and it has a powerful and big body. Its tail is hairy and its paws are big. The dog has only two colors: The first is black with a white patch on its chest, and the other is what we call *dörvön nüdtei* ('with four eyes').[45]

According to the program's host, the Mongol dog not only boasts an aesthetically pleasing appearance but also exhibits the following admirable moral characteristics:

> It not only looks after the livestock and protects the household, but it also does not leave young animals, such as lambs and goat kids, without protection. In stormy weather, the dog leads its owners and livestock back to the safety of the household. Wolves are afraid of its barking.[46]

The entire program unfolded as an animated contest among its participants, each vying to outshine the others in their praise of Mongol dogs. Among the guests was Tömörjav, the passionate director of the Agricultural Institute, who ardently advocated for the visual and auditory prowess of Mongol dogs. He emphatically pointed out, 'European dogs can only see up to 300 meters, whereas the Mongol dog boasts an eye-popping vision range of 500-700 meters'. Following a prerecorded interview with another enthusiast extolling the virtues of Mongol dogs, the host gracefully concluded the program. She reminded listeners that 'it's widely believed that dogs of pure lineage are a rare find anywhere, and the Mongol dog is a shining example of pure breed'.[47] This broadcast captured the nation's attention, especially considering

---

45 Terbish, 'The Mongolian dog as an intimate other', 156.
46 Ibid.
47 Ibid.

that every household was equipped with a mandatory radio, which was customarily kept turned on at all times to receive news and directives from the people's government.

In subsequent radio and television programs as well as newspaper articles, Mongol dogs continued to receive lavish praise. This adoration showed no signs of diminishing as time passed.

Historically, as previously noted, the first written reference to domesticated dogs can be found in *The Secret History of the Mongols*. According to modern nationalists, the domesticated dogs mentioned in this historical account were a 'pure' breed of Mongol dogs. However, the imperial annals do not provide specific details about whether Mongols kept different breeds. It only makes mention of 'Tibetan dogs' (*tobudut noqat*), characterized by their large, shaggy coat and ferocious nature, bred in the Tibetan mountains to guard livestock from predators.[48] The imperial annals underscore the reputation of Tibetan dogs for their ferocity in the expanding Mongol empire.

Interestingly, the dog known today in Mongolia as the *banhar*, often considered a 'pure' Mongol breed, does not appear under its name in historical records. Nevertheless, this absence does not necessarily imply that this breed, possibly under a different name, did not exist. In fact, there is some evidence from later periods suggesting that this dog was kept by the Mongols in the Ilkhanate state founded by Hülegü.[49]

Furthermore, *The Secret History of the Mongols* sheds light on another breed of wild dog known as *tsoovor* or Asiatic wild dog (Cuon alpinus).[50] Mongols recognized these creatures for their strong sense of social cooperation and their collective defense of their lairs. Notably, Genghis Khan's grandson, Kubilai, the founder of the Yuan Dynasty in China (a period not covered in *The Secret History of the Mongols*), maintained an extensive collection of canines. Marco Polo documented Kubilai's possession of a diverse array of dogs, including hunting dogs, retrievers, greyhounds, and the formidable mastiff dogs (essentially Tibetan dogs). Additionally, among these working dogs, the Great Khan also kept a 'little dog' as a companion, likely a Pekingese.[51] It is worth emphasizing

---

48   *The Secret History of the Mongols* §141.
49   Gonchigiin, *Nüüdelchdiin Nohoi, II Devter*, 24-27.
50   *The Secret History of the Mongols* §78.
51   Polo, *The Description of the World*, 227.

that throughout history, particularly in the imperial era regarded as the Golden Age by today's nationalists, Mongols kept a diverse range of dogs, with no evidence supporting the classification of these dogs into categories of pure or superior breeds versus mixed or inferior breeds.

In more recent times, pre-revolutionary Mongols held the Pekingese breed in high regard without attaching notions of disloyalty or inferiority to them. Pekingese dogs were celebrated as some of the most charming and faithful canine companions,[52] challenging the contemporary nationalist perspective on 'non-Mongol' dog breeds.

In today's Mongolia, amidst ongoing discussions concerning purity and contamination, numerous societies, clubs, and enterprises are dedicated to preserving the 'pure' Mongol dog.[53] Dog enthusiasts also annually host the prestigious *Mongol Dog Competition*, exclusively for dogs of 'pure' Mongol lineage.[54] Dogs that deviate from the 'pure' Mongol breed standard are referred to as *erliiz nohoi* ('hybrids') or dogs with 'impure' lineage. In nationalist discourse, these *erliiz* dogs are often depicted as the antithesis of the 'pure' Mongol breed. They are deemed unsuitable for the challenging Mongolian climate and are considered lacking in bravery, loyalty, clairvoyance, physical endurance, and the instinct to care for livestock.

However, this contradicts my own experiences with *erliiz* dogs, of which Sharik is a typical example. He was a simple mongrel with short legs, a long body, and yellow fur. Despite his 'inferior' physical appearance and humble pedigree, he not only had iron balls, bravely confronting and often overpowering much larger dogs, but also proved exceptionally loyal to his owners. Additionally, he adapted remarkably well to Mongolia's harsh weather conditions. If he had lived in a nomadic camp close to livestock, I am certain he would have excelled as a guard dog, displaying strong instincts to protect his household, including both humans and livestock.

---

52 Humphrey, 'Some notes on the role of dogs', 14-15.
53 Notable organizations include The Society for the Study of the Mongol Dog, Mongol Nohoi Banhar, and Arslan, alongside dog-related businesses such as Ih Mongol, Alma, Asar Basar, Hotoch, Has, Goviin Haltar, and Dornod Mongol.
54 Dog enthusiasts also run a less prestigious event, the Champion Dog Competition, where participants are non-Mongol breeds. For instance, the 2018 show featured 403 dogs representing 30 different breeds.

Erliiz dogs parallel *erliiz* citizens, who are portrayed in a similar nationalist discourse as physically weak, conspiratorial, and worst of all, as possessing dual allegiances, thus serving as a soft underbelly of the Mongol nation. Their loyalty is believed to lie not with mighty Mongolia, protected by the Eternal Blue Sky, but with foreign nations, particularly China.

Conclusion

Humans, as primates possessing a bicameral (divided) brain with a small frontal lobe and large hormonal glands, exhibit a fascinating ability to hold mutually contradictory beliefs, a phenomenon known as 'cognitive dissonance'. Humans can also simultaneously be 'irrational' (or to nurture an 'inner chimp' to use Steve Peters' concept) and 'rational' as well as harbor conflicting emotions, such as love and hate, toward the same individual. This is eloquently depicted in the song 'I Hate You Then I Love You' by Celine Dion and Luciano Pavarotti.[55]

However, this inherent cognitive duality, far from being a weakness as some might argue, is a testament to the complexity of human reasoning, incorporating both our long evolutionary heritage in the animal kingdom and the 'humanizing' effects of culture. Rather than a failure, this unique ability to embrace conflicting beliefs and emotions serves as a vital mechanism, enabling humans to navigate the complex jungle of social interactions. It allows individuals to forge deep connections and sustain relationships despite contradictions and conflicts.

Just imagine a world where we lacked the power of cognitive dissonance and the ability to be both rational and irrational, and to

---

55   Here are some excerpts from the lyrics:
I'd like to run away from you
But if I were to leave you I would die
I'd like to break the chains you put around me
And yet I'll never try
No matter what you do you drive me crazy
I'd rather be alone
But then I know my life would be so empty
As soon as you have gone...
I hate you
Then I love you, I love you more
For whatever you do
I never, never, never
Want to be in love with anyone but you.

feel both reverence and ambivalence towards others. We wouldn't have soulful songs like 'I Hate You Then I Love You', no fictional stories or myths essential for literature and art, and definitely no religions or ideologies that hold together large, complex societies. In short, there would be no culture as we know it. We would be just another primate species, like our distant forebears, scrapping for survival, food, and the chance to copulate, competing with other members of the animal kingdom.

What fundamentally sets *Homo sapiens* apart is our unique ability to imagine and create a shared complex reality, sustained by our exceptional storytelling power. Our stories, reflective of our cognitive duality and rich imagination, can lead to diverse practices, the meanings of which can easily be lost in cultural translation.

Take love or esteem for others as an example. These emotions often result in admiration for the loved person. Love and admiration can be expressed differently across cultures, shaped by various stories and traditions. In European societies, love and admiration might manifest through romantic gestures such as heartfelt poetry, giving a guinea pig as a birthday present, or sharing good wine, food, and laughter. In Papua New Guinea, however, these emotions could be expressed in a vastly different way, such as through cannibalism.

In some societies that historically practiced cannibalism, including Papua New Guinea until the latter part of the twentieth century, this act was not performed out of a belief in the inferiority of the consumed. On the contrary, those consumed were often seen as fellow humans, frequently possessing superior qualities and powers. The stories told within these cultures justified the act by suggesting that one could acquire the powers of others by ingesting their flesh. It is not surprising, then, that forensic anthropological studies show that cannibalism was widespread in ancient human societies across the world.[56]

Symbolic cannibalism, which is another form of cannibalism, encompasses rituals where human remains or their representations are metaphorically consumed for various purposes. A notable example can be found in the Christian ritual of Communion, where the ingestion of bread and wine symbolically represents the flesh and blood of the

---

56 Gibbons, 'Archaeologists rediscover cannibals'.

God-turned-Sapiens entity. This ritual is rooted in a biblical story of divine love, where God, omnipotent, compassionate, and wise, endeavors to redeem humanity from its sins by no other means than by subjecting his son to crucifixion, a gruesome ordeal of limb impalement and agonizing death. Recognizing this act of violent sacrifice as a gift of divine mercy and love, and by symbolically partaking in the body of the crucified, believers seek salvation and eternal life.

This raises a question: If humans can simultaneously love and hate other humans and consume them, both literally and symbolically, why not extend these complex emotions and practices to animals perceived as human-like, half-human, or human-originated? The answer, unequivocally, is affirmative.

A Tale of Love and Hate?

This chapter shows the contradictory treatment of dogs in Mongol culture, where these animals are perceived as 'transitional beings', embodying both human-like and animal qualities. Cosmologically, they exist in a state of perpetual transformation, inching closer to becoming one of us. Hence, dogs are treated by humans in a manner reminiscent of how we treat one another. Not only is dog meat believed to have the power to give humans the vital breath of life by curing respiratory diseases, but these animals evoke a complex interplay of emotions, encompassing both love and hatred, reverence and ambivalence. However, unlike human-to-human relationships, where conflicting emotions often arise from shared history, interests, and unresolved issues, the love and hate directed towards dogs are largely ritualized and cosmologically compartmentalized. In Mongol culture, the love and reverence for dogs stems from their companionship, invaluable assistance in economic activities such as protecting livestock, aiding in hunting, and serving as alarm systems, as well as their perceived spiritual powers and human-like qualities. On the other hand, the hatred and ambivalence towards dogs finds its roots in beliefs surrounding their impurity and potential danger, concepts often defined within a cosmological framework.

During the socialist era, when cosmology was ridiculed as superstition and the cosmological bond between humans and dogs was severed, emotional and physical intimacy with dogs persisted, especially for pets and working dogs. Amidst this change, previously imposed bans and restrictions were lifted, allowing domesticated dogs to share living spaces and meals with people.

In stark contrast, stray dogs, stripped of their spiritual significance, were systematically hunted down in the name of public health and hygiene, labeled as impure animals from the perspective of modern veterinary science. This example demonstrates that the concept of impurity can be both cosmologically and 'scientifically' justified, and in both cases, it serves as an effective technology to mark certain beings as inferior or dangerous, channeling hate and fear towards them.

Viewed through a broader lens, this duality also serves as a metaphor for humanity's tendency to exploit and commodify what it reveres, highlighting the inconsistencies in how humans value nature and non-human beings. As explored in the following chapters, Mongols exhibit this duality in their relationships with other animals, such as marmots, cats, and camels.

If we return to state socialism, it was also during this period that canines ceased to be perceived as transitional or spiritual beings and were ideologically categorized as either 'good' (domestic) or 'bad' (stray), mirroring the divisive classification of the human population itself into two antagonistic classes—pro-revolutionaries/the people versus anti-revolutionaries/the enemies of the people.

Changing attitudes towards dogs in Mongolian society serve as barometers of political and cultural shifts, offering insights into the evolution of societal values. When religious beliefs are suppressed, dogs lose their spiritual significance; conversely, with the resurgence of religion, the spiritual importance of dogs is reinstated. In fact, this dynamic applies to other animals as well, as will be explored later.

In today's Mongolia, where hybridophobia (fear of individuals with mixed Mongol heritage) is prevalent, dogs have been categorized into three distinct groups in nationalistic narratives: (1) dogs of 'pure' Mongol lineage, (2) dogs with foreign ancestry, and (3) dogs with 'polluted' or 'impure' blood, referred to as *erliiz*. The distinction between dogs with foreign blood and *erliiz* hybrids is often blurred. Many dogs not conforming to the traditional Mongol appearance are indiscriminately grouped together, contrasting sharply with the 'pure' Mongol breed. These 'non-Mongol looking' dogs, especially hybrids, are perceived as inferior and are often targeted by thugs and violent individuals who don't believe in the bad karma resulting from mistreating dogs—a legacy of state socialism. This violent behavior towards stray animals is also indicative of today's low cultural tolerance intertwined with aggressive masculinity, where a man's willingness to use his fists in response to an insult or to prove his point is perceived as a sign of respectability and having balls. The transition from violence against allegedly inferior men to violence against animals or vice versa is distressingly swift. The inferiority associated with hybrid dogs also aligns with the skepticism directed towards hybrid individuals, who are often viewed as having a dual nature and being untrustworthy and unpatriotic.

A lesson that can be drawn from this is that the discourse surrounding *erliiz* (hybrid) dogs and people parallels broader conversations about inclusion, purity, and the fear of 'contamination' in human societies. What emerges is the destructive potential of purity myths and the importance of embracing hybridity as a source of resilience and diversity.

The collapse of state socialism in Mongolia not only unleashed a powerful wave of nationalism and religious revival but also introduced freedom of speech alongside a free-market economy. However, this transformation didn't erase socialist-era beliefs; instead, it created a diverse marketplace consisting of old, new, and mixed ideas for people to choose from. This variety of ideas and worldviews is often produced and peddled by diverse actors, including the state, religious groups, NGOs, businesses, public figures, and social media.

For example, social media platforms like Facebook, Instagram, YouTube, and Twitter, widely used in Mongolia, became a melting pot of local traditions, culture, and global influences, notably from the West. Western concepts, especially popular among the younger generation, seeped into Mongolian social media trends. The anthropomorphism of dogs took distinctive forms in Western countries like the United States, Canada, and the UK, where there is a fast-growing canine-focused industry. Dogs are welcomed with open arms in accessory shops, canine daycare centers, and doggie spas. Beyond this, dogs have even become social media influencers, accumulating followers, merchandise deals, and movie appearances. When their time comes, there are specialized dog cemeteries where they can rest in peace. Another interesting trend is the growing popularity of 'neuticles', prosthetic testicles for neutered or castrated dogs. Interestingly, the demand for these artificial balls stems from dog owners' concerns about preserving their pets' self-esteem post-surgery.[57] While in Mongolia, there are many people ready to spoil their pooches as badly as their Western counterparts, there are only a handful of places in Ulaanbaatar where dog lovers can purchase special treats, accessories, and toys for their four-legged companions. Public spaces such as restaurants, pubs, medical centers, and shops are often closed to dogs. The country also might need a nudge to catch up with the growing 'neuticles' culture in the West, but as the saying goes, 'every dog has its day', even in a remote place like Mongolia.

Shamanic Stories, Zoophilia, and Sexuality

Inter-species mating, also known as cross-species reproduction, involves sexual interactions between individuals from distinct species. This phenomenon is relatively rare in the animal kingdom, especially among unrelated species, such as between sea lions and penguins, though it occurs more frequently among closely related species, like different species of doves or dolphins. Factors driving such interactions may include displays of dominance, social bonding, mistaken identity, scarcity of suitable mates within one's own species, or environmental pressures. While these interactions are observable, the motivations behind them are often inferred by researchers and can be challenging to prove definitively.

Bonobos—our closest evolutionary cousins alongside the chimps— are renowned for their highly sexualized behavior. They frequently engage in sexual activities with individuals of the same sex, opposite sex, and even with other primates as a means of reducing tension, resolving conflicts, and strengthening social bonds. Hence, their reputation as a peaceful species. For bonobos, engaging in sex is as casual as a handshake for humans. Their sexual repertoire is wide-ranging and strikingly familiar, including passionate tongue kissing, deeply staring into each other's eyes, practicing oral sex, playing with each other's genitalia, masturbating, and even fashioning sex toys. When engaging in heterosexual sex, bonobos also often adopt the face-to-face 'missionary

---

57   Bell, *Silent But Deadly.*

position'—a behavior not observed in any other primate, including chimps,[58] who perceive staring as an act of aggression and typically adopt a ventro-ventral copulatory position, which is a fancy way of saying that the male mounts the female from behind in the 'doggy style'. However, despite their seemingly unrestrained 'make love not war' behavior, there is no documented instance of bonobos engaging in sexual activities with animals from entirely different species, such as elephants, antelopes, or reptiles. We can only speculate that bonobos refrain from attempting initiating sexual contact with elephants, antelopes, and reptiles, partly because they do not encounter social conflicts or alliances with these groups of animals that would necessitate such behavior. In contrast, human sexuality is fundamentally different from mating behavior in the animal kingdom; it is an extraordinarily fluid phenomenon shaped as much by human culture as by psychology.

Human sexuality is intertwined with layers of political, religious, social, economic, aesthetic, fetishistic, and carnal dimensions. Humans are also unique in their propensity to categorize, penalize, and establish moral standards around their sexual desires and activities. Hence, various cultures, as documented by anthropologists, not only exhibit a variety of marriage patterns (monogamous, polygamous, same-sex, group, endogamous, exogamous, temporary) but also lay claim to a staggering array of sexual positions, techniques, rituals, values, ideas, fetishes, fantasies, phobias, identities, rules, roles, and prohibitions. Engaging in sex with animals, also known as zoophilia, is just one among many activities on the extensive list of human sexual behaviors. No wonder, humans have surpassed even our hyper-sexualized bonobo cousins—or any other species, for that matter—by copulating with an even wider range of creatures, from chickens to dogs to donkeys to dolphins. Since sex with animals can provide valuable insights into human behavior and societies, let's conclude this chapter by looking at Mongol society from yet another intimate angle—exploring how, throughout their history, Mongols have perceived sex with animals in general, and dogs in particular.

In Mongol culture, the first allusion to what a modern reader might interpret as sexual activity with a dog appears in *The Secret History of*

---

58   Cooke, *Bitch*.

the Mongols in the story about Alan Goa's pregnancies, as introduced at the beginning of this chapter. The imperial annals note that she was impregnated by a supernatural entity ('a yellow man') that entered her *ger* through the roof opening in the form of a ray of light and left in the morning in the shape of a dog. The story vaguely describes what occurred inside the *ger* during the reproductive nights by putting the following words into Alan Goa's mouth: 'a shining yellow man... stroked my belly; and his brilliance dissolved into my womb'. When this supernatural entity left, 'he would crawl out with the beam of the sun and moon like a yellow dog'.[59] Many Mongolists who have studied *The Secret History of the Mongols* agree that the primary protagonist of this impregnation story was 'a dog'. To understand its meaning, we must step into the shoes of the Mongols' shamanic ancestors and attempt to set aside our contemporary values and identities.

In the shamanic traditions of this region, the relationship between humans and animals has been marked by deep respect and a belief in spiritual interconnectedness. This is manifested through the ability of shamans or humans to transform into animals and vice versa, as well as through the practice of interspecies unions. These unions, as described in shamanic stories, can lead to the creation of unusual offspring, hybrid beings, powerful individuals, or even entire clans. Such narratives are largely symbolic rather than indicative of zoophilia as it is understood today. They also suggest a fluidity of shamanic identity, which stands in stark contrasts to modern Mongol notions of fixed identities.

Although shamanic traditions are diverse, with various indigenous groups across Eurasia having their unique stories and rituals, one common theme that unites them is the incorporation of beliefs attributing spiritual qualities to animals, which in turn are interconnected with human life. Thus, in various shamanic stories, certain animals could be associated with human fertility or serve as progenitors to clans, as in the story of Alan Goa, where her pregnancy results in the establishment of the Borjigid lineage. According to this reading, in this particular story, the dog is to be understood as a symbol and instrument that connects the world of the mortals with that of the gods. It is most certain that in the past, many Mongols took the story of Genghis Khan's ancestry at

---

59   *The Secret History of the Mongols* §21.

face value and believed that his legendary ancestress was impregnated by a celestial dog. In this context, this particular scene of impregnation would have been regarded as sacred rather than zoophilic in the modern sense. This story, rich in animal symbolism, was likely employed to legitimize the Borjigid lineage, specifically Genghis Khan's authority and divine rule. Given this powerful canine symbolism, it is not surprising that, in the thirteenth century, Mongols also genuinely believed in the existence of a nomadic tribe where women were beautiful humans and their husbands were dogs. Plano Carpini noted a Mongol saying from that time: 'Your father or brother was killed by the dogs'. In this story, the dogs referred to were the canines from the tribe, living alongside human women, who were said to have defeated the otherwise invincible Mongol cavalrymen.[60]

However, it is important to recognize that the presence of shamanic stories involving dog-progenitors does not necessarily imply that all Mongols viewed these tales solely as metaphysical expressions of the divine human-animal union and refrained from engaging in actual sexual intercourse with dogs. Shamanism, as was practiced among the Mongols, after all, did not explicitly prohibit sexual interactions with dogs or other animals. The absence of recorded accounts or written materials detailing such affairs should not be taken as evidence that such encounters did not occur. Quite the opposite, it is highly plausible that shamanic stories featuring dog-human offspring or tales about tribes where women shared their beds with dogs, not to mention the high status of canines in shamanic cosmology, could have inspired certain nomads—whose identities are now lost to the sands of time—to engage in lovemaking with canines. Moreover, it should be noted that certain zoophilic acts, particularly in the context of shamanic traditions, could symbolize rebellion against societal norms or attempts to claim spiritual or supernatural power.

Indirect evidence suggesting that some Mongols, whether out of rebellion, spiritual ambition, or pure carnal desire, engaged in sex with animals can be found in the *Mongol-Oirat Regulations* of 1640. This set of laws officially established Buddhism as the state religion among the Halha Mongols and Oirats, at the expense of other religions, particularly

---

60   Dawson, *The Mongol Mission*, 23.

shamanism.[61] Notably, this historic code of laws includes a provision that expressly prohibits sexual acts with animals, with a prescribed penalty of a 'fine of five heads of cattle'.[62] Although the code does not specify which animals are forbidden for such activities, it is evident that dogs, goats, and sheep were of primary concern, being the most commonly associated animals in such practices. In other words, the existence of this prohibition implies that there were instances of individuals engaging in sex with four-legged beauties, prompting the need for such legal regulation.

It is intriguing to observe a unique aspect of this prohibition within a code of laws influenced by Buddhism. Notably, Buddhism, at its core, does not explicitly address the issue of going to bed with animals in its teachings. Instead, it casts all forms of sexual desire in a negative light, linking them to worldly suffering. From this perspective, sex in any form or shape is viewed as an obstacle to achieving complete awakening or Buddhahood, considered the ultimate goal for every human being. However, Buddhism also recognizes that most humans may get their teeth into worldly pursuits and not necessarily achieve *nirvana* in this or even in many future lifetimes. Therefore, it promotes ethical principles with a focus on alleviating suffering and shaping relationships and moral conduct. The overarching Buddhist principles of compassion and non-harm extend to all living beings, including animals. Consequently, these principles can be applied to view zoophilia as an activity that not only inflicts harm and exploitation upon animals but is also considered morally inappropriate.

Given that Buddhism does not explicitly address zoophilia, one might wonder why the *Mongol-Oirat Regulations* of 1640 specifically prohibited sexual intercourse with animals. In my view, the inclusion of zoophilia in these regulations can be attributed to a combination of factors. First, Buddhism, which had been declared the state religion among the Halha Mongol and Oirat fiefdoms, played a role in discouraging the mistreatment of certain animals, including dogs,

---

61 Despite the official prohibition of shamanism, Buddhism incorporated a myriad of local shamanic deities and spirits, who, having donned a Buddhist mantle, continued to oversee their localities and address the specific needs of local populations.

62 Golstunskii, *Mongolo-Oiratskie Zakony 1640 Goda*, 86.

which held significance in shamanic rituals. Second, if unions with certain animals, such as dogs, were believed to enhance one's shamanic powers and divinity, Buddhism had every reason to suppress practices that sustained shamanic cosmology and worldviews. Third, during that period, some Oirat groups embraced Islam, particularly those living on the fringes of Muslim-majority areas in Central Asia, where they became aware of the prohibition of zoophilia under Islamic law (*sharia*). This awareness and concern may have contributed to the inclusion of zoophilia in the *Regulations*. These three explanations can complement each other, providing a more nuanced understanding of the historical context surrounding this prohibition.

It is worth noting that the *Mongol-Oirat Regulations* were a unique set of laws promulgated under exceptional circumstances, containing distinctive bans, notably zoophilia. This distinctiveness can be discerned when we compare the *Mongol-Oirat Regulations* to later codes of laws that were formulated under more typical circumstances, after society had become firmly oriented toward Buddhism. None of these subsequent laws make any mention of zoophilia. This absence is not necessarily an indication of its existence or non-existence but rather implies that zoophilia was *not* a matter deemed significant enough to warrant legal attention or concern during those periods. The only other code of laws that specifically addresses zoophilia is the *Zenzeli Regulations* of 1822, which were designed for the Kalmyks (Oirats) in Russia. These regulations aligned with Russian law, where zoophilia was prohibited. The prescribed penalty for zoophilia in both the *Zenzeli Regulations* and Russian law was a fine of one head of cattle, accompanied by 50 lashes administered with a whip.

The transition from shamanism to Buddhism in Mongol society, as discussed in this chapter, led to the demotion of dogs from heavenly creatures to earthly entities due to their incorporation into Buddhist cosmology. Appreciating this shift, which might not sound terribly sexy, is crucial to understanding how canines became anthropomorphized in the modern sense. This shift resulted in dogs' ambiguous status and their use as insults, attributed to their newly perceived human-like qualities. Hence, in today's Mongolia, implying that a dog had sexual relations with someone's ancestors is considered an insult, whereas from a shamanic perspective of the thirteenth century, such references would have been complimentary.

Historical Mongol laws and shamanic stories suggest that zoophilia was never a significant concern for Mongols, which explains its notable absence from all Mongol legal codes, with the exception of the extraordinary *Mongol-Oirat Regulations*. Allow me to elucidate this point with another example. In certain societies, engaging in sexual intercourse with animals is sometimes perceived as an initiation rite for young men. A contemporary example can be found in Turkey, where I lived for several years until 2006. Particularly in rural regions, some teenagers and young men reportedly experience their first sex with donkeys. During my stay in the country, I got to know several young men from rural Anatolia who claimed to have witnessed their peers penetrate donkeys, although, tongues in cheek, they denied personal participation. Instances of this behavior indeed occasionally make headlines in Turkish national newspapers and social media. Not surprisingly, there are also reported cases of middle-aged or older men, well past their teenage years, who continue to engage in such practices, suggesting that the desire they harbor for jackasses remains steadfast and doesn't necessarily diminish over time. When we engage in sexual intercourse, we fuse together our senses of touch, sight, smell, and sound, catapulting ourselves, if only for a moment, to cosmic heights and divine happiness that transcend this mortal existence. In that instant, we feel connected to the entire universe and the cosmic divinity itself. Just as beauty is said to be in the eyes of the beholder and desire in the heart of the seeker, sexual pleasure too is a subjective experience that can be derived equally—so the argument goes—from a moaning human soulmate or a squeaking rubber doll or a braying donkey. Notably, during my time in Turkey, certain sex shops in Istanbul even offered inflatable donkeys for sale to accommodate citizens with such preferences.[63]

By contrast, in Mongolia, engaging in sexual acts with animals has never been considered a rite of passage for teenagers because sexual relationships outside of wedlock were permitted, which enabled

---

63   In my humble opinion, Turkey should be granted full entry into the EU, a door that Turks have been patiently knocking on for several decades. I believe that the inclusion of Turkey in the EU would undoubtedly enrich the diverse tapestries of Europe's cultural and social life.

teenagers to engage in intimate relationships with human partners. Mongolia's traditional values have long supported sexual activity without attaching any social stigma to sexually active individuals. Additionally, it should be noted that Buddhism's anti-sex doctrines primarily target the Sangha, the monkish community, and not necessarily the laity, upon whose reproduction, donations, and labor the Sangha has historically depended for its survival and prosperity. In fact, the more the laity procreates, donates, and toils for the monks, the better. This stands in stark contrast to Muslim-majority countries like Turkey. Consequently, zoophilia has remained an exception rather than the norm in Mongol society, rarely necessitating specific legal regulations.[64]

In matters of sexual intercourse, Mongols with a preference for animals typically go for either a dog or a sheep or a goat, as mentioned. If Mongols had kept donkeys, there might have been those among them who would have approached jackasses as well. After all, as members of the *Homo sapiens* ('wise men') species, humans are quite similar, and irrespective of their country of origin or religious beliefs, people tend to find imaginative ways to satisfy their sexual urges and fantasies. Let alone sleeping with flesh-and-blood animals, Sapiens can even imagine having sexual relationships with fictional entities such as gods, spirits, and the like. To the best of our knowledge, only humans can do this with entities that they have never seen, touched, smelled, or kissed.

A contemporary example from Mongolia illustrates this aspect of human behavior. In Mongolia, some men observe sexual abstinence before embarking on hunting trips. This practice is rooted in the belief that, by symbolically marrying the enchanting daughter or sister of the shamanic Lord of the Forest, the act of hunting becomes a temporary 'marriage alliance' between the hunter and the female shamanic spirit. To demonstrate his commitment to this spiritual 'bride' and ensure a successful hunting expedition concluded with a bloody kill, the hunter refrains from engaging in sexual intercourse with a human female. This concept of hunters simultaneously having wives in both the spiritual and human realms—which necessitates the temporary separation of these two categories of females through sexual abstinence with humans before the 'hunting-marriage' with spirits—not only reflects ancient

---

64   Terbish, *Sex in the Land of Genghis Khan.*

polygamous patriarchal norms from the era of shamanism but also underscores the remarkable creativity of our species. Similar myths and rituals involving humans flirting or forming sexual unions with fictional entities can be found in cultures worldwide, spanning from Ancient Egyptian and Greek civilizations to Hinduism.

Such myths can be categorized alongside zoophilic myths involving animals as agents of divine intervention, reflecting humanity's aspiration to transcend ordinary boundaries and merge with powerful forces of nature or divinity. In the Alan Goa story, for example, the celestial dog symbolizes divine fertility and transcendence, rather than merely physical union. This parallels humanity's broader impulse to mythologize desire as something that connects the mortal to the divine.

Human cultures excel at both nurturing sexual fantasies and suppressing them, frequently invoking religious reasons. For instance, Abrahamic religions such as Judaism, Christianity, and Islam are founded on the doctrine of original sin, positing that humanity inherited a sinful nature due to humanity's mythical progenitors Adam and Eve's disobedience in the Garden of Eden. This concept of original sin has often been linked to human desires, including sexual ones, resulting in the discouragement of premarital or extramarital relations as sinful. By stressing sex's procreative purpose exclusively within marriage, certain denominations also advocate celibacy for specific groups of humans, such as nuns and clergy members.

During my time in Turkey, I came to know numerous young men who took Islamic teachings about the sinful nature of sex and desire very seriously. One of them, my friend Fatih, was a genuinely good-natured person but often appeared deeply unhappy and spiritually tormented despite his devoutness. He performed the prescribed prayers five times a day, steered away from Western music, and promptly switched off a movie if a male protagonist approached a woman too closely (something Fatih interpreted as an impending romantic kiss)—all of which were meant to keep Turkish Muslim men out of trouble and supposedly make them happy. Fatih also strongly disapproved of some of his fellow countrymen indulging in homosexual fellatio or copulating with donkeys, a topic that made him as sick as a dog, not only because these activities violated sharia law but also because they were unproductive sex and had a perverting influence on those involved. Once, Fatih confided in me about his desire for a family and a couple of children to continue his lineage. Given his puritanical view on sex, unsurprisingly, he told me of his intention to have sex with his future better half only twice (proportionate to the number of planned children), viewing it solely as a mechanical means of procreation rather than a source of pleasure. Aside from his apparent lack of basic knowledge about human reproduction (a couple may need to engage in intercourse more than once to achieve pregnancy) or female psychology (women also have sexual urges and would expect physical intimacy with their husbands), what struck me about Fatih's attitude is that when I questioned his steadfast anti-sex stance, he would gesture upwards in consolation and roll his sorrowful eyes in pleasure, indicating that in Allah's paradise, he believed he would have eternity to enjoy the companionship of seventy-two beautiful virgins. It is in moments like these that one truly appreciates Karl Marx's description of religion as 'the opium of the people'.

It is not only religious doctrines that can shape societal attitudes toward sex and exert a profound influence on people's worldviews and carnal desires. In totalitarian regimes, ideologies such as Leninism-Stalinism—which seek to exert total control over all aspects of human life, and which can be described as 'the sedative of the masses'—can also leave a lasting impact not only by numbing people's critical thinking but by suppressing their sexual urges and behaviors. This influence was clearly visible in socialist Mongolia, which embraced an anti-sex worldview not very different to that of Fatih's.

Guided by the principles of the Communist Party in the Soviet Union, the People's Revolutionary Party of Mongolia regarded sex as a strictly utilitarian act, primarily viewing it as a mechanical means of procreation confined to the institution of marriage. The Party effectively stripped citizens of their sexuality, particularly women, and reduced them to a proletarian force within society. Consequently, sexual intercourse was expected to be mechanical, devoid of any experimentation, overindulgence, or deviation such as the 'doggy style' and other dodgy positions. In public discourse, there was no space for the genitalia to rear its shameful head either, even in the pages of biology textbooks on human anatomy, where human reproductive organs were explained vaguely by drawing parallels with those of other animals.

Ironically, this stringent stance unintentionally gave birth to a certain type of personality shaped by the political system: the citizenry was sexualized—albeit in a de-romanticized and vulgarized manner that reduced sex to its most basic function. As a result, sex became a preoccupation for many individuals who publicly demonized it but secretly cherished and intensely fantasized about it, seizing every opportunity to engage and indulge in it. Thus emerged the stereotypical socialist citizen who thought one thing, said another, and did yet a third. One might call this person *Homo Sovieticus Mongolicus,* a mirror image of *Homo Sovieticus* but adapted to Mongolia's pastoral life and deep-rooted Buddhist cosmology and heritage.

One of my cousins was a vivid example of this political species. He was the youngest son of my paternal aunt in Dundgobi Province and the one who performed a funerary rite for Sharik. He might not have been exactly the mold from which the People's Revolutionary Party would have cloned model citizens to populate the proletarian paradise on the steppes. Nevertheless, he was a humble and exemplary laborer with a special fondness for military songs and sausages, which he carried in his pants pocket much like Westerners carry snacks or chewing gum in theirs. Despite acting in public as if he was asexual, he was, at heart, a bonobo-style libertine—the kind who wouldn't take 'no' for an answer. In his private life, he pursued female members of the proletariat with unrelenting determination, always wearing a perpetual grin that seemed to work wonders. Unlike the well-off sugar daddies in the People's Revolutionary Party, who could financially support women in exchange for intimate favors, he was broke and always on the lookout for casual encounters that wouldn't cost him a penny. Once, after it rained 'cats and dogs' for several days in Ulaanbaatar, the road leading to the bus stop in our neighborhood became submerged in floodwaters. Having paid a visit to my father and quickly self-medicated with penicillin in our bathroom for a sexually transmissible disease, my cousin noticed a young woman struggling to navigate through a muddy puddle on his way to the bus stop. Grinning like a Cheshire cat, he offered her assistance by giving her a piggyback ride to a dry area, not out of kindness of his heart but because he saw this as an opportunity to initiate an affair with her. Later, he told me that he managed to arrange a 'doggy style' rendezvous with her in a public park. My cousin was what people call *jingeriin nohoi*, literally meaning 'the male dog of the bitches'. This term is used to describe a promiscuous man who single-mindedly pursues women for sexual encounters, regardless of consequences, even if it means becoming a real pain in the ass. His favorite anecdote was as follows: *A single woman gives birth in the countryside to a baby boy. Immediately after entering the world, the boy looks angrily at his mother's lover and starts poking the man's forehead repeatedly with his tiny fingers, saying, 'How does it feel when someone pokes you every night like this?'* One day, my cousin and I decided to explore the National Art Museum in Ulaanbaatar, where a series of paintings, *One Day in Mongolia*, depicting various parts of the country in different seasons, created at the turn of the twentieth century by the renowned Mongol artist Sharav the Joker, caught his attention. As we carefully examined the pre-revolutionary masterpiece depicting various daily activities of nomads, my cousin turned red with embarrassment and struggled to contain his giggling for quite a while. His reaction was easy to follow—he poked his finger at the couples engaged in passionate sexual intercourse depicted in the artwork. Although he lived a secret life as a womanizer, the mere sight of sexual images and symbols in public displays was enough to trigger conflicting emotions in him.

It would be unfair to pin the label of *Homo Sovieticus Mongolicus* only on men—many women were equally skilled at leading double lives that didn't quite match their public image or communist modesty. Take another of my distant relatives, for example. She was a libertine with a flair for romantic drama, who had a talent for attracting men as easily as a magnet attracts iron balls. A single mother, she dated men like it was a sport—only to fall disastrously in love every time. Compared to her, even Halle Berry's character, Leticia Musgrove, from *Monster's Ball* (2001)—with her troubled personality and uninhibited sexuality— would seem like a picture of innocence. One evening, I overheard her on a date. She began with awkward silence and nervous giggling, which soon progressed into her puissantly demanding that the man 'eat her pussy'. At some point, she mounted her lover and started ferociously jumping on him, moving with the same intensity as a woman riding a horse at full gallop. Apparently, she hurt his manhood, and he moaned in what seemed like a mix of pleasure and pain. She pledged eternal loyalty to him, chirped X-rated profanities, and passionately copulated all night long, only to transform into a political animal the next morning, pretending she had never met him before.

One can anticipate that in this puritanical socialist regime, practices viewed as hindrances to the social duty of procreation, such as homosexuality, masturbation, and zoophilia, were condemned as unnatural, immoral, unhealthy, unpatriotic, and anti-ideological activities. Decreed as contrary to the innate nature of *Homo Sovieticus Mongolicus*, homosexuality was not only stigmatized but also criminalized on ideological grounds, positing that there was no legitimate place for anal sex in the annals of the socialist Fatherland. Masturbation was also deemed a dangerous perversion of solitary self-gratification and believed to lead to various health-related issues, including impotence, memory loss, and genital and back pains.[65] However, the truth is that if the supposed harms attributed to masturbation were fact-based, my cousin, who believed that the keys to happiness were in his hands and was also a frequent masturbator, would have been an impotent weakling suffering from memory loss and back pain, which was far from his actual condition. Both the anti-homosexuality law and anti-masturbation views were copied from the Soviet criminal law or imported from the Soviet code of ethics. In a similar vein, although the authorities did not emphasize this topic, engaging in sexual activities with animals was considered unproductive and selfish, believed to jeopardize the mental health and sanity of those who engaged in this 'unnatural' vice.

In Mongolia, societal perspectives on zoophilia, much like views on other forms of sexual activity, have undergone significant changes over time. Initially, the ideas of human-animal union had their roots in ancient shamanic stories and hunting rituals. Later, within the context of Buddhism, zoophilia was seen as an activity attaching the fornicator to the chain of rebirth and suffering. Eventually, under state socialism, which was ideologically sustained by the Leninist-Stalinist 'sedative of the masses', it was medicalized as a psychological disorder. This example suggests that human desire is culturally framed and can either be suppressed or liberated based on prevailing ideologies.

---

65   Ibid.

3. The Marmot

In the summer of 1347, a devastating and unprecedented deadly disease broke out in the port city of Constantinople, the vibrant heartbeat of the Byzantine Empire. The Grim Reaper spared no one, claiming the souls of both the humble and the influential, including the teenage son of Emperor John VI Kantakouzenos, considered God's chosen ruler and his viceroy on Earth. This calamity cast a dark shadow over the once-thriving city, claiming countless lives in its wake and instilling widespread panic that paralyzed the metropolis.

In fact, the plague struck two other major Byzantine cities, Pera and Trebizond, simultaneously. Not only that, other European port cities such as Venice, Genoa, Mallorca, Marseille, Sicily, and Cyprus were also affected by the plague, which ravaged through the continent, wiping out entire communities in its path. Between 1347 and 1351, approximately 25 million lives were lost in Europe alone, later earning the epidemic the grim moniker, the Black Death. Globally, the plague's toll is estimated to have ranged from 75 to 200 million lives. To put this into perspective, this represented about a quarter to more than half of the total world population at that time. In today's world, this figure would be equivalent to approximately 1.7 billion to 4.4 billion people. The Black Death's impact was so profound that it reshaped the economic, political, religious, and demographic landscapes of the affected societies, triggering significant environmental changes. The staggering death toll led to the abandonment of settlements and untended fields, allowing forests and wilderness to reclaim these once-cultivated lands sustaining thriving communities.

While contemporaries in Europe attributed the plague to celestial alignments, divine wrath, or scapegoated groups like Jews, modern epidemiological research identifies the true culprit: *Yersinia pestis*, a

    https://doi.org/10.11647/OBP.0450.03

bacterium responsible for the plague. This zoonotic disease spreads to humans primarily through the bite of an infected flea, direct contact with an infected animal, or, in its pneumonic form, via respiratory droplets from an infected individual. Although both zoonotic, plague differs fundamentally from COVID-19, as it is caused by a bacterium rather than a virus. Recent research suggests that *Yersinia pestis* may have arrived in Constantinople and other port cities on grain shipment boats from the Black Sea region after the Golden Horde Mongols lifted their siege on the port city of Caffa in Crimea in 1347. During the siege of Caffa, Mongol soldiers were reportedly afflicted by the disease, suggesting that the plague was rampant in this crucial trade node, through which shipments of grain arrived in Southern Europe. After the Mongol siege ended, it is believed that fleas infected with *Yersinia pestis*—latching onto black rats and possibly the bodies of sailors—hitchhiked their way to European destinations aboard merchant grain ships, bringing the plague to the continent.[1]

Strikingly, the role of marmots, cute-looking creatures carrying deadly fleas, in this tragic story remained little noticed until recently. Despite being hunted by Mongols and their ancestors for centuries, if not millennia, marmots historically served as one of the primary carriers of the plague across Inner Asia. There are several possible scenarios for what might have happened in Caffa under the Mongol siege. It is highly plausible that the two-year siege of the port city actually delayed the arrival of the plague on European soil via grain shipment boats until the siege was lifted.[2] During the siege, it is possible that Mongol cavalrymen became infected with the plague from local sources. Another possibility is that the Mongols, already infected by sick marmots, either introduced or supplemented the existing plague in Caffa. In any case, when the Mongols lifted the siege, Caffa is believed to have opened the floodgates for the devastating pandemic that ensued once the merchant boats, loaded with grain, arrived at their intended destinations across Europe.[3]

Following the structure which we have adopted throughout this book, this chapter examines the human-marmot relationship in two

---

1   Benedictow, *The Black Death, 1346-1353*.
2   Barker, 'Laying the corpses to rest'.
3   Benedictow, *The Black Death, 1346-1353*.

conceptually parallel yet closely interlinked contexts: cosmology and historical reality. Divided into four parts, the chapter explores various facets of this relationship, where the marmot figures both as a cosmological being embedded in cultural imaginations and as a biological species intertwined with the history of Mongol society. Part I explores the marmot's place within cosmology and its use in traditional medicine. Part II delves into the plague in Mongolia's history and its treatment by modern medicine. Part III explores both scientific and pseudoscientific perspectives on the plague and the marmot throughout Mongolia's socialist and post-socialist eras. The Conclusion wraps up the chapter and provides reflections on potential future scenarios concerning the plague.

Part I

The Marmot in Cosmology and Traditional Medicine

Once upon a time, when the earth was scorched by seven suns and life was parched by a devastating drought, there lived an archer named Erhii Mergen, meaning 'Erhii the Skillful'. He took upon himself the daunting task of remedying this dire situation. Erhii vowed that unless he brought down the suns, he would sacrifice his very humanity by cutting off his thumbs and turning into a rodent. With dogged determination, he relentlessly pursued the suns, skillfully shooting them down one by one from the heavens. However, when aiming at the seventh and final sun, he missed, resulting in his transformation into a marmot, destined to dwell underground in darkness.

This popular Mongol legend, which has several versions, narrates the origin of the marmot and explains certain characteristics of this rodent.[4] The marmot has some body parts referred to as *hün mah*, or 'human meat', reflecting its human origin. It possesses four claws, a consequence of Erhii the Skillful's sacrifice in severing his own thumbs. In the Mongolian language, the human thumb is also called *erhii huruu*, or 'Erhii finger', in homage to Erhii.

---

4   Potanin, *Ocherki Severo-Zapadnoi Mongolii*, 179-80.

The Marmot in Cosmology

In contemporary times, although the explanation of the marmot's human origin has been dismissed as a myth, many Mongols continue to take *bolson yavdal* stories seriously. In these stories, the marmot, imbued with the enigmatic essence of potent 'human meat', assumes various cosmological forms. To understand the marmot's diverse cosmological forms, the concept of a chimera proves insightful. Derived from the Greek term, 'chimera' denotes an entity formed from disparate elements. Anthropologist Carlo Severi employs this term to describe religious images and artefacts, defining chimera as 'an amalgamation, within a single image, of the varied features of multiple beings'.[5] Unlike the monstrous chimeras in Greek mythology or the composite creatures found in medieval European bestiaries, the Mongol marmot aligns more with Severi's concept. It can be seen as a combination of various beings, with diverse features in a single image.

Multiple forms or aspects of the marmot are revealed through *bolson yavdal* stories in which the marmot figures: as an actual living marmot, as a Marmot Lord (*Noyon Tarvaga*), as a 'horse marmot' (*morin tarvaga*), and as a nonhuman spirit being (*lusyn am'tan*). These multiple aspects of what Mongols perceive when they think of the marmot do not organically turn into one another (in other words: shape-shift), nor do they directly communicate with each other in a cosmological sense. The image of the marmot embodies fantastical, as well as physical aspects of this animal. To perceive its different aspects or forms, one needs to deconstruct the chimera-marmot with the help of *bolson yavdal* stories that portray the marmot as a representative of multiple supernatural forms. In 'ordinary' locations marmots are generally not expected to appear in diverse supernatural forms. However, in certain sacred places marmots are believed to emerge in various forms and are protected by local supernatural entities, making them dangerous to hunt. Hence, nomads not only avoid hunting in such perilous places but also refrain from harming any marmot that behaves or appears uncharacteristically, such as albino marmots, even in 'ordinary' locations.

---

5   Severi, *The Chimera Principle*, 67.

An illustrative *bolson yavdal* from the socialist era, set in a location teeming with marmots, recounts the story of a man who purportedly killed a Marmot Lord (*Noyon Tarvaga*, a deity revered as the guardian of marmot colonies). Such 'Lord' or 'Master of the Animal' figures are common in hunting societies worldwide, often manifesting as giant representatives of specific animal species, as exemplified by *Noyon Tarvaga* in the Mongolian context. According to the story, on a scorching summer day, when idleness pervaded his home, a man ventured out to hunt marmots. Having killed several marmots and tasted blood in his mouth, the man couldn't believe his luck and decided to continue killing as many animals as he could. Happy as a dog with two tails, he shot dead one marmot after another, unable to stop, all the while wondering whether he could take down the local Marmot Lord. Finally, he spotted an uncharacteristically huge marmot poking its head just out of a burrow and sent a bullet right through its forehead. Triumphant with a howling success, the man returned home, only to witness his children falling gravely ill, one after another. Panic-stricken, he sought help from a neighbor, a seer. Following the seer's counsel, the man meticulously prepared a marmot carcass, filled it with specified materials, and conducted a magical ritual at the very spot where he had slain the Marmot Lord. It was only after this ritual that his children recovered.

Across Mongolia, a rich array of *bolson yavdal* stories can be heard, recounting how Mongols faced supernatural consequences—such as illnesses and even death—for harming unusual marmots and those protected by the supernatural, which do not exist in nature but live on in people's fertile imaginations and the stories they share.

In another related story said to have happened in the socialist era, a man, who had abstained from meat for a considerable time, developed an intense craving for marmot meat—a desire termed *mahsah* in Mongolian, derived from *mah*, or 'meat'. Despite warnings from friends against hunting near a certain sacred mountain, the man dismissed the prohibition as mere superstition. With the anticipation of a delicious meal, he aimed his rifle at what he perceived as a living barbecue (*horhog*) on four legs. However, every time he prepared to shoot, his vision blurred, revealing a colossal, hazy black hand shielding the marmot. Undeterred, he persisted in chasing marmots, but the mysterious vision also persisted, prompting his retreat in fear.

That night, he had nightmares. Seeking counsel, he approached a local elder, who was a monk in his youth. After hearing the man's account, the elder imparted wisdom: 'You are fortunate not to have harmed any marmots, for what you witnessed was the spiritual guardian of the sacred mountain safeguarding its creatures. But now, having angered the deity, it will pursue you and your family. Before it's too late, relocate your family where the deity's influence cannot harm you'. Troubled and alarmed, the man heeded the elder's advice, moving to a new place where his nightmares ceased, and life regained its equilibrium. I learned of this *bolson yavdal* story from my mother, who had heard it from her father, originally from Western Mongolia.

However, not all marmots are dangerous to hunt. A particular type of marmot that appears to be potentially spiritually beneficial for hunters is known as the 'horse marmot' (*morin tarvaga*), often found in 'normal' places. These are indeed larger than average marmots. When their skins are removed, they reveal yellow fat instead of the white fat found in regular-sized marmots. Hunters who have killed these 'horse marmots' often interpret it as an auspicious sign, heralding good fortune and abundance, and indeed, many *bolson yavdal* stories are about nomads who have benefitted from these marmots.

That said, not all Mongols approve of hunting marmots. Elders, in particular, warn against disturbing marmot colonies, not only due to the risk of disease but also because they believe these creatures hold ancient knowledge of the land and are deeply connected to its spiritual energy. Any unnecessary disturbance of marmots, especially excessive hunting, is thought to disrupt this natural balance, potentially provoking nature's wrath. Some even believe that such disruptions may awaken dormant forces, leading to the spread of plague or other misfortunes that affect both the environment and human life.

My father was one of them. He never ate marmot meat himself and often rebuked his younger kinsmen for going marmot hunting. Following the collapse of state socialism, which coincided with droughts, harsh winters, and the spread of various zoonotic diseases, he attributed these hardships primarily to the fact that people had begun hunting marmots excessively, disturbing the delicate balance of nature.

Many Mongols also hold a belief in the existence of 'marmot persons' (*tarvagan hün*), a term that carries a couple of meanings. Firstly, it refers to diminutive individuals with conditions like dwarfism, and secondly, it denotes mythical 'tiny' people believed to be the same size as actual marmots. In *bolson yavdal* stories, mythical 'marmot persons' dwell underground in spiritually significant locations.[6] They are believed to ride miniature horses, don Mongol traditional attire, and safeguard ancient treasures, much like leprechaun fairies in Irish folklore. Although tales of these beings have always captivated herding communities, a significant incident in the early 1990s marked a turning point.

It was an ordinary day in post-socialist Ulaanbaatar, much like any other. Bureaucrats crammed into state offices, shuffling stacks of paper, factories hummed along in their daily grind, national shops opened with empty shelves, and prostitutes lined up in the central Lenin Park. What began as an unremarkable day quickly took an unexpected turn. A truck driver on the outskirts of the city claimed to have seen a 'marmot person', dressed in a traditional robe and hat, carrying a small knife, running across the road before diving into a burrow. By midday, the story had become national news, spreading like wildfire and turning the sighting location into a go-to spot for curious crowds and TV crews. Bureaucrats left their offices, workers deserted their factories, and students skipped school, all drawn by the allure of witnessing this bewildering event. I vividly recall this episode from my high school days, when our teacher sternly warned us against truancy. Despite the admonition, some classmates couldn't resist the temptation, driven by the desire to witness a national news story unfold. My younger sister, two years my junior, watched her classmates hatch a plan to lure the elusive 'marmot person' out of the burrows and bring him to their class for a closer medical examination. Needless to say, no one ever saw the marmot person again, as if the earth had quietly inhaled and taken him with it, leaving only a whisper that spread from mouth to mouth.

Traditional Knowledge of the Plague

Let's explore how Mongols understood the plague and the benefits of marmot meat—a knowledge rooted in cosmological thinking and religious dogma.

As nomads, whose livelihood and survival depend on animals, Mongols possess an intimate knowledge of their herd animals, including

---

6   In some regions of Mongolia, these beings are not referred to as 'marmot persons' but as 'tiny people' (*jijig hün*).

their anatomy. They must deal not only with injuries and diseases that affect their livestock but also with those that can be transmitted to humans, including foot-and-mouth, brucellosis, anthrax, rabies, and others. True to their self-designated name meaning 'wise hominin', *Homo sapiens*, as exemplified by Mongol nomads, often demonstrate wisdom when diagnosing and treating illnesses in the animals they rely for sustenance and care, necessitating practical knowledge, reasoning, and effective solutions.

However, historically, when it comes to diagnosing human diseases, people lacked proper understanding until the advent of modern medicine. This problem with traditional medicine arises from at least two factors. Firstly, unlike animals, humans can articulate their symptoms and provide detailed information about their ailments. Therefore, diagnosing human diseases requires a deeper understanding of human anatomy, psychology, and complex needs. Secondly, human diseases are often social constructs: their classification and treatment are influenced by religious, social, and other factors unique to different societies. In the past, our ancestors relied on limited medical knowledge, different conceptions of 'health' and 'well-being', superstitions, and beliefs rooted in mythology when treating illnesses. As a result, traditional methods of healing often fell short in accurately diagnosing and treating a myriad of human ailments.

To understand how Mongols might have perceived and treated the plague, it is useful to first examine the fundamentals of traditional Mongol medicine, which is primarily derived from the Tibetan medical tradition, supplemented by local folk practices. Traditional Mongol medicine incorporates symbolic elements and concepts that do not align with modern scientific understanding. Reflecting the Buddhist philosophy that views the universe and all living beings as intimately interconnected, this system adopts a holistic approach, seeing human health as intricately linked to cosmic elements and energies.

These include the five elements—Earth, Water, Fire, Air, and Space—as well as the three energies, Tripa, Lung, and Pekan. Illness is traditionally understood as a result of imbalances among these elements and energies, and the goal of treatment is to restore harmony within the body by addressing these symbolic factors.

Reflecting an understanding of health within its cultural and religious framework, this system lacks the microbiological knowledge central to modern medicine. For instance, it is unaware of microorganisms, which comprise 99.99 percent of all the organisms on the planet and play critical roles in causing diseases and maintaining bodily functions, such as digestion. Additionally, its reliance on symbolic generalizations, universal associations, and magical rituals can limit its efficacy in treating certain illnesses.

For instance, if a patient is diagnosed with a disease understood to be caused by 'the lack of Water', the medical practitioner might try to restore balance by increasing Water levels through specific substances and healing techniques believed to enhance the patient's 'fluidity'. It is worth noting that, similar to diseases being attributed certain elemental qualities (Fire, Water, etc.), the classification of 'medicinal' substances, herbs, and meats is also based on symbolism. This way of cosmological thinking underscores the potential pitfalls within the system, as 'medicinal' substances may be categorized not solely based on their physiological effects but often influenced by mythical stories and religious doctrines.

To illustrate this point, let's take a brief detour to examine a specific case from the late nineteenth and early twentieth centuries, when Mongolia faced a widespread syphilis epidemic that affected all social classes and genders. The sole available treatment to restore the balance of energies in the patient's body and rid it of syphilis was offered by monks specialized in Tibetan medicine. This disease, characterized by skin lesions and damage to soft tissues, was seen as an ailment linked to cosmic imbalances in both Tripa (associated with the Fire element) and Pekan (associated with Water and Earth) energies, rather than being attributed to a tiny bacterium called *Treponema pallidum*.

Based on this symbolic diagnosis, monastic treatments for syphilis involved the ritualized burning of incense (representing the Fire element), washing patients with holy water (representing the Water element), and reciting health-bringing prayers. In the initial stages, monks often administered high doses of mercury (associated with the Earth element), a practice resulting in patients losing teeth and hair, enduring severe and prolonged diarrhea, developing mental illness, and experiencing an overall deterioration of health, yet offering limited effectiveness. In the later stages of syphilis, which was inevitable given the nature of the initial treatment, when patients developed soft tissue damage in the face and brain, causing bone lesions, and felt basically ready to be airlifted to the next life, the advanced monastic treatment was enhanced with poplar (associated with the Air element) and the root of sarsaparilla (associated with the Fire element) to turbocharge the process.

Among these 'medicinal' substances, mercury—associated with the mystical power of Buddhist Tantra and believed to balance the three fundamental energies (Tripa, Lung, and Pekan) —was the most dangerous. Treating syphilis with high doses of mercury, an extremely toxic element, merely superficially burned away syphilitic lesions, while seriously poisoning the patient's body. Guiding the treatment process with theories about balancing these three energies was as insightful as explaining the disease with the nursery rhyme 'Three Blind Mice', ultimately leading the treatment down a blind alley. Consequently, when Mongolia's living god, Javzandamba Hutugtu VIII, contracted syphilis, the monastic doctors were unable to treat him. If any mortal at his audience had dared to look at his blessed face, they would have noticed that the living god's blank stare into the air was not meditation, but a sign that he had lost his eyesight, thanks to progressive syphilis. Even the erection of a towering eighty-four feet statue of Avalokitesvara, a bodhisattva embodying the compassion of all Buddhas, in the brand-new temple of Megzed Janraiseg ('Eye-Opening bodhisattva') built in 1913 in Urga, proved futile in halting the deteriorating eyesight of the promiscuous monarch. In this case, all the combined powers of the Buddhas and bodhisattvas, the mystical forces of Tantra, mercury, and the medicinal knowledge diligently passed down from infallible elders through generations proved to be of little help in treating the divine Javzandamba Hutugtu.

However, it does not do justice to Buddhist medicine to accuse it alone of utilizing symbolism. In medieval Europe, for example, medical practices were influenced by misogynistic and patriarchal values intertwined with phallic symbolism, particularly in their approach to women's health. The pharmacopoeia of that time was notably infused with phallic-looking ingredients such as cucumbers, horns, and various gourd varieties. These items were routinely prescribed for women's gynecological ailments, grounded in the belief that a sick woman simply required a remedy reminiscent of an erect penis. Thus, prescribing a suggestively shaped vegetable was thought to suffice in addressing women's health concerns.[7] Given the state of medicinal knowledge at that time, patients often faced a higher risk of dying when treated by doctors than if they were left alone to allow the body's natural healing processes to take over.

It would not be inaccurate to assert that 'traditional medicine is to modern medicine as astrology is to astronomy'. This analogy implies that traditional medicine, like astrology, often relies on symbols, gods, the alignment of stars, tradition, and magic without necessarily adhering to the rigorous scientific methods employed by modern medicine or astronomy, which include systematic observation, measurement, experimental verification, and the formulation, testing, and continuous modification of hypotheses based on new empirical evidence. That said, I wish to make one important point without sounding overly critical of traditional medicine or too eager to embrace all the claims of modern science. While traditional medicine in Mongolia, particularly the Tibetan-inspired approach, has not always lived up to its self-promoted image of infallibility and has room for improvement, its holistic view of health—emphasizing the interconnectedness of body, mind, and spirit—and certain herbal remedies have demonstrated effectiveness and are increasingly being integrated into biomedical practices. Conversely, as modern medicine advances, it has at times faltered with misdiagnoses, overprescription, and unforeseen side effects, revealing the complexity of human biology and highlighting our ongoing gaps in understanding. However, as it continually improves through meticulous research, self-correction, and collaboration, scientifically-grounded medicine is poised to gain even deeper knowledge of human biology and psychology, developing increasingly personalized and efficient treatments—something that cannot be said for non-biomedical, indigenous medicine.

If we are to return to the topic of the treatment of the plague, although we do not have precise knowledge of how the Mongols historically understood the cause of the plague, we have no reason to doubt that they perceived it similarly to other diseases. They likely interpreted it through a religious lens, where illnesses were often attributed to disrupted energy balance, displeased gods, or jealous spirits. However,

---

7   Gilbert, *The Very Secret Lives of Medieval Women.*

a poor understanding of the cause of a disease does not always lead to equally ineffective methods of containment. Containment measures, such as fleeing to the steppe for their lives or quarantining after infection, may not save the afflicted individuals but can minimize the disease's spread, constituting a positive outcome when viewed from a societal perspective. As early as the thirteenth century, Mongols were recorded to have isolated themselves from outsiders during disease outbreaks. The reason for this behavior was a belief that an evil spirit or some harmful wind might accompany strangers or outsiders.[8]

The first Mongol documented to have acknowledged the connection between the plague and the marmot is the Tu (Mongour) monk and polymath Sum-pa mKhan-po Ishi-Baljur (1704-87), who referred to the plague as 'marmot poison' (*tarvagany hor*).[9] While this monk might not have had knowledge of the spread and epidemiology of *Yersinia pestis*, he correctly recognized that contact with sick marmots made people gravely ill or 'poisoned', which fits with Mongol Buddhist medical tradition that categorizes plague and rabies as diseases related to a poisoning of the body (*dug nad*) that requires the restoration of the balance of energies. Hence, the Mongol name for the plague, presumably coined no later than the eighteenth century, is 'disease of marmots' (*tarvagany* övchin) or 'marmot plague' (*tarvagany tahal*).

Having some knowledge about the association of certain diseases with animals does not imply the ability to cure them, especially within the context of magical medicine. There is no evidence to suggest that Mongols were able to cure marmot plague victims, and local doctors were reportedly ineffective against serious zoonotic diseases, just as they were against venereal diseases that are now curable with antibiotics.

One ritual that has been traditionally performed by Mongols and continues to this day in the treatment of serious diseases is called *seterleh*, which may offer some clues about how the plague was treated before the introduction of modern medicine. This ritual involves the consecration of a dog or livestock from the patient's family herd by a Buddhist monk. In exchange for the life of the afflicted person, the consecrated animal is spared from future slaughter and dedicated to the gods. These consecrated animals, believed to be under the protection

---

8   Rubruck, *William of Rubruck's Account of the Mongols*.
9   Atwood, *Encyclopedia of Mongolia and the Mongol Empire*, 345; Norov, 'Mongolian Buddhist scholars work on infectious diseases', 5.

of supernatural powers, roam freely, are treated well by humans, and are expected to die a natural death. Some medicinal rituals also involve actual animal sacrifices to the gods, but dogs were spared due to the ban on their sacrificial slaughter (see Chapter 2). However, attempting to cure serious illness by bribing gods with a dog or offering a scapegoat is as effective as asking Santa Claus for presents or praying to a tooth fairy for wealth and health.

A commonly known method of preventing the plague involved letting sick marmots cure themselves. A nomad would place saksaul (*Haloxylon ammodendron*) as an offering at the entrance of a marmot burrow. However, the healing power of this desert-steppe plant is rooted in religious myth rather than pharmaceutical qualities. According to legend, a swallow once discovered an elixir that could cure sick marmots. While flying with the elixir in its beak, a bumblebee stung the swallow, causing the elixir to drop onto a saksaul bush. This event miraculously imbued all saksaul plants with healing powers, as it often occurs in religious myths. Consequently, there is a widespread belief that during a plague outbreak, a knowledgeable marmot would bite off some saksaul and bring the plant to its burrow. However, attempting to suppress the plague within the marmot population using this method, with the hope of preventing its transmission to humans, is as effective as expecting church mice to resurrect the dead with holy water and a cross.

The most efficient traditional method for protecting oneself from the plague involved a preventative measure based on the observation of marmot behavior. Hunters keenly observed the behavior of sentinel marmots, who acted as lookouts at burrow exits, alerting the rest of the colony to approaching predators or other dangers. In Mongol belief, these sentinel marmots can communicate not only with their colonies but also alert hunters about the spread of disease through signs of illness. If a sentinel marmot doesn't make a loud warning call to the colony and seems oblivious to danger, or appears sluggish with slow or unsteady movements, this indicates to the hunter that it may be diseased and should be avoided. A marmot crossing the grassland steppe on its own, rather than remaining near burrows, is another sign that something is wrong. Such solitary marmots are to be avoided and not targeted for hunting.[10]

10　Fijn and Terbish, 'The survival of the marmot'.

The Use of Marmot Parts in Traditional Medicine

In traditional medicine, almost no part of the marmot—bones, pelt, meat, fat, and internal organs—goes to waste. People wear marmot anklebones as talismans against malignant spirits, bad fortune, and disease. Women seeking pregnancy or those already pregnant and aiming for a healthy gestation are often advised to wear anklebone talismans. A mixture created by grinding marmot bones and diluting them in holy water is believed to be beneficial for healing fractured bones.

In the not-so-recent past, women who experienced multiple miscarriages were encouraged to carry the tail of a female marmot as a talisman. Similarly, in some cases, men carried a male marmot's fluffy tail—often tucked inside their underwear—believing it could enhance their reproductive vitality. However, these tails could also harbor infected fleas, posing a serious health risk. This beautiful tradition is being revived today in some places, but there is a caveat for those practicing or thinking of practicing it: if not careful, instead of stiffening the penis, one could end up contracting *Yersinia pestis*. Additionally, the tails of 'horse marmots' are sometimes hung inside *ger*s to ward off diseases and misfortunes, while back braces made from marmot skin are believed to alleviate back pain. Needless to say, the efficacy of these methods remains scientifically unproven; one might as well attach a skunk's tail to one's underwear or wear amulets made of rat's teeth to improve fertility and ward off disease.

In Mongol cuisine, marmot meat is used in baked or boiled dishes, but in traditional medicine, various body parts may be consumed raw. The most potent meat, believed to be beneficial for one's health, is the so-called *hün mah*, or 'human meat', which includes the collarbone, small reddish meat from the marrowbones, some small pieces attached to the marmot's kidneys, meat around the neck, and the lymph glands. Believed to be parts of the mythological archer Erhii the Skillful, these mouth-watering bits can potentially harbor the plague, directly delivering the consumer to the bosom of *Yersinia pestis*. While considered a taboo to partake in everyday life, as it would equate to cannibalism, *hün mah* is revered for its purported medicinal properties precisely due to its taboo nature. It is believed to be beneficial for various ailments, such as injuries, gallbladder problems, kidney issues, thyroid disorders, osteoporosis, and pancreatic conditions, among other illnesses.

In traditional societies, taboo substances are often viewed as potent medicine. Rooted in religious and spiritual concepts, taboos are linked to mystery and secrecy, and the act of using these substances challenges societal norms believed to be meant for ordinary mortals. Hence, in some cultures, breaking certain taboos is thought to bring the practitioner supernatural transformative experiences associated with healing or spiritual growth. No wonder, taboo substances are typically derived from rare or dangerous sources, seen as harnessing the power of nature and gods. Traditional societies pass down knowledge and practices through generations, and substances like the marmot's 'human meat', or mercury, or any number of other dangerous substances, used for healing over time, become deeply ingrained in cultural heritage, reinforcing their perceived medicinal value.

The least dangerous way of administering marmot meat for 'medicinal' purposes is to eat boiled marmot liver, believed to be good for fractured bones. Although boiling marmot organs is the best way to avoid direct contact with *Yersinia pestis*, as the bacterium dies in boiling water, its medicinal effectiveness in healing broken or fractured bones is likely no more effective as chewing bull's testicles or sucking on a lollipop. After all, both provide some nutrients that may contribute to tissue repair and growth.

Marmot fat is used for healing wounds or burns, and, when processed, it serves as a remedy for respiratory conditions such as breathing difficulties, impaired lung function, and other respiratory symptoms. Imagine the following scenario: A man armed with marmot fat applies it to a burn on his hand, hoping for miraculous healing overnight. Unsurprisingly, the burn persists, appearing red, swollen, and blistered, causing him considerable discomfort. Slightly disappointed, the man takes a deep breath, hoping the marmot fat might help with his breathing difficulty. With a sigh, he realizes it's yet another folk remedy that fails to fulfill its promises, at least as far as he is concerned. 'Maybe it just works alright on other people; otherwise, how do you explain the ancient wisdom passed down from infallible ancestors concerning the miraculous healing powers of marmot fat?' thinks the man to himself, trying not to get entangled in his caravan of thoughts. He concludes, 'The same ancestors who knew everything there was to know about the universe. They even knew that the world is flat and is supported by four giant elephants that stand on an even bigger and fatter turtle swimming across the universal ocean. If they knew about this, how could they not know about such trivial things like the healing quality of marmot fat?'[11]

Eating marmot meat is regarded by many Mongols as a medicinal therapy in itself. The preparation of *horhog*, a traditional dish, involves a meticulous preparation. The process unfolds as follows: first, the marmot carcass is suspended from a pole, gently swaying in the breeze. To ensure cleanliness and to sear it from the outside, a blowtorch is deftly wielded, flames dancing as they purify the carcass by eliminating any remaining fur and fleas. Meanwhile, rocks, glowing red from the heart of the fire, are carefully chosen and inserted into the marmot's headless neck cavity. This method allows the meat to cook from the inside out, infusing it with flavors as ancient as the legend of Erhii the Skillful itself. The opening, now filled with hot rocks, is securely sealed with rope, trapping the heat and the essence of the cooking process. Once the marmot is thoroughly cooked, nomads gather around to relish the choicest pieces of meat and exchange news or *bolson yavdal* stories. The hot rocks assume a new purpose, becoming tools for therapeutic juggling, their warmth seeping into the hands of those who skillfully manipulate them. These warmed stones are also strategically positioned on the body to alleviate discomfort. Furthermore, sitting on these warm stones with bare buttocks is employed by some as a remedy for conditions such as radiculitis and various forms of cold. Next time you encounter Mongols sitting on stones, naked from the waist down but clothed above, don't ridicule them or assume they are trying to communicate with the spirits of the earth. Consider it an improvised nomadic approach to hot stone therapy, similar to practices in Scandinavian countries, with the only difference being the absence of saunas, requiring nomads to utilize whatever materials are at hand.

---

11   While applying marmot fat or any other animal fat is not a recommended method for modern wound care, Mongol herders employ a traditional practice to address the following condition in herd animals in the summer. In situations where animals have not shed their winter hair, indicating a struggle to gain weight for the upcoming winter, herders cook a broth with a high concentration of marmot fat. According to nomads, this marmot fat broth improves the condition of underweight animals, assisting them in shedding their winter coat and gaining weight. Though this practice requires scientific investigation, there is a possibility that the high concentration of fat, containing acids, cholesterol, and other nourishing substances, may contribute to the well-being of underweight animals.

Hunting the Marmot

Traditionally, hunters used bows and arrows or handheld weapons like bolos to capture marmots.[12] Fire was also employed to smoke marmots out of their burrows or block their escape routes, facilitating easier retrieval.

In the nineteenth century, the introduction of Russian-made rifles revolutionized hunting strategies. Hunters could now wait near marmot burrows, shooting them as they emerged, or approach them closely and take precise shots. The latter technique was observed by Russian scholar Sevyan Vainshtein in Tuva at the close of the nineteenth century. Notably, Tuva, a Russia's ethnic republic but once part of Mongolia until 1911, is now recognized as a favorite hunting ground for Vladimir Putin. There, he has been photographed in various 'sexy' chest-beating poses, such as sitting half-naked on horseback, sunbathing bare-chested, or holding a rifle while shirtless. Vainshtein's observations included hunters not bare-chested like Putin but clad in unique costumes. These outfits comprised a white jacket made from goat or deer hide, paired with a cone-shaped hat featuring horns or long ears, resembling a mammal's silhouette. If Putin had adhered to the local hunting dress code, photographs of him resembling a horny animal would have been more fitting. This attire was specifically designed to startle and agitate the marmot initially. The hunter would hold a stick with fine white hair on the end, twirling and jerking it alluringly to simulate the tail, keeping the aroused marmot still long enough for the hunter to aim and fire the rifle. Similar hunting costumes from the Paleolithic era have been discovered in Siberian rock engravings, highlighting the ancient origins of this hunting costume and technique, albeit with a bow and arrow.[13]

More recently, in 1989, British ethnomusicologist Carol Pegg observed the marmot hunt as a kind of 'dance' in Western Mongolia. This 'dance' involved running in circles, abruptly stopping, and then resuming until the hunter was pegged within close proximity to the marmot.[14] If executed correctly, the marmot didn't flee but sat barking, akin to an

---

12 Braae, *Among the Herders of Inner Mongolia,* 443-44.
13 Jacobson-Tepfer and Meacham, *Archaeology and Landscape in the Mongolian Altai,* 49, Fig. 3.38; Vainshtein, *Nomads of South Siberia,* 182.
14 Pegg, *Mongolian Music, Dance and Oral Narrative,* 246.

intrigued spectator in a deadly performance, responding to the hunter's movements. This method, known as *hoshgoruulah*, or 'making a marmot bark', might also involve specially trained dogs following the hunter or being held on a leash, enhancing the deception. Some herders used non-threatening herd animals such as sheep or camels to discreetly approach marmots.

Another tactic involved horsemen galloping toward the marmot, forcing it into a burrow. Reminiscent of scenes from Western movies depicting Native American warriors using tricks to ambush a wagon of terrified settlers, one horseman would dismount and lie on the ground with a rifle, while the other continued galloping, tricking the marmot into believing the danger had passed. When the curious marmot checked, the hunter would shoot it.

The least labor-intensive method employed traps or snares made from materials like wire or rope, strategically placed near the marmot's burrow entrance.

Similar to many traditional activities centered around interacting with nature and the animal kingdom, hunting was steeped in religious significance. Hunters engaged in rituals to seek approval from deities for their marmot hunts and to shield themselves from supernatural forces. These rituals included the use of containers or homemade vessels known as *anchny ongon* to attract spiritual entities that would assist in the hunt. Moreover, some hunters would drip blood from the captured marmot onto their firearms, believing that it transferred the prey's life force onto the weapon, thereby enhancing the fortune (*hishig*) of future hunts. However, this practice also meant that they were directly exposed to the risk of contracting the plague.

While marmot hunting took place as it does today throughout Mongolia, the most valuable thick pelts were found in the forested and mountainous regions of Northern and Western Mongolia. In rural communities, knowledge about hunting marmots was typically passed down from fathers to sons. Marmot hunting was seasonal, occurring in late summer and autumn when marmots were heavier and fattier in preparation for hibernation. These traditional techniques and knowledge, passed down through generations, some of which were recorded by scholars like Vainshtein and Pegg, continue to be practiced by hunters today.

Sacred Places

Many Mongols are wary of places believed to be under supernatural protection. These include 'wrathful places' (where protectors are unpacified shamanic spirits), sacred locales (guarded by powerful and ill-tempered Buddhist deities), cemeteries (inhabited by ghosts), and haunted grounds (a playground for various malevolent spirits and beings), which are all considered exceptionally dangerous. Nomads avoid hunting marmots or any game in these perilous places and try not to enter them without good reason, harboring an instinctive, animal-level fear of such areas.

When nomads venture into these areas—whether in search of lost cattle, to take a shortcut, or for any number of other reasons—their behavior closely resembles that of chimps venturing beyond their own territories. Chimps become animated, but upon entering the neighbors' territory, they suddenly become quiet, cautious not to attract attention. If they encounter foreigners, they make a considerable commotion, screaming, twirling branches, and drumming on trees. This seemingly exaggerated behavior can be explained by the fact that it is usually during such encounters that chimps venturing into their neighbors' territory get attacked, raped, or killed. In a similar vein, upon entering a 'foreign' territory—a wrathful shamanic land, or a location not under full Buddhist jurisdiction, or an area guarded by exceptionally angry Buddhist deities, or a haunted place—Mongol nomads exercise caution, refraining from singing or speaking loudly to avoid detection by potentially unfriendly and 'lethal' supernatural entities. If they believe they have encountered such entities, they chimp up by reciting powerful Buddhist mantras, attempting to intimidate and ward off any unfriendly forces. While subtler than screaming and twirling branches, the essence of the nomads' actions remains the same, reflecting the closeness between humans and chimps.

Let's not forget our other close evolutionary cousin—the bonobo. In stark contrast to territorial chimps, when bonobos encounter unfamiliar members of their species, there might be initial screaming, but soon it resembles less a battleground and more a picnic where everyone is having sex with each other. The Mongols also can exhibit bonobo-like behavior when encountering non-human entities, such as gods and spirits, in 'ordinary' places where they seek supernatural cooperation. In Chapter 2, we explored a shamanic hunting tradition where a hunter envisions his hunting trip as a temporary 'marriage' to the enchanting daughter or sister of the shamanic Lord of the Forest. To demonstrate his dedication to this spiritual 'bride' and ensure a successful expedition, the hunter refrains from engaging in sexual intercourse with a human female, whether it is his wife or girlfriend, prior to the expedition. In essence, his entire hunting experience transforms into an imaginary love affair with the unseen spirit.

These examples illustrate how humans may perceive the same landscapes differently depending on the religious lenses they view them through and whether they anticipate supernatural hostility or cooperation.

The Impact of Buddhism on Animals and Locations

Before the advent of Buddhism, as noted in Chapter 2, shamanism endowed animals with spiritual powers, placing them on par with humans. As cosmological equals or near-equals, humans and animals communicated directly through rituals, during which animals often offered themselves as a 'gift of meat' to humans. This was especially true for wild animals, including marmots. Some remnants of this worldview still persist today among certain groups, such as the Darhad in Northern Mongolia, who venerate shamanic spirits of nature.[15]

---

15   The history of shamanism among the Darhad is complex. They inhabit the Shishget region in Hövsgöl Province, historically one of Mongolia's most remote areas. During the Manchu Qing period, the Darhad Great Ecclesiastical Estate (*Darhad Ih Shavi*) existed in the flat steppe areas of Shishget, belonging to the Javzandamba Hutugtu, the head of Mongolia's Buddhist establishment. Despite this, Buddhism and shamanism coexisted, with the former relegating the latter to the fringes of society, particularly towards the taiga forest. During the socialist period, Buddhism in Shishget was systematically and harshly persecuted. In contrast, shamanism, already marginalized and not viewed as a political rival to the socialist regime, was kept under pressure, with individual shamans being allowed to practice their trade, as long as they did it in secrecy behind closed doors. After the collapse of state socialism, there was a resurgence in shamanism, accompanied by various shamanic spirits and ghosts of forgotten shamans reemerging. See Peredsen, *Not Quite Shamans*; Hangartner, *The Constitution and Contestation of Darhad Shaman's Power.*

One of the main changes introduced by Buddhism was the substitution of shamanic spirits (*ongod*) with Buddhist deities or the incorporation of these spirits into the Buddhist pantheon, which enabled them to assume roles as new guardians of their traditional territories. The only exceptions are the afore-mentioned sacred places believed to be protected by unpacified shamanic spirits or hungry ghosts.

During this transformation across Mongolia, without shamanic spirits to elevate their status and with humans placed above the animal kingdom by Buddhism, wild animals lost their powers in the new Buddhist world. Consequently, their ability to protect themselves by instilling fear in humans diminished, and humans no longer felt the need to communicate with them directly. Instead, Buddhism required humans to communicate with Buddhist or shamanic-turned-Buddhist deities. The only sanctuary offering wild animals some supernatural protection from hunters became these sacred places. Hence, in the majority of *bolson yavdal* stories, the clashes between wild animals, such as marmots, and humans resulting in misfortunes occur in these types of locations. Otherwise, hunting or even poaching in ordinary Buddhified places does not constitute a spiritual offense.

Part II

History: The Marmot, the Plague Control, and Modern Medicine

A man becomes infected from a sick marmot he hunted. Initially, he is exposed to the bubonic form when handling the dead marmot and putting its severed tail inside his underwear, thus acquiring its fleas. Then, he unknowingly exposes himself to the septicemic form while skinning the marmot with his injured hands. Just before cooking the raw meat, he ingests a small piece of fatty tissue attached to the marmot's kidneys for medicinal purposes, thus acquiring the digestive form of the plague. The man, content with the process, believes he successfully juggled three balls with one hand, reaping triple benefits: (1) improving his health through the consumption of raw meat as prescribed in folk medicine, (2) enjoying a delicious dinner, and (3) enhancing his manhood by cushioning his penis with a pad made from the marmot's tail. However, not long after, he experiences nausea and begins coughing (pneumonic form). A race ensues among these forms of plague to determine which will claim the victim's life first.

This is one possible—albeit exaggerated for emphasis—infection scenario where a man acquires all four forms of plague by handling a sick marmot in various ways and exposing himself to *Yersinia pestis*, the plague bacterium.

Yersinia Pestis

There are two kinds of marmot in Mongolia: *Marmota sibirica* and *Marmota baibacina*. Referred to as *tarvaga* in Mongolian, both kinds host the bacterium *Yersinia pestis*.

Yersinia pestis, responsible for causing plague in humans, has afflicted civilizations across Eurasia since ancient times. Evidence suggests that the bacteria were present in the Eurasian population about 4000 years ago. In an archaeological site near the Volga River, ancient teeth extracted from the skeletons of a human couple contained traces of the bacteria.[16]

In the annals of modern epidemiology, the bacterium was first identified in rats as the primary carriers of the disease. In 1898, Paul-Louis Simond conclusively argued that the plague is transmitted to humans when fleas, infected with *Yersinia pestis*, jump from a rat to a human and bite the human.

In addition to rats, marmots are another primary natural host of *Yersinia pestis*, serving as a transmitter of the plague to humans. This classifies the plague as a zoonotic disease, similar to COVID-19 and others that originate in animals and then jump to infect the human population. The plague manifests in four forms: bubonic, pneumonic, septicemic, and digestive.

The bubonic form is transmitted from infected marmots to humans through marmot fleas. This form is called bubonic because it can lead to buboes at the lymph nodes, neck, armpits, and groin. Bubonic plague is not typically transmissible between humans, as for it to occur, the bacteria must be directly introduced from the source of the infection

---

16   Spyrou et al., 'Analysis of 3800-year-old *Yersinia pestis* genomes'.

into the target body. If the victim neither recovers nor succumbs to the bubonic form in about a week, the disease could progress to their lungs, transforming into the pneumonic form and becoming transmissible through the air from an infected person to another. By becoming airborne, it increases its transmission potential.

The initial bubonic form could also progress into the septicemic form, where the disease enters the victim's bloodstream. At this stage, mottled blue-black patches may appear all over the body, signifying extensive hemorrhaging.

All three forms are highly lethal, often mutating from bubonic to pneumonic and/or septicemic during a plague outbreak. If left untreated with modern methods, the survival rate for the bubonic form is about twenty percent. The pneumonic form presents the most distressing demise, with a person typically spending days coughing up blood until they drown in it. In contrast, the septicemic form offers a faster and relatively easier way to go to the heavens, with a survival rate of zero percent.

Beyond bubonic, pneumonic, and septicemic types of plague, there is a fourth type—digestive plague. This plague is contracted by consuming the raw meat or fat of an infected animal, such as the marmot. When infected, the human victim's symptoms not only fail to significantly differ from the bubonic form, but also various forms may strike the victim in various combinations. Consider the above-recounted possible infection scenario, which could be adapted into a movie story titled *A Million Ways to Die in Mongolia*, drawing inspiration from the movie *A Million Ways to Die in the West* (2014).

Beyond the marmot, *Yersinia pestis* can also be carried in Mongolia by various rodents, including jerboas, ground squirrels, pikas, hamsters, and gerbils, none of which are consumed by Mongols today. Historically, however, it is documented that Mongols consumed jerboas and ground squirrels, blissfully unaware of the lethal repercussions, as reported by Muslim, Russian, and Mongol sources in the thirteenth century. Interestingly, mammals such as corsac foxes, Siberian polecats, and mountain weasels have also been found infected by plague bacteria, likely contracted from entering and sometimes sheltering in marmot burrows.[17] Since the plague is part of a larger ecosystem, eradicating it is nearly as impossible as catching a rainbow; different strains can appear in spectra of species and become dispersed among them at any time.

The unique relationship between marmots and fleas (*O. silantiewi*) is influenced by the intercontinental climate on the Mongolian Plateau, which is dry with extreme temperature fluctuations. *Yersinia pestis* has adapted to marmot hibernation, during which marmots plug up their burrows with soil, organic matter, and their own feces. During hibernation (typically from October-November to March-April, depending on seasonal conditions), marmot flea larvae feed on the blood by damaging the skin around the marmot's mouth, eyes, and anus. When a flea ingests *Yersinia pestis*, the bacteria multiply, obstructing the flea's gastrointestinal tract. Consequently, fleas disgorge some bacteria into any marmot they bite.[18] The plague can remain dormant within marmot burrows for over a year.

The Marmot in History

Archaeological evidence from various sites suggests that marmots have held cultural significance and served as a popular food source on the Mongolian Plateau for millennia. One of the most revealing discoveries comes from Southern Siberia near Lake Baikal, where marmot bones were found in graves dating back to the Early Neolithic period (between 10,000 BCE and 6000 BCE). Particularly striking was the excavation of 643 marmot incisors at one site and 152 incisors at another. This abundance of marmot teeth implies their diverse applications, including their use as decorative elements in clothing and jewelry.[19] One can almost visualize a Neolithic person strutting around, proudly wearing a marmot tooth necklace or a similar ornament, showcasing the ancient craftsmanship and presumably other ideas associated with the ornamentation of their time.

Within the present-day borders of Mongolia, marmot-tooth pendants were discovered in burial sites at Chandmani Uul in Northwest Mongolia, dating back to the period transitioning from the eighth to the fifth

---

17 Galdan et al., 'Plague in Mongolia'.
18 Orloski and Lathrop, 'Plague: a veterinary perspective'; Suntsov, 'Recent speciation of plague microbe'.
19 Masuda et al., 'Ancient DNA analysis of marmot tooth remains'.

centuries BCE.[20] Moreover, evidence from summer campsites originating from the Xiongnu period sheds light on the seasonal consumption of marmots. Marmot bones found at these sites exhibit distinct cut marks, indicating their significant role as a food source during specific times of the year.[21] These discoveries collectively underscore the integral part marmots played in the cultural, culinary, and artistic dimensions of ancient societies inhabiting the Mongolian Plateau.

The earliest documentation of marmot hunting and consumption among the Mongols can be traced back to *The Secret History of the Mongols*, which recounts the story of Höelün and her sons, including Temüjin (the future Genghis Khan), and how they made a living after being abandoned by their people following the death of Höelün's husband, Yesügei. Apart from fishing and hunting jerboas, Höelün's sons relied on marmot hunting for sustenance.[22] As Genghis Khan grew older, the metaphor of marmot hunting, which had aided his family's survival during his challenging childhood years, became a recurring theme. This is evident in a decree he issued in 1205 to his loyal general, Sübedei, a key figure in the Mongol Empire's expansion, to hunt down and capture three godless fugitives, Godu, Gal, and Chilagun: 'If they [Godu, Gal, and Chilagun] have wings and fly up into heaven, then you, Sübedei, will you not become a falcon and fly to catch them? If they become marmots and dig with their claws into the earth [to hide], will you not become a spade sounding them out and reaching down to strike them?'[23]

Muslim and Christian observers who traveled as envoys to Mongol territories or served as vassals to the Mongols also documented the Mongols' consumption of marmots. Plano Carpini, who journeyed to Mongol territories as a papal envoy of Pope Innocent IV, provides the following information:

> They (Mongols) eat dormice and all kinds of mice with short tails. There are also marmots there which they call sogur and these congregate in one burrow in the winter, twenty or thirty of them together, and they sleep for six months; these they catch in great quantities.[24]

---

20 Atwood, *Encyclopedia of Mongolia and the Mongol Empire*, 440.
21 Houle and Broderick, 'Settlement patterns and domestic economy of the Xiongnu in Khanu Valley, Mongolia'.
22 *The Secret History of the Mongols* §89–90.
23 Ibid. §199.
24 Dawson, *The Mongol Mission*, 100.

Foreigners frequently expressed strong disdain for the Mongols' penchant for marmots, a meat consumed not only by ordinary Mongols but also served on the imperial table. As these foreigners rendered their observations on paper, they must have still been under the impression of how, wide-eyed and bewildered, they watched the Mongols devour large rodents with gusto, their eyes closed. In a fourteenth-century culinary book titled *Yin-shan-cheng-yao* ('Proper and Essential Things of the Emperor's Food and Drink'), a list of animals that delighted the Mongol Yuan Emperor's palate included marmot meat.[25] This culinary compilation of fine dining, presented to the last Yuan Emperor, Togon Tömör, in 1330 by Hu Ssu-hui, the chief imperial dietary physician, reflected the imperial preference for marmot delicacies.

Marmots were not merely hunted for their meat; their fur and pelts were also highly valued by the Mongols, who used them for clothing. An illustrative instance occurred in 1285 when General Bayan, the conqueror of South China under Genghis Khan's grandson Kubilai, returned to Mongolia after quelling a crisis caused by the rebellion of several frontier Mongol princes. Faced with severe supply shortages in Mongolia, Bayan instructed his troops to augment their diet with steppe roots and their clothing with marmot skins, which required hunting a large number of rodents.[26]

Marmot fur and skin were also used as offerings to the supernatural. The *Yuan-shi*, the official dynastic history of the Mongols composed in 1370 during the succeeding Ming court, documents that during the Yuan dynasty, the Mongol Emperor erected ancestral temples in Beijing, where offerings included marmot pelts, alongside furs from other wild animals.[27]

After the fall of the Yuan dynasty in 1368, which redirected the Mongols' focus to their ancestral land of Mongolia, this enduring practice of marmot hunting and consumption is detailed in the *Halha Jirum*, an eighteenth-century code of laws. It included a specific provision that prohibited hunters from abandoning marmots inside their burrows after smoking them. Hunters were required to excavate the deceased or injured marmots.[28]

---

25   Buell, 'Pleasing the palate of the qan', 58, 65.
26   Atwood, *Encyclopedia of Mongolia and the Mongol Empire*, 38.
27   Jagchid and Hyer, *Mongolia's Culture and Society*, 38, 40, 45.
28   Zhamtsarano, *Khalkha Dzhirum*, 38.

The Plague in the Times of the Mongol Empire

After uniting all the steppe tribes in 1206 through dynastic ties, military campaigns, and diplomacy, Genghis Khan went on to create the largest land empire in history, which was further expanded by his descendants. However, the Mongols' impact on the conquered territories extended beyond violence and destruction. They were prolific city builders, facilitated trade and cultural exchange, promoted religious tolerance, and introduced administrative innovations, establishing what is known as Pax Mongolica or the 'Mongol Peace'. This period ushered in political stability and connectivity across Eurasia by uniting previously disconnected regions and warring peoples under a single Mongol rule.

Drawing parallels from our experience with the COVID-19 pandemic, we understand all too well that globalization and connectivity also facilitate the rapid spread of diseases. Pax Mongolica was no exception. It accelerated commercial and demographic exchanges across vast territories, fostering conditions conducive to the spread of diseases.

While the Mongols lacked an understanding of germ theory or disease transmission mechanisms, they recognized the concept of contamination and the importance of isolating themselves from outsiders during times of illness. This awareness is evident in accounts from William of Rubruck, a Franciscan missionary who visited Mongol territory in 1253-55. According to his observations:

> When anyone sickens he lies on his couch, and places a sign over his dwelling that there is a sick person therein, and that no one shall enter. So no one visits a sick person, save him who serves him. And when anyone from the great *ordu* (someone from one of the great households) is ill, they place guards all around the *ordu*, who permit no one to pass those bounds. For they fear lest an evil spirit or some wind should come with those who enter. They call, however, their priests, who are these same soothsayers.[29]

It is clear from this passage that the Mongols self-isolated and connected illnesses with spiritual imbalance and, to protect themselves from sick individuals, they tried to distance such people.

---

29 Rubruck, *William of Rubruck's Account of the Mongols.*

The nomadic lifestyle that Mongols led offered little opportunity for a plague or any infectious disease to develop into anything resembling an epidemic, let alone pandemic, affecting large populations. There would have been isolated outbreaks and deaths, concluding the matter. However, when the Mongols embarked on their conquest campaigns, outbreaks could escalate into epidemics among the sedentary populations they were conquering. This provided the plague with more opportunities to spread to a broader populace. During the empire-building phase, disease-avoidance practices mentioned by Rubruck would not have been confined to nomadic camps but would have also been implemented on a large scale during military campaigns.

During the conquest of Baghdad in 1258, Genghis Khan's grandson Hülegü led a force of 100,000 men marching west from Mongolia. Following Mongol military protocol, Hülegü brought his own food supplies, including livestock and substantial quantities of grain escorted by rats, as well as dried meats, including cured marmot.[30] Vulnerable to attacks by plague-bearing rodents both from within and outside the army, this vast military campaign resembled a metaphorical sitting duck, susceptible to the invisible pathogen from the very start. Historical records indicate that in 1257, Hülegü's army had to relocate its camp at least five times while preparing to assault the city. These actions may reflect the Mongols' attempts to reposition themselves, possibly to contain or stay ahead of outbreaks of disease. In the course of the actual siege in 1258, numerous city dwellers were reported to have died of 'pestilence'.[31] Whether this army brought the plague from Mongolia or contracted it en route to Baghdad remains unclear. Whatever the case, according to some scholars, this moment marked the transfer of the Black Death from the East.[32]

However, determining the exact origin of the Black Death remains a formidable challenge because it likely involved complex patterns and a multitude of variables. The disease might have originated from several species of rodents simultaneously, including rats and marmots. According to Monica Green, an authority on the subject, the strain of the bacterium that caused the Black Death originated in Central Asia

---

30   Montefiore, *The World*, 344.
31   Frankopan, *The Earth Transformed*, 294.
32   Montefiore, *The World*, 344.

a century before reaching Europe, implying that the Mongols began spreading it in the thirteenth century wherever the hooves of their military horses reached.[33] If this theory holds water, various local outbreaks across Eurasia that came under Mongol rule emerged from Central Asia and were spread by the Mongols as they moved around; these local outbreaks occurred intermittently for more than a century. The Black Death could have resulted from the convergence of these various local epidemics facilitated by events such as the movement of armies and refugees, cross-continental grain trade and shipments hitch-hiked by rodents, and the Mongol horse relay system (which not only allowed swift communication but also facilitated the efficient transportation of pathogens across the vast Mongol Empire). The 1340s also marked one of the most tumultuous decades in global military history, with wars erupting not only in Europe but also in territories dominated by the Mongols and North Africa—regions severely affected by the Black Death in the first wave. Engaging in wars imposes strain on conflicting sides, even in the best of times, but during this particular period, the challenges faced by all warring parties would have been exceptionally demanding, implying that respective populations would have been exhausted and more susceptible to diseases. Each variable served to magnify the problems caused by other variables, leading to a cascading effect, with the Black Death representing culmination.

Periodic outbreaks of the plague affected most parts of the Mongol Empire and its off-shoots, both before and after the Black Death. In the Yuan, which likely suffered the most due to its large populations residing in dense settlements, a series of epidemics struck Henan province from 1313, with coastal provinces experiencing outbreaks in 1345-46. The most devastating wave occurred in 1351, spreading throughout Yuan China yearly and lasting until 1362, leading to a catastrophic population decline.[34]

In the Chagatai state, besides the outbreak of the plague in the 1250s, evidence of the epidemic surfaced in Nestorian Christian graves dating back to the late 1330s, a decade before the outbreak of the Black Death in Europe. Discovered near Issyk-Kul in 2022 (now in Kyrgyzstan), this

---

33   Green, 'The four Black Deaths'.
34   Atwood, *Encyclopedia of Mongolia and the Mongol Empire*, 41.

burial site contained human teeth samples containing *Yersinia pestis* DNA.[35]

The impact of the plague was also deeply felt in the Golden Horde. Özbeg, the ruler of the Golden Horde, had expanded into Europe and designated Caffa as Genoese territory and Tana as Venetian territory in Crimea. However, tensions escalated after Özbeg's death in 1343, leading to a Genoese killing of a Muslim that, in turn, prompted Özbeg's son, Janibeg, to besiege Caffa. Upon Janibeg's return in 1346, the plague struck his camp, resulting in a devastating loss—twelve percent of the Golden Horde's population is believed to have succumbed to the disease.[36] Saray, the capital of the Golden Horde, was again stuck by the plague in 1364.

The plague not only spread extensively across Mongol-controlled territories but also far beyond. Once it reached Europe, the death toll was of biblical proportions, claiming fifty percent of England's six million people, seventy-five percent of Venice's population, and ninety-eight percent of parts of Mamluk Egypt in North Africa. Furthermore, pandemics continued to resurge over the next centuries, perpetuating the devastation, albeit to a lesser extent.[37]

The Plague in the Ecological History of the Mongol Empire

In the thirteenth century, the Mongols' head-spinning military success relied not on superior technology or wonder weapons but on efficient organization, iron discipline, and hardy Mongolian ponies, which enabled the Mongol Empire to expand at breakneck speed in all directions. Constantly on the move and wielding unparalleled striking power, Mongol cavalrymen were like medieval 'terminators', materializing without warning in the most unexpected places, descending upon their enemies with the sudden, ferocious force of a thunderstorm unleashed from a clear sky. However, the Mongol expansion may not have been solely due to Genghis Khan's leadership genius and the skills of his troops; recent research indicates that climate played a significant role. Between 1211 and 1225, a period corresponding to Genghis Khan's rapid

---

35 Spyrou et al., 'Analysis of 3800-year-old Yersinia pestis genomes'.
36 Montefiore, *The World*, 364-65.
37 Ibid., 364.

ascent and his military successes, the typically cold and arid Mongolian Plateau experienced unusually heavy rainfall and mild temperatures. Although this did not transform Mongolia into a tropical paradise, the warmer climate spurred the growth of essential grasslands, leading to an expansion in the size of livestock herds, especially those of ponies, providing a solid foundation for the Mongol Empire.

In Mongolia, children start riding horses at around the age three or four, and in no time, they become adept horse riders. For many nomads, their horses become like an extension of their limbs, offering stability and speed. Hence, when mounted, nomads feel like a fish in water—they can eat, drink, flirt, party, fight, and take a nap without dismounting. Nomads become so accustomed to constant riding that when nature calls while in the *ger*, they prefer saddling up instead of walking a short distance to defecate. Horsemanship, true for contemporary Mongols, echoes the historical habits of Mongols in the past.

Under Genghis Khan, each Mongol cavalryman owned multiple ponies (at least two, usually four to seven remounts), enabling them to ride without stopping, and the additional grass resulting from the warmer climate provided the energy required for the Empire's remarkable expansion.[38] Genghis Khan effectively harnessed this abundant supply of horses to create the most formidable cavalry force in history.

This radical climatic change at the regional level, unprecedented in more than a thousand years, occurred against the backdrop of global warming from about 950 CE to 1250 CE, also known as the Little Optimum. This period resulted in an extended growing season, leading to a more reliable food supply and a subsequent global population increase over those three centuries. This growth, in turn, spurred a significant surge in urbanization, creating paradises for germs and other contagious diseases.

In Mongolia, the mild climate and flourishing grasslands not only facilitated the growth of horse herds but also supported a population explosion of various species, including those carrying the plague, such as marmots. The impact of this change on *Yersinia pestis* and the fleas that carry it, remains unclear. However, what is becoming increasingly

---

38   Pederson et al., 'Pluvials, droughts, the Mongol Empire, and modern Mongolia'.

apparent, thanks to the latest developments in medicine and science allowing us to examine DNA, is that an event called polytomy occurred sometime around the 1250s. It appears that *Yersinia pestis* diverged into three and subsequently four distinct lineages (a process called polytomy) at that moment. The bacterium that caused the Black Death can be traced back to that climactic event that geneticists have called the 'Big Bang', which marked the end of the Little Optimum.[39]

The Little Optimum, however, does not imply the absence of climatic fluctuations during this period. Periodic droughts, cold spells, and abundant rainfalls occurred, intensifying especially from the end of this period. These changes would have affected the pathogenic landscape and posed challenges to rodent species such as marmots by weakening them and making them more susceptible to the plague bacterium. While the Mongols may have thrived in optimal climatic conditions under Genghis Khan for empire building, the regions facing Mongol attacks did not necessarily share the same auspicious climate for resisting invasion. Central Asia, for example, had already been grappling with prolonged drought and water scarcity before the Mongol invasion, affecting resistance negatively. At the beginning of the fourteenth century, the Eurasian landmass underwent a sharp cooling trend marked by cold and humid conditions, resulting in more outbreaks of the plague, extensively documented in Chinese annals and potentially impacting regions beyond.

In the turbulent period prior to and during the 1340s, marked by the Black Death, Europe also faced adverse weather conditions, leading in lower crop yields. This not only weakened the population, making them susceptible to diseases, but also exposed them to overseas grain shipments, which carried rodents hosting the plague.

This climatic fluctuation with unpredictable weather formed the backdrop against which all other events unfolded, as mentioned above—plague outbreaks, harvest failures in certain regions making them dependable on foreign grain shipments, the weakening of the populations in affected areas, the political unification and internal splitting of the Eurasian landmass, and large-scale wars.[40]

---

39   Green, 'Putting Asia on the Black Death map'; Green, 'The four Black Deaths'.
40   Frankopan, *The Earth Transformed*, 302–14.

The Plague in Mongolia's Post-Imperial History

The Yuan dynasty in China collapsed in 1368 amid widespread social unrest and a weakened, corrupt central government. The situation was exacerbated by outbreaks of diseases, famine, natural disasters such as droughts and floods, and price inflation, all of which fueled rebellions. This event marked a pivotal moment not only in Mongolia's history but also in the annals of epidemics and pandemics. As the Yuan court retreated to Mongolia, the Mongol state deflated into a regional power, losing its symbolic influence over other Genghisid states and their offshoots in Russia, Persia, and Central Asia.

These Genghisid states also grappled with profound challenges in the aftermath of the Black Death. The Golden Horde in Russia, for example, plunged into anarchy in 1359 before its capital, Saray, was once again struck by the plague in 1364. This period coincided with the extinction of the Batu line after 1360 and of the Orda line a bit earlier, setting the stage for ceaseless struggle for the leadership among the descendants of their brothers. This gave rise to the 'Time of Troubles', involving several khans concurrently holding sway. The heightened competition for power and domination reflected a stark reality: there were fewer rewards and benefits available than in the past, and resources were rapidly dwindling.[41]

In addition to existential struggles, these Genghisid states underwent Islamization, leading to significant changes in dietary habits, including the prohibition of consuming 'impure' animals like marmots in adherence to Islamic laws. This religious and cultural transformation, coupled with the fragmentation of the Islamized Genghisid states into smaller polities, restricted the flow of goods, people, and pathogens. Consequently, these changes potentially impeded the spread of local epidemics into global pandemics, marking a departure from the earlier period of Pax Mongolica when interconnectedness facilitated the movement of diseases on an intercontinental scale.

In post-Yuan Mongolia itself, Mongols reverted to their traditional lifestyle while splintering into numerous groups and fiefdoms, periodically attempting political reunification by means of sword and

---

41   Ibid., 311.

arrows. In 1640, the Halha Mongols and the Oirats, each consisting of a patchwork of fiefdoms, made peace with one another and established an alliance in response to the threat posed by the rising Manchu Qing dynasty. However, this alliance among militant and mutually suspicious fiefdoms proved as fragile as a marriage in a loveless, dysfunctional family and was just as destined to fail. Following tensions among the Halha fiefdoms and between the Halha and the Oirats, the Oirats, led by the ambitious Galdan Boshogtu Khan, invaded Mongolia in 1688, pillaging and burning the holiest of Buddhist temples. This prompted many Halhas flee to Inner Mongolia, which had been conquered by the Manchu Qing in 1634-36. In Inner Mongolia, the Halha refugees appealed to the Manchu Emperor Kangxi for protection, a situation reminiscent of a group of mice quarreling with another group of mice and seeking refuge from a hungry cat. After considerable hesitation, the 'cat' acquiesced to the 'mice's' plea for protection. In 1691, at the (not-so-great) Doloonnuur Convention, the Halhas officially submitted to the Manchu Emperor for full protection, marking the commencement of spending next two centuries in a metaphorical mousetrap.

Under Manchu Qing rule, various Mongol groups were pacified, divided, and confined to fixed territories, limiting their interactions and exchanges. Over the six centuries from post-imperial disintegration to submission to the Manchu Qing dynasty until the early twentieth century, there were no significant plague epidemics in Mongolia. Localized outbreaks persisted, but Mongols presumably managed to control the plague using familiar methods: by relocating, avoiding areas with confirmed or suspected plague outbreaks, staying away from strangers, and quarantining themselves when afflicted by the plague.

Compared to the imperial period, Mongolia also experienced relatively stable climate conditions from the fourteenth century to the twentieth century, with less radical changes. That said, due to its continental nature the country did witness some fluctuations and variations in its climate over this period. The sixteenth and seventeenth centuries saw relatively warm and wet conditions, while the eighteenth century brought colder and drier weather. The nineteenth century, on the other hand, was marked by severe winters (known as *dzud*) and dry summers, posing significant challenges for the nomadic herding communities. These fluctuations inevitably impacted the ecosystem and the prevalence of plague outbreaks in the region. In certain years, there were presumably more cases of infected nomads than in others. However, due to the country's landlocked position and its division into disconnected territories and sub-territories, and considering Mongols lived in small nomadic communities, the plague never escalated into an epidemic, even if there was a possibility for it to do so.

All this changed on the eve of Mongolia's proclamation of independence from the Manchu Qing in 1911 when the plague caused a regional outbreak, known as the Manchurian Plague. The plague spread in a social context that breached Mongolia's relative isolation, allowing the bacterium to travel from the Mongolia-Manchurian border by rail and eventually infect densely populated settlements in China. The outbreak was precipitated by the development of new dyes by the German chemical industry that could transform cheap marmot fur into imitation sabre, otter, and mink fur, increasing the demand for marmot skins. This attracted a large number of migrant Chinese unskilled laborers to the Mongolia-Manchurian border region who began hunting marmots indiscriminately. These inexperienced hunters not only handled infected marmots casually but also lived and slept in cramped and unhygienic conditions—ideal hotbeds for disease. From there, it was a small step to the outbreak of the plague, which started in the autumn of 1910. By January 1911, more than 10,000 people had died in Manchuria. Manchuria's railway network facilitated the disease's spread as thousands of migrant laborers returned to their homes for the New Year Festival. By the time it finally waned in March-April 1911, the Manchurian Plague had claimed more than 60,000 lives. The situation could have been much worse had it not been for the prompt measures taken by the authorities armed with modern medical knowledge, who established makeshift plague hospitals and imposed strict quarantine.[42]

The Control of the Plague During the Socialist Period

The Manchu Qing's plunge into an existential crisis animated Mongolia's elites to take advantage of the situation, akin to mice starting to play when the cat is away. Mongolia liberated itself from the self-imposed shackles

---

42 Spyrou et al., 'Analysis of 3800-year-old *Yersinia pestis* genomes'.

of the Manchu Qing in 1911, only to submit itself to another foreign empire, the Soviet Union, a decade later, remaining only nominally independent. This new period marked another phase of isolation for Mongolia, as it became cut off—this time by the Soviet Union—from the rest of the world.

Despite the challenges faced by this landlocked country, there was a benefit from a broader regional health perspective. Mongolia's geographic isolation meant that potential plague outbreaks were scientifically monitored and confined to one of the world's most sparsely populated regions with the help of modern epidemiological knowledge and procedures imported from the Soviet Union.

The fight against the plague began in earnest in 1931, inaugurated by the publication in Ulaanbaatar of the first popular book on the dangers and causes of the plague.[43] This was followed by the establishment in the same year of the Marmot Plague Control Laboratory in Ulaanbaatar, with help from the Soviet Union. Initially run by Soviet experts, the laboratory underwent expansion and transformation, becoming the Marmot Plague Control Center in 1940. This evolution involved the integration of more Mongol personnel into its operations. Under the guidance of Soviet doctors and epidemiologists, the Marmot Plague Control Center developed a systematic approach, employing cutting-edge techniques to combat contagious zoonotic diseases. Whenever provinces or smaller administrative units reported confirmed or suspected plague outbreaks, swift isolation measures were implemented. Those who had contact with plague patients were quarantined, and patients received antibiotic treatment in regional hospitals.

Given the politicization of every aspect of life under socialism, the control of the plague had a comprehensive ideological aspect which went hand in hand with its practical aspect. Its ideological goal was to instill a rational, scientific way of thinking on the population and fight against traditional medicine and superstition, defined as the enemies of scientific progress and hence communism. It was in this environment that the marmot was stripped of its mythical chimera-skins and labeled as a biological species harboring a dangerous zoonotic disease. This

---

43   *Chium-a Kemeku Tarbagan-u Miljan Ebedchin-u Tuhai.*

mirrored the way dogs were similarly divested of their cosmological roles and reduced to germ carriers (see Chapter 2).

Despite these measures, plague cases were recorded almost every year during the socialist period, indicating that the *Homo Sovieticus Mongolicus* wasn't following the Party instructions to the letter. The high mortality rate in confirmed cases resulted not only from citizens failing to fully heed the Party's advice to stop eating raw marmot meat or using marmot tails to pamper their penises, but also from the power of misplaced human optimism—the belief that contracting the plague or being unlucky is something that happens to others, not to themselves. This misplaced optimism among Mongol comrades is humorously illustrated in the following joke:

> A herder commits a banal crime against the socialist state and is duly sentenced to death. The day before his execution, his wife visits to bid him a tearful goodbye. With misplaced optimism, the man reassures her, 'Don't cry, my love. There's no certainty the execution will proceed tomorrow. Even if it does, there's no guarantee the firearms won't malfunction. And even if they don't, there's no guarantee the bullets will find their mark. And even if they do, there's no guarantee I won't survive. So, don't worry. I'm sure nothing serious will happen to me and everything will be alright'.

To this should be added the fact that, the sparse distribution of healthcare facilities across Mongolia's vast territory made it challenging for infected nomads to receive timely medical care. This challenge was further compounded by the presence of plague foci covering extensive areas of the country. Nevertheless, the modern plague control system ensured vigilant monitoring of local outbreaks, effectively bringing them under control and preventing their spread to neighboring provinces and beyond.

The Marmot as a State Commodity

From the socialist state's viewpoint, marmot hunting carried substantial economic significance, bringing much-needed foreign currency to Mongolia's coffers. This demand for marmot skins was largely driven by foreign markets. However, industrial-scale hunting had commenced before the socialist regime was established, kicking off in the late nineteenth century to meet the growing demands for marmot skins in Russia and China. The surge, as mentioned, was fueled by revolutionary skin processing techniques pioneered by the German chemical industry.

For instance, between 1906-10, Mongolia exported a staggering thirteen million marmot pelts to Russia, a stark contrast to the mere 30,000 exported in 1865.[44] This commercial success, however, had a darker side. On the other side of the Mongol-Manchurian border, intensive marmot hunting by Chinese unskilled laborers, eager to cash in on the bounty, inadvertently caused the outbreak of the Great Manchurian Plague in 1910-11.

Upon seizing power, the Mongolian people's government capitalized on the marmot-skin craze in 1920s Germany, transforming marmot skin export into a major trade item. During the socialist period, Mongolia's annual marmot skin trade averaged over 1.2 million skins.[45] While demand eventually decreased slightly, it persisted, continuing to impact marmot hunting in Mongolia. The state's annual purchases of marmot skins from hunters declined from over a million to fewer than 700,000 between 1960 and 1990, although this still constituted a significant quantity.[46]

Under socialist rule, the state monopolized all economic activities, including the procurement and pricing of marmot skins, which became heavily regulated in the 1930s. Private hunters were banned from profiteering by selling marmot skins on the black market, as skins were declared a state-owned resource. Many collective farms had mobile shopping units called *agant* that sold, among other items, bullets and had quotas for procuring marmot pelts each year, established to regulate the number of marmots harvested annually. While many nomads hunted marmots and sold the skins to these *agant* shops, some were employed as full-time hunters by the state and provided with salaries and equipment.

While setting annual quotas for marmot skins, the state also sought to control wildlife populations by preserving the country's natural habitats through the establishment of protected areas where hunting was strictly prohibited. These designated zones served as essential sanctuaries for

---

44 Summers, *The Great Manchurian Plague*, 119-20.
45 Wingard and Zahler, 'Silent steppe'.
46 Atwood, *Encyclopedia of Mongolia and the Mongol Empire*, 229.

wildlife, ensuring that the broader environment remained wild and thriving.

In theory, communist society was envisioned as a utopian state where the needs of every laborer and herder would be fully satisfied. However, in practice, it was marred by chronic shortages and distribution failures. In Mongolian, many phrases draw upon the nomadic heritage and center around animal husbandry and hunting. One particularly vivid expression is 'a fox dies of hunger by looking at the bull dangling its testicles'. This phrase conjures an image of a hungry fox staring at a bull's loosely hanging testicles, hoping they might drop off soon, offering a satisfying meal. It is used to illustrate situations where someone clings to an unrealistic hope for too long. During the socialist era in Mongolia, most citizens found themselves in a similar situation to these hungry foxes, relying on the economically impotent socialist state to provide them with a satisfying life. However, rather than passively waiting for metaphorical juicy testicles to fall onto their dinner plates, some enterprising *Homo Sovieticus Mongolicus* took matters into their own hands. This proactive approach gave rise to an underground economy, an attempt to compensate for shortages in goods, food, and monetary income. However, grabbing destiny by the balls also had its darker side, as corruption became pervasive, fueling various illicit activities, including widespread poaching across Mongolia, even within wildlife sanctuaries. Those involved in poaching seemed motivated to improve their living conditions, rather than outright undermining the existing system. Similarly, other activities considered anti-communist or illegal— such as secretly conducting religious rituals, chopping off dead dogs' tails, stealing state property, prostituting, offering to be sugar daddies or sugar mamas, and many other actions—were integral parts of everyday life for many otherwise law-abiding citizens in the socialist country.

In Post-Socialist Mongolia

In 1990, Mongolia made a decisive shift away from state socialism, embracing a free-market economy and open borders that allowed its citizens to travel abroad and permitted foreigners to enter the country without restrictions. Rejecting communist ideology, the government adopted a new democratic constitution in 1992, championing consumerism, entrepreneurship, political freedom, freedom of movement, and human rights—freedoms that had previously been denied to the populace. However, this epochal transition wasn't all smooth sailing. Mongolia faced unprecedented instability, along with a significant rise in poverty and unemployment, reflecting the challenges encountered by other former socialist nations transitioning to market-oriented systems. During this tumultuous period, the only sectors keeping Mongolia's economy afloat were those based on the country's abundant resources. Gold mining and the export of marmot skins, primarily to Russia and China, emerged as vital industries immediately after socialism's demise.

The marmot skin trade, a sector driven by individual entrepreneurs rather than the state, played a crucial role not only in sustaining the livelihoods of numerous families across the country but also in the initial accumulation of private capital that individuals would later invest in other sectors, thus contributing to the diversification of Mongolia's economy. This trade created a chain of individuals involved, starting with hunters who sold skins to middlemen, prompting many to rush to provinces in hopes of purchasing skins cheaply and reselling them at a higher price in Ulaanbaatar to traders traveling abroad. This development paralleled a gold rush in the country, as people flocked to the abandoned or depleted gold mines in hopes of striking it rich.

In the early 1990s, I found myself swept up in the 'marmot skin rush'. During my summer vacations from high school, I collected marmot skins from local hunters in Dundgobi Province and resold them in Ulaanbaatar. Despite the hard work and stress involved, I barely made any profit. Intense competition made acquiring marmot skins difficult, and losses during transportation from Dundgobi to Ulaanbaatar, along with purchasing low-quality skins, wiped out my meager gains. Despite this, I thoroughly enjoyed the experience because I gained independence and learned valuable networking and problem-solving skills. The only individuals who reaped real profits were traders transporting skins to Russia or China in large quantities. However, engaging in cross-border trade, especially with Russia, was daunting due to widespread corruption at border controls and the need for trustworthy partners in Russia. The challenge was amplified by the dog-eat-dog environment during Russia's plunge into wild capitalism, where contract killings were commonplace, and hitmen even advertised their services in the local press.

Having decided that marmot skin business wasn't my calling, I ventured into shuttle trading between Ulaanbaatar and Russia. This was in 1993 when I, still a teenager, made trips to Russia. Without the funds for serious import-export operations, I started small. Armed with Mongol leather coats and trendy leather bags that were all the rage in Russia at that time, I hopped on a bus from Ulaanbaatar to Russia, eager for new adventures.

During this era, shuttling by bus between Ulaanbaatar and Siberian towns in Russia was incredibly popular in Mongolia. Multiple buses made the journey daily. Mongol shuttlers typically traveled to Russia with two types of goods: Mongol produce, such as marmot fur coats and hats, leather coats, and leather bags; and Chinese products, including low-quality, inexpensive items like clothing, shoes, and duvets. In return, people brought back food stuffs, condoms, Soviet military jockstraps (an underwear for protecting the vulnerable part), Soviet military coats, and various miscellaneous items they bought in the Russian flea market.

Passing through Russian customs unscathed required having the balls of a brass macaque, an entrepreneurial nose, and a fair amount of luck. While it was mandatory to declare every item brought into Russia, the wildly exorbitant taxes imposed by Russian customs officials were enough to ruin any shuttle trade expedition. Hence, many tried to avoid declaring all their items and resorted to hiding goods in various places. During my first business trip, I vividly recall witnessing several Mongol businesswomen, dressed in marmot fur coats for sale, trying to conceal goods in their brassieres and underwear. At the Russian customs, Mongols, especially men, caught attempting to smuggle merchandise, were unceremoniously subjected to kicks and punches by officials and border guards. Though I personally escaped mistreatment, I anticipated a punch, as most men on our bus seemed to be receiving one or two. Perhaps my tender age and my proficiency in Russian spared me, or maybe I was just lucky, or gave the impression that I had the brass balls of a macaque. Who knows?

The situation in the Russian market was no better. The Mongols had to play a constant game of evasion with predatory Russian tax collectors and policemen, who regularly raided the open market where Mongols displayed their goods. During one such raid, the Mongol vendors, many sporting marmot fur coats for sale, scattered in all directions like marmots fleeing from indiscriminate hunters. This starkly contrasted with the treatment shown to some Japanese tourists who had arrived on a bus, accompanied by a police escort, and stopped at the hotel entrance opposite the open market. These tourists received all signs of courtesy from the bus driver and hotel doormen, not to mention the Russian passersby who admired how well-groomed and well-dressed the Japanese appeared, flaunting their expensive cameras and watches. As I stood there observing the Japanese tourists, a Russian male Sapiens standing beside me, also keeping an eye on the tourists, offered his opinion that Mongols would be treated with respect when we too became 'proper humans' like the Japanese.

On the return journey at the Russian-Mongolian border, a long column of both Russian and Mongolian vehicles awaited entry into Mongolia. All Russians were allowed to jump the queue and pass controls swiftly, while the Mongols were instructed to wait for further notice. Frustration grew among the Mongols who were unhappy with the blatantly unfair treatment. Some of them shouted a few questions at the Russian border officials about how long they would have to wait and tried to shame the Russians by reminding them that Mongolia was the second socialist country in the world, after the Soviet Union. This sentimental bullshit from former imperial subjects must have been the last straw that broke the camel's back, and in no time, the feared Russian riot police, the OMON, arrived on the scene. Without warning, the cops started indiscriminately beating those standing closest to the border gates. I saw men and women running away, holding their bleeding heads with their hands. This was a horror scene out of a Soviet movie where Nazis beat occupied people. The Mongols were not admitted into the border controls area until the next day as a punitive measure. During the night, I had a chance to converse with a couple of male Russian prison runaways who were avoiding the police. They approached our bus under the cover of darkness to ask for food and cigarettes. This experience led me to a conclusion, further substantiated during my subsequent research in Russia: in this country, individuals, especially foreigners from former 'brotherly' socialist countries, have more to fear from the police and officials than from gangsters. When

Russians, especially officials and those in uniform, are empowered with a hammer, both real and metaphorical, they typically treat everyone else like nails that need to be struck to instill order. Today, whenever I come across news detailing the mistreatment and torture of the local civilian population in the occupied territories of Ukraine by Russian soldiers, secret police, and officials—whom the Russian occupants regard as inferiors or even worse, as traitors to Greater Russia—I know where this chauvinistic and cruel behavior comes from.

In the 1990s, one of my paternal cousins was a successful marmot skin trader, shuttling between Ulaanbaatar and Russia by train, skillfully ensuring his skin shipments reached their destination unscathed amidst corrupt customs officials, gangsters, policemen, and Russian ultranationalists, earning him the reputation of a small-time marmot fur kingpin. He was the elder brother of the man who performed the funerary rite for Sharik and also the person to whom my father used to send dog meat to treat his respiratory disease. Initially, my cousin, the marmot fur kingpin, went to the Soviet Union to study the communist theory at university in the late 1980s. His goal was to become an intellectual and climb the ranks of the Party hierarchy. He possessed the correct philosophical mindset and moral position to succeed as a party apparatchik. Whenever he read Marx's and Lenin's opuses on dialectical materialism—he once confided in me—he 'thought of pussies', and whenever he had sex, he found himself thinking about dialectical materialism. As endorsed by the socialist state, he also practiced the correct face-to-face 'missionary position' and not the bourgeois 'doggy style' or similar dodgy positions. However, in the aftermath of the Soviet system's disintegration, this golden boy of communism was bitten by the capitalist bug that drove him to become an entrepreneur. Cool as a cucumber and fluent in Russian, he frequently traveled between Mongolia and Russia, transporting several thousand marmot skins in one go, in the process making a small fortune. Many who knew him were envious of his larger-than-life personality and unabashed playboy lifestyle: he was always surrounded by sugar babies, was perpetually drunk, dined and wined in the fanciest restaurants, and carried stacks of cash he never failed to show off. If we are to apply the communist critique of capitalism, my cousin converted commodities (marmot skins) into filthy lucre, amassed wealth, purchased high-end services, and actively contributed to class inequality and the perpetuation of bourgeois, hedonistic forms of self-gratification. Despite his industriousness, rather than directing his energy towards more productive pursuits and investing his money in gold mining or a similar venture, my cousin indulged in a morally destructive lifestyle. As his maternal uncle, my father often advised him to stop these excesses, but alas, it was like casting pearls before swine.

My cousin was not alone in succumbing to greed and losing sight of his values. The entire society resonated with an insatiable entrepreneurial spirit, unrestrained sex, unchecked violence, pervasive fear, and a survival instinct, having abandoned the moral compass established during the socialist period. In the age of chaos when the world seemed turned upside down, socialist-era heroes—such as toilers, herders, intellectuals, and elderly statesmen—no longer held the spotlight. Instead, society started to admire figures like cutthroat entrepreneurs, gangsters, and high-end escorts, who became the new role models, dangling their newfound wealth and fame like unreachable prizes before the impoverished masses. My cousin stood as a living embodiment of this shift, reflecting the changing values of the age.

Mongolia's marmot population has faced significant challenges over the years due to both legal and illegal hunting practices. During the socialist era, overhunting was a persistent problem, but the situation worsened after the liberalization of hunting regulations following the collapse of state socialism. In the mid-1990s, the price of marmot pelts surged due to rising international demand, which, combined with relaxed gun control laws and increased car ownership, made marmot hunting more accessible and widespread. By the early 2000s, the annual number of marmots hunted exceeded three million.[47] This unsustainable level of hunting led to severe biodiversity loss and regional extinctions, culminating in what has been dubbed as a 'marmot crisis'. As a symbol of the marmot's significance, there are now two monuments dedicated to the marmot—one is in the town of Nalaih and the other in the village of Bayan-Uul, Dornod Province, where in both places the marmot has disappeared due to overhunting.

---

47 Wingard and Zahler, 'Silent steppe'.

While marmots are potential vectors for diseases like the plague, ecologists recognize them as a 'keystone species' in the grassland ecosystem. Marmot activities help sustain biodiversity and ecological resilience, meaning that their decline negatively impacts the entire ecosystem.[48] This mirrors Mongol cosmological themes of harmony and imbalance, where marmots serve as indicators of environmental health.

In response to the critical situation, in 2006 the Mongolian government enacted a law prohibiting marmot hunting, aiming to protect the species and rein in the greed of hunters and entrepreneurs. Simultaneously, the government has taken proactive measures to reintroduce marmots in areas where they have gone extinct. For example, in Sühbaatar Province, authorities initiated marmot reintroduction efforts in 2006, 2011, 2012, and 2019. Similar initiatives are also underway in other parts of the country.

Despite this, enforcing the hunting ban has proven incredibly challenging due to rampant corruption, understaffed law enforcement, and cultural preferences for marmot meat, not to mention economic gains to be made from the marmot pelt trade. Tragically, every year or so, several people die in Mongolia from contracting the plague. The revival of religion, including Buddhism and shamanism, claiming ownership over wildlife, didn't appear to have influenced hunters to kill fewer animals. On the contrary, many hunters sought to strike deals with deities and nature spirits by bribing them with rituals, offerings, and prayers to ensure continued blessings and successful hunts. This is not dissimilar to acts of bribery or strategic exchanges seen in chimp societies, where our distant cousins offer grooming and other valuable resources to increase their chances of receiving food or sexual access in return.

Part III

Science, Pseudoscience, and the Plague

In the early-1990s, as Mongolia embraced religious freedoms and pseudoscience, a man in our neighborhood became renowned for his healing powers, practicing divination, and assisting people in winning the lottery. Miracles that he allegedly performed were on everybody's

---

48   Yoshihara et al., 'Effects of disturbance by Siberian marmots'.

lip, and many sought him out for a session. One day, luck was on our side, and the man agreed to grace our humble flat with his charismatic presence and perform magical health-related rituals. Apparently, he liked the way we treated him and the special food my mother cooked for him so that he ended up staying in one of our bedrooms for a month. Although he preferred to be left alone in the room, where he spent most of his time sleeping like a marmot, eating, releasing gazes of the least salubrious origin, leafing through pornographic newspapers, and enjoying himself, I had plenty of time to observe him and even ask a few questions about his magical powers. A former laborer with special interest in the occult, he found fame overnight after he started healing people with cosmic energy. In his new trade, he used various Buddhist implements (a rosary, a statue of Buddha), sacred objects (stones for divination, consecrated coins), holy water, marmot ankle bones, along with a calculator (to calculate some celestial equations)—not to mention his sweet tongue: his most potent tool. During his month-long stay in our flat, we grew so accustomed to his therapeutic presence that his departure to sofa-surf in another family's flat left us missing him.

Given the nature of humanity—a species closely related to chimps and bonobos—we are social primates whose beliefs and actions are shaped not only by analytical thinking but also, and more significantly, by our gut feelings, intuition, and herd mentality. We often adopt ideas and beliefs uncritically from the groups we belong to—whether neighbors, religious communities, political affiliations, or peer groups—often without realizing it. While we sometimes engage in analytical thinking (what Daniel Kahneman refers to as 'System 2' or 'slow thinking'), most of the time, we rely on quick, intuitive thinking (termed by Kahneman as 'System 1' or 'fast thinking'; Steve Peters calls it the 'inner chimp'[49]).

Given our fallible nature as a species, no human creation is free from biases, subjective errors, or misinterpretations. This applies to institutions including religion, politics, and even science. However, there is a crucial distinction between religion and science, as mentioned earlier. While religion is built on the premise of infallibility, science acknowledges its mistakes and is founded on self-correcting mechanisms designed to refine and improve knowledge.

---

49 Kahneman, *Thinking Fast and Slow*; Peters, *The Chimp Paradox*.

Science does not exist in a vacuum; it is susceptible to external influences not only because it reflects the personalities and biases of scientists but also because it is intertwined with other social institutions. This is particularly evident in authoritarian regimes, where scientific disciplines often become subservient to political agendas. In such environments, knowledge production can be stifled, allowing unscientific ideas, myths, and falsehoods to flourish under the guise of science. Additionally, science can be manipulated by spiritual movements and charismatic individuals, turning it into pseudoscience rather than a pursuit of truth.

This raises important questions about the susceptibility of science to manipulation and influence by rigid belief systems—whether Leninist-Stalinist ideologies, religious dogmas, or spiritual movements—in both autocratic regimes (such as socialist Mongolia) and transitional societies (such as post-socialist Mongolia). This section explores the relationship between power, science, and pseudoscience, using the example of Mongolia during its socialist and post-socialist periods. It sheds light on the circumstances under which Mongolia sought to manage the plague situation.

Stories, Religion, and Communism

As discussed earlier (see Chapter 1), in human culture, nearly every belief, concept, or social activity is rooted in and communicated through stories, which serve as the foundation of culture. Stories—whether myths, religious dogmas, cosmologies, ideologies, *bolson yavdal* stories, national histories, genealogies, or rumors—don't need to convey the truth or accurately represent reality. Most are subjective interpretations at best and falsehoods at worst, with their primary function being to foster cooperation among people by offering different types of information that resonate with various groups. Despite their fictional nature, these stories exert a tangible and unifying force on our lives as long as we believe in them.

Viewing stories in this way helps us understand that human cultures essentially revolve around fictions and subjective interpretations that gain materiality and tangibility through their incorporation into daily life. These fictional stories become embedded in the material world through rituals, politics, art, clothing, sexuality, morality, architecture, the media, and other aspects of society.

Let's take religion as an example. In a narrow definition, religion is built upon stories that legitimize a set of beliefs, practices, and moral values, often by attributing them to supernatural entities such as gods, spirits, and the like. In Christianity, God is considered the ultimate source of legitimacy and truth, guiding human actions through divine commandments and teachings found in religious stories inscribed in holy texts like the Bible. Despite containing numerous falsehoods about the age of the Earth, the origins of humanity, the causes of diseases, and historical events, as well as promoting questionable moral positions such as misogyny, homophobia, xenophobia, and slavery,[50] Christianity has united large numbers of people. Like other religions, it has done so by integrating its teachings into all aspects of its followers' lives, from the cradle to the grave, instilling shared interests, goals, and identities. If the primary function of religion were to represent reality correctly and seek the truth, it would be difficult to explain why its fictional texts, full of untruths, create and maintain large communities of millions and, in some cases, billions.

In its broadest definition, religion doesn't require gods, as long as it offers an all-encompassing story conferring 'natural' legitimacy on human norms and actions. According to this definition, communist ideology is also a kind of religion. Despite their outward differences, communist ideology, *in essence,* is no different from Christianity, Islam, or any other traditional religion in that it too offers an all-encompassing story where the 'natural' laws of 'dialectical materialism' and 'relentless class struggle' play a similar role to personal God in Christianity and Islam or the impersonal forces of karma and dharma in Buddhism. Just like traditional religions, communist ideology provides an explanation for the meaning of life, the nature of reality, and the relationship between humans and the environment, aiming to guide social evolution toward its predestined goal of achieving communism—an earthly paradise. In other words, according to this communist narrative, humans have no choice but to obey and follow these 'natural' laws (which are invented by human storytellers). It is no coincidence that communist

---

50 Hitchens, *God Is Not Great;* Dawkins, *The God Delusion.*

ideology, despite being based on materialist philosophy, exhibited all the hallmarks of traditional religions, including having prophets (Karl Marx, Friedrich Engels, Vladimir Lenin), holy texts (works of the Founding Fathers of the communist theory), an institution to safeguard and impose knowledge (the Communist Party), heretics (all people or groups deviating from the prescribed state beliefs), rituals (mass rallies, ideological education sessions, birthdays of communist leaders), pilgrimage sites (mausoleums housing mummified leaders), miracles (delivered by Soviet science and technology, as well as charlatans like Trofim Lysenko[51]), witch-hunts (leading to mass arrests, show trials, and executions), and justification for global war (with the heretical capitalist world and its minions). Communist ideology—or 'communist religion', based on myths, dangerous fantasies, and falsehoods—served as the foundation of Soviet culture and influenced millions of people worldwide. If the primary function of this ideology were to accurately represent reality and seek the truth, it would have collapsed before winning over entire nations.

The same can be said about any other social order, including liberal democracy. As a cultural product, liberal democracy doesn't need to objectively reflect reality or exclusively promote the truth, even though it claims to do so—much like all other social organizations. Its primary function is to unite people through shared myths and fictions, such as those concerning nationhood, equality, inalienable human rights, meritocracy, and so on. These myths and fictions can sometimes take a blatant and more nefarious form, such as the narrative of a nation being invaded by immigrants, immigrants causing crime surges, or other countries stealing jobs. Leaders who spread such falsehoods and anti-foreign rhetoric may rally support by fostering societal division between supporters and opponents—a tactic that can occur even in democracies. From a broader cultural perspective, the best social orders are not those that most accurately seek and promote the truth, but rather those that most effectively unite people. In this regard, communism was one of

---

51   The Soviet agronomist and pseudo-scientist Trofim Lysenko (1898-1976), favored by both Joseph Stalin and his successor Nikita Khrushchev, formulated unsound agricultural theories based on deception and fantasy. His theories and policies significantly contributed to the Soviet Union's agricultural failures, resulting in food shortages and famine.

the most effective regimes in history in achieving near-totalitarian unity, although from the perspective of individual citizens, it was likely one of the worst.

The question of which socio-political system provides its citizens with the greatest happiness and comfort is a separate issue. Since the primary objective of culture is to unite people, there is no guarantee that regimes offering better lives and more freedoms, such as liberal democracy, will ultimately prevail over systems like communism or its authoritarian copycats. We saw this in the aftermath of the collapse of the Soviet system when almost all former socialist countries experimented with liberal democracy. Yet, over time, many, including Russia and the Central Asian 'stans,' reverted to authoritarian regimes. In today's Russia, Putinism exemplifies how authoritarian regimes can foster national unity and justify invading neighboring countries based on myths, fantasies, and outright falsehoods, all while relying on mass surveillance and propaganda.

Returning to communism in the Soviet Union, from which Vladimir Putin claims to draw inspiration, the regime's fictional aspects were exposed in all their nakedness in its early years, before there was sufficient time to conceal and institutionalize them. Leading Bolshevik figures, including revered names such as Alexandr Bogdanov (an early political rival of Lenin), Leonid Krasin (the People's Commissar for Trade), and Anatoly Lunacharsky (the People's Commissar for Education), openly proposed a program of God-building (*bogostroitel'stvo*). They hoped this state-sponsored program would replace the rituals and myths of the Orthodox Church with the creation of an 'atheistic religion' that would accommodate new secular rituals and myths.

This plan for replacement was not envisioned to make the new secular religion any less powerful. Early Bolshevik leaders, many of whom were formidable intellectuals, knew well the immense power that rituals and myths exert on the human body and mind by entrenching themselves in people's ways of life. You don't need an anthropologist to tell you that rituals and myths not only unite us with others, but they also help rearrange social relations, as at a wedding, or help us through our most difficult times, such as funerals. If myths or stories are like building blocks that hold human culture together, then rituals are like the glue that holds these blocks together, and a human life without either would be inconceivable.

This secular belief system, as envisioned by the Bolshevik God-builders, was intended to be based on the ideas of the pseudoscientific movement of cosmism. Now, let's briefly look at cosmism and the myths that underpin it, as they are crucial not only for understanding Soviet culture's relationship with pseudoscience but also for analyzing post-socialist Mongolia.

Russian Cosmism

Cosmism emerged in Russia in the late nineteenth and early twentieth centuries as a response to the rapid scientific and social changes in the country, where the power of gods was diminishing. It sought to systematize groundbreaking scientific discoveries and provide a new, holistic story about the universe, encompassing everything from atoms to human societies and galaxies. Influenced by Western occult and theosophical ideas as well as Russian folk superstitions, cosmism emphasized human agency, technology, the occult knowledge, and scientific progress as the means to achieve immortality, create perfect humans, and conquer the cosmos teeming with innumerable alien civilizations.

Based on an idealistic belief in science and the power of humankind to tame and change nature, cosmism offered a holistic and anthropocentric view. According to cosmism, the universe consists of energy flows, and humans are intimately connected not only with their planet but with the endless expanse of the universe through myriad cosmic energies and waves. These waves transfer not only heat but also miraculous qualities such as collective intelligence, wisdom, memories, healing powers, and even sensibilities. Some cosmists even believe the universe to be a gigantic living organism. Endowed with the power of creation and destruction through modern science, humans have a duty to conquer and perfect the universe, assuming the role traditionally ascribed to gods. This must be accomplished by pursuing scientific progress, developing powerful technologies, eradicating diseases, overcoming biological limitations, and ultimately attaining immortality.

Alexandr Bogdanov was the head of Proletkult, an early Soviet movement aimed at creating a new proletarian culture. A polymath and theorist deeply fascinated by the sciences and cosmism, he conducted experiments delving into the possibility of achieving eternal youth and defeating the Grim Reaper itself through blood transfusion. Notably, Lenin's sister, Maria Ulyanova, was one of the guinea pigs in his trials. Tragically, Bogdanov's audacious experiment in blood transfusion proved fatal, leading to his untimely death.[52]

Even Lenin could not escape the influence of cosmism, if not in life then in death. The Soviet Immortalization Committee, established to organize his funeral, chose to preserve his body—a decision heavily influenced by the People's Commissar for Trade, Leonid Krasin, a fervent follower of cosmism and advocate of the secular God-building program. This decision found favor among cosmists and kindred spirits, who envisioned not only Lenin's corpse inspiring the proletarian cause but also the potential for future science to resurrect him. Lenin's tomb, designed as a cube by Kazimir Malevich, the cosmist artist who proposed the shape, was believed to offer an escape from death.[53]

Yet, the initial phase of harmony in cosmism-Bolshevik relations started to wane in the 1930s as scientific disciplines rapidly unified under the ideology of Leninism-Stalinism. The occult aspects of cosmism were suppressed by Stalin, though certain elements found their way into Soviet science, art, propaganda, and politics. Particularly, its God-building mission influenced the creation of the Lenin cult and the Stalin cult. While Lenin discouraged cult-building during his lifetime, Stalin orchestrated his own cult. Presenting himself as Lenin's faithful disciple and chosen heir, Stalin propagated the notion of collective miracles through Soviet science and technology. In Soviet stories he came to be described in divine terms—omnipotent, omniscient, and benevolent Father of Nations. Criticizing Stalin was deemed heretical, and countless

---

52 Terbish, *State Ideology, Science, and Pseudoscience in Russia*.
53 The mummification of Lenin's body established a tradition across the socialist world. Among the first supreme leaders of socialist countries to undergo this process by specialists from the 'Lenin lab' in Moscow was Mongolia's Choibalsan in 1952. Others included Bulgaria's Georgi Dimitrov in 1949, Czechoslovakia's Klement Gottwald in 1953, Vietnam's Ho Chi Minh in 1969, Angola's Agostino Neto in 1979, Guyana's Lindon Forbes Burnham in 1985, and North Korea's Kim Il-Sung in 1994, followed by his son Kim Jong-Il in 2011.

individuals lived and died in dread of the Father who could capriciously select anyone for sacrifice. Stakhanovite 'shockworkers' claimed that the mere thought of Stalin drove them to work harder and love him even more. Many households had red corners devoted to the worship of Stalin. During World War Two, Soviet soldiers charged into battle shouting, 'For the Motherland! For Stalin!' Even a specific 'Stalinist salute', similar to the Nazi salute, was introduced where comrades raised their hand to the level of their head as a gesture of allegiance and respect to Stalin. If Stalin was the Almighty, his engineers, doctors, and technocrats were viewed as wizards of a burgeoning earthly paradise, where man-made miracles were expected through science, technology, and the conquest of nature. When Stalin passed away, it was akin to Nietzsche's moment of the death of God—met with disbelief and shock. People from all walks of life, whether they worshipped or hated him, wept and mourned. The writer Ilya Ehrenburg, who witnessed Stalin's coffin at the state funeral, captured the public mood in his memoir *People, Years, Life* (*Lyudi, Gody, Zhizn'*) by describing Stalin's corpse as: 'The god who died from a stroke at the age of 73, as if he were not a god but a mere mortal'.[54] After Stalin's death in 1953, his corpse was placed beside Lenin's in the mausoleum. But instead of being resurrected by future Soviet scientists, the corpse was unceremoniously removed in 1962 during Khrushchev's rule amidst Soviet stories vilifying Stalin.

Science, Superstition, and Conspiracies Under Communism

Humans are an inherently superstitious and conspiratorial species, largely due to our natural tendency to seek patterns and detect agency in our surroundings. This inclination is deeply rooted in our neural architecture, which is designed for fast and energy-efficient decision-making, often requiring the simplification and generalization of information. As a sense-making mechanism, this neural system— what Kahneman refers to as 'System 1' or 'fast thinking'[55]—allows us to perceive the world as more coherent, simple, and predictable than it actually is. This likely provided an evolutionary advantage to our ancestors, who lived in a world where quick thinking could make all

---

54 Paperno, *Stories of the Soviet Experience*, 28.
55 Kahneman, *Thinking Fast and Slow*.

the difference between obtaining food or becoming food themselves. However, this same mechanism also gives rise to cognitive biases, superstitions, and conspiracy theories, as we attempt to impose order and meaning on what might otherwise seem chaotic, unpredictable, or threatening. For example, rather than deliberating whether a slinking shadow in the bushes is a tiger, it is safer to assume that it is and flee—an illustration of 'negativity bias', which is the tendency to focus more on negative or threatening information. Similarly, superstitions arise when people believe that certain actions or rituals can influence outcomes, even in the absence of empirical evidence. Given that we all share the same *Homo sapiens* biology, even the most fervent atheists and scientifically-minded individuals cannot fully escape this aspect of human nature.

As a product of humanity, culture reflects and amplifies these inherent tendencies. Individually, people often form more confident and coherent views when they know less about a subject. Similarly, at a cultural level, the simpler the ideas that unify a community, the stronger their unifying effect—hence why myths and fictions that caricature reality can be more effective at fostering unity than complex, nuanced truths. This tendency helps explain why, throughout history, many successful politicians have connected with followers by offering easily digestible, often sensational stories designed to provoke strong emotions like fear or hope. Such messages frequently combine falsehoods, conspiracies, exaggerated claims, and subtle grains of truth—a tactic observed in various historical and political contexts where individual leaders or entire propaganda machines use simplified narratives to create unity and solidarity, often at the expense of objective reality and truth.

Under Khrushchev's leadership, the Soviet Union achieved the milestone of sending the first human into orbit, thus realizing cosmism's prediction of 'conquering the cosmos', while investing massively in science with the intent of demonstrating the Soviet Union's technological leadership, ideological superiority, and societal advancement. Consequently, Soviet cosmonauts were presented by state propaganda as paragons of model Soviet citizens—if not perfect humans—and as harbingers of the impending era of scientific communism. As poster boys of the atheistic regime, cosmonauts were selected not only for their physical endurance, technical expertise, and appearance, but for their unshakable ideological commitment.

Nevertheless, much like broader Soviet culture and society, the beliefs and actions among these shining beacons of perfection were infused with rituals and superstitions. For example, both before and after their flights, cosmonauts adhered to over two dozen superstitious practices, including the ritual of urinating on the wheel of the bus that transported them to the launch site at the Baikonur Cosmodrome—a tradition started by Yuri Gagarin out of necessity before his historic flight.[56] Subsequent cosmonauts repeated this ritual not only as a tribute to the first man to venture into space but also as a superstition aimed at ensuring the success of their own missions. The only exceptions were the two Soviet female cosmonauts, Valentina Tereshkova and Svetlana Savitskaya, who were physically unable to perform the ritual as their male counterparts did without compromising their dignity.

Despite its rhetoric, the Soviet system never eliminated superstitions, myths, or conspiracy theories. This was not only because all human cultures are based on myths and fictions, but also because the way the system operated exacerbated the situation. The Soviet system simplified complex social realities and sought secret puppeteers behind events, continuously generating conspiracy theories. It also propagated myths about the West through state propaganda, infusing paranoid thinking into every aspect of society and politics. The state's encouragement of conspiratorial thinking in a society notorious for its secrecy and suppression of truth led many Soviet citizens to develop their own unsanctioned explanations and conspiracy theories about the world, sustaining beliefs in the hidden, the unknown, and the paranormal.

Communism is not so different from conservative religious societies—such as medieval Europe during the Inquisition or present-day Afghanistan under the Taliban—in terms of producing myths, fictions, and superstitions. Hypersensitive to the slightest criticism, all three regimes issued special decrees to impose severe punishments on heretics or nonconformists, whether through Soviet secret police orders, *autos de fe* during the Inquisition, or Islamic fatwas. What distinguishes communism, however, is its emphasis on worshiping humanity and science rather than gods and ancient traditions. In the communist story, collective humanity serves as a source of inspiration and meaning, while

---

56   Lewis, *Cosmonaut: A Cultural History*, 148-49.

science and technology hold a central and revered position, regarded as indispensable tools for transforming the world into an earthly paradise. While it is true that Stalin could not have built a totalitarian society without modern technologies—such as the telegraph, radio, telephone, television, mechanized vehicles, and airplanes—that endowed the Soviet regime with advanced capabilities for surveillance, discipline, and brainwashing, this does not mean that science in the Soviet Union adhered to the fundamental principles of objectivity, impartiality, and truth-seeking. Instead, science was monopolized and politicized by the Communist Party's high priesthood, becoming a powerful extension of the state's utopian ideology and a tool to reinforce the regime and its falsehoods.

Many middle-aged and elderly Mongols, who grew up under state socialism, often argue that the Soviet Union, despite its many shortcomings, was an industrialized behemoth with the largest scientific community in history. While this is true, it does not absolve the regime of its many sins. It is important to reiterate that science in the Soviet Union was subject to the whims of individual leaders, potentially turning it into a powerful instrument of mass punishment and control. For example, psychoanalysis and genetics—one field that treats humans as individuals rather than as a gray mass, and the other a discipline with the potential to improve agricultural productivity—were both banned on Stalin's orders. Only scientific disciplines that generated power for the Communist Party without explicitly threatening the social order were encouraged to seek the truth and received state support. These were primarily fields such as rocketry, nuclear physics, engineering, mathematics, chemistry, and medicine, which had the potential to contribute to the glory of the Motherland and the Soviet defense industry geared towards waging a holy war against the heretical West and its liberal democracy. Even these disciplines remained inefficient. The Soviet Union developed rocketry, jet propulsion, the atomic bomb, and radar, managing to maintain only a small gap between its weapon systems and those of the West, primarily by stealing scientific discoveries on an industrial scale. According to a 1979 KGB internal report, produced at the height of communism, more than half of the projects run by the Soviet defense industry were based on intelligence stolen from the West. In 1980, hooked on stolen Western technologies like a lifeline, the Soviet Military-Industrial Commission

(VPK) compiled a list of 3,617 'acquisition tasks' for the KGB, of which 1,085 were completed within a year, allegedly benefitting 3,396 Soviet research and development projects.[57] This helped the Soviet Union maintain its image as a 'superpower'—though perhaps 'super-thief' might have been a more fitting title.

In contrast, fields such as historiography, the theory of communism, political science, sociology, philosophy, literature, and the arts—areas with the potential to undermine the Soviet system by exposing its lies, frauds, and myths—were tightly controlled. Professionals were forced to blindly adhere to the principles of Socialist Realism, personally approved by Stalin. Those who didn't were imprisoned, tortured, or executed. Despite its name, Socialist Realism was not intended to portray social reality as it existed in the (gloomy) present, but rather as an idealized, imaginary reality shaped by the Party's narrow perspective. This insistence stemmed not only from the fact that Party leaders lived in abundance and privilege, detached from the daily struggles of ordinary people, but also from the belief that all truth had already been revealed by the Founding Fathers of communist theory. As a result, historical, theoretical, or social inquiries were not meant to uncover new knowledge or challenge existing myths, but rather to provide supplementary evidence for what had already been established in Marx's and Lenin's opuses on dialectical materialism. Socialist Realism could just as well have been termed Fabricated Realism.

Consider the following popular Soviet slogans: 'Socialist Realism: The Truth of Life Through the Lens of the Party!', 'Through Socialist Realism, We Build the Future of Communism!', and 'The Path to Communism is Painted with the Brush of Socialist Realism!' Now, read these slogans as they truly should have been, where Socialist Realism is replaced with Fabricated Realism: 'Fabricated Realism: The Truth of Life Through the Lens of the Party!', 'Through Fabricated Realism, We Build the Future of Communism!', and 'The Path to Communism is Painted with the Brush of Fabricated Realism!'

While the Soviet Union was overtly future-oriented, aiming to establish communism, the very mechanism of knowledge production and dissemination that drove it toward this goal was already ossified

---

57   Andrew, *The Secret World*, 689-92.

and past-oriented, conducive to churning up or allowing untruths, myths, and inefficiencies to flourish in society. This example not only showcases *Homo sapiens'* creative power of imagination to square circles and create imaginary worlds but also underscores how science can be co-opted by totalitarian regimes when they suppress or manipulate scientific discoveries to conform to their own political stories and narrow agendas. When science is subjugated in such a fanatical manner, unable to challenge the sacral dogmas and myths of the governing regime, it can impede societal progress, limit individual freedoms, and hinder the advancement of human understanding. These consequences were unmistakable hallmarks of socialism in the Soviet Union and its satellite, Mongolia.

Science in Socialist Mongolia

In a swift parallel to events in the Soviet Union, Mongolia embraced totalitarianism, instigating mass terror during peacetime and promoting the cult of personality in the persona of Choibalsan. Taking inspiration from Stalin's Great Purges, the Mongolian dictator launched his own wave of purges aimed at cleansing society of both old ideas and heretics. This led to the arrest and execution of thousands on largely trumped-up charges. The victims included not only aristocrats, monks, and monastic doctors, custodians of old knowledge, but also members of the emerging intelligentsia. Virtually all pioneers of modern Mongolian prose, linguistics, and history, instrumental in spreading the communist story, faced arrest and execution, for deviating from the principles of Fabricated Realism.

Unlike the Soviet Union, however, Mongolia lacked scientists—or 'technical intelligentsia', as this group was referred to in the Soviet Union—due to the country's backwardness. This absence made it impossible to target non-existent scientists for ideological heresy. For the first cadre of scientists, it was a stroke of luck that their rise coincided with the cessation of the purges in 1939 and the death of 'Mongolia's Stalin', Choibalsan, in 1952, who, following the cosmism-inspired Soviet tradition, was mummified by specialists of the 'Lenin Lab' in Moscow and placed in a tomb on the main square in Ulaanbaatar, which was a replica of Lenin's death-defying tomb on Red Square. Despite pervasive state control over every aspect of life, including scientific disciplines, in Mongolia the Party's interventions in emerging 'hard' sciences such as medicine, epidemiology, mathematics, and others were limited. This was not due to a lack of desire by the Revolutionary Party's high priesthood to fully control scientists, but primarily because they lacked the scientific expertise necessary for meaningful arbitration.

As a result, scientists enjoyed a certain degree of freedom to engage in purely scientific pursuits, as long as they maintained a facade of adherence to Leninist-Stalinist dogma and expressed dogged loyalty to the Party. This structural latitude paved the way for tangible achievements at the newly established Marmot Plague Control Center in Ulaanbaatar, which operated with relatively little intervention from individual leaders. The Center launched a vaccination initiative in rural areas using an anti-plague vaccine developed in the Soviet Union and implemented various preventive and life-saving measures.

In broader terms, science in socialist Mongolia was characterized by duality. On one hand, it was formally aligned with the utopian state ideology, with certain disciplines either stifled, banned, or co-opted for state propaganda. On the other hand, the 'hard' scientific fields offered practical benefits to the populace. This was particularly true for medicine and agriculture, which dealt with the biological well-being of people and animals. These fields managed to make impressive progress, enhancing the prestige of science in the eyes of the people. This approach mirrored the Soviet model, where science was selectively used as a tool for both propaganda and practical progress.

Aliens, Spirituality, and Pseudoscience in the Post-Socialist Period

In the early 1990s, Mongolia was captivated by a televised emergency. In a dim studio, a young woman, her voice trembling and her face tense as if she was about to defecate, recounted her recent encounter with aliens from outer space. Her ordeal revolved around an object she claimed to have found in the countryside, only to later realize that it belonged to extraterrestrial beings. One evening, the aliens descended on her *ger* and abducted her, demanding that she returned what didn't belong to her. Despite possessing intergalactic transportation technology, the aliens apparently couldn't locate their lost item without subjecting a female representative of a species just half a chromosome away from being a chimp to a terrifying ordeal. The woman decided to share her extraordinary story with the rest of the country. Many credulous citizens, including myself, who trusted state TV on providing truthful news, believed her account and were scared shitless.

This program was followed by another TV broadcast, featuring Dashtseren, the personal astrologist and advisor to Mongolia's first post-socialist President, Ochirbat. The state astrologist was shown standing on a hill, his arms open as if welcoming someone, reminiscent of a scene from the movie *Titanic*, in which Jack (played by Leonardo DiCaprio) stands at the bow of the ship with his arms outstretched, embracing the winds as if he's flying. Alas, Dashtseren was mimicking a radio receiver to capture messages from cosmic aliens. The audience, once again glued to the blue screen, eagerly awaited the moment when the state astrologist would be contacted by an alien spaceship. Lump in my throat, I anxiously watched this news with my family, but nothing transpired for a considerable time. Dashtseren looked increasingly fatigued, gulped down some water, and then stripped off his clothing, revealing to the nation on camera strange strips on his chest that extended down to his private area—evidence, he implied, of his impending contact with cosmic aliens. Heroically, he then declared, 'That's what happens when you try to contact aliens!' before succumbing to complete exhaustion. Eventually, the TV program had to be halted, diverting to other more urgent down-to-earth issues that Mongolia was grappling with.

Dashtseren, a former driver, gained fame after the demise of socialism, much like many other characters from that period. Thanks to his powerful clairvoyance, he was granted the official title of 'State Seer' by the President and given a residence in a state-protected gated complex just a stone's throw from the Palace of Government. There, the national treasure spent his days engaged in divination and advising Mongolia's leadership. In another related incident, in 1993, a passenger plane flying from Ulaanbaatar to Western Mongolia disappeared mid-air, prompting a rescue operation. What made this operation extraordinary was the fact that Dashtseren dashed to the rescue operation team to offer his swift help in locating the missing plane. To the relief of the anxious public, the State Seer was reported by the national media to have assembled a group of Mongolia's two hundred most powerful seers, shamans, and astrologists. They spent two weeks attempting to determine the whereabouts of the missing plane. Despite collectively divining round the clock and even making tours along the missing plane's route on a specially designated plane—all while with his good name at stake—Dashtseren failed miserably in this important task, leading him to announce to the astonished country that the plane had been abducted by aliens. Much to his embarrassment, the plane wreckage was found on the fifteenth day of disappearance by a group of rescue alpinists, aided by locals, in the Marz Mountain in Western Mongolia.

Following the collapse of state socialism, Mongol politicians and nationalists pledged never to replicate Russia's model again, driven by a surge in anti-Russia sentiments fueled by newly released revelations of atrocities perpetrated within the shadows of the Soviet Empire. These revelations included purges modeled after the Stalinist Great Purges in the Soviet Union, the fabrication of national history, and the total control of Mongolia by the Soviet Union.[58] Despite their fierce anti-Russian rhetoric, many Mongols, including self-appointed democrats, nationalists, and seers who were themselves products of state socialism, never ceased to see the world through socialist lens and never completely abandoned following events in Russia. An illustrative example is the parallel between abduction stories in post-socialist Mongolia and the revival of cosmism in Russia.

As noted previously, although the pseudoscientific movement of cosmism was suppressed during Stalin's era in the 1930s, some of its stories permeated Soviet art, politics, and eventually, counterculture. This movement persisted in underground intellectual circles, resurfacing during perestroika when its energetic, universalist, and humanist ideals found a place in Mikhail Gorbachev's policy of 'new

---

58 However, this doesn't mean that being a Soviet satellite or colony was an entirely negative experience, during which Mongolia gained nothing of value. The country secured its formal independence, underwent rapid modernization, effectively combated venereal diseases, implemented modern education and healthcare systems, and significantly improved life expectancy and overall quality of life—all under Soviet supervision and with its assistance. Dismissing all Soviet legacies would mean disregarding modern Mongolia's achievements and its deep connection with its northern neighbor. The Soviet Empire engaged in a wide range of activities in Mongolia, providing ample examples to support both negative and positive perspectives.

thinking'. Prominent figures like Gorbachev, Eduard Shevardnadze, and Alexandr Yakovlev, along with other Communist Party bosses, stressed the crucial importance of global unity and universal values in their speeches, announcements, and writings, contributing to the resurgence of cosmism and its popularization among the masses. Thus, Gorbachev advocated for the 'formation of an integrated universal consciousness' describing it as 'a form of spiritual communication and rebirth for mankind'. Yakovlev, a key intellectual shaping Gorbachev's perestroika reforms, used cosmist language to affirm that 'the world is becoming ever more aware of itself as a single organism'. Shevardnadze, the Soviet Foreign Minister, underscored in the best tradition of cosmist thinking that all nations 'share a place where individual national efforts unite into a single energy field'. Adamashin, the Soviet Deputy Foreign Minister, echoed this sentiment, pointing out that 'physicists have long realized the unity not only of the world but of the entire universe'.[59]

The notion of universal unity wasn't merely rhetoric uttered from the high Politburo platforms; it manifested as a reality in the skies when widespread UFO sightings were reported throughout the Soviet Union. These sightings often occurred near the nation's treasured sites, including military bases, nuclear power plants, and other strategic locations. Significant events, such as a UFO landing near a major Soviet military installation in Voronezh in 1989, a sighting over the Chernobyl atomic plant in 1991, and reports of UFOs flying over Chelyabinsk, a Soviet military bomber training base, and many more, received extensive coverage through state news agencies and newspapers across the Soviet Union.[60]

Given Mongolia's deep political, economic, and other ties with the Soviet Union, it didn't take a crystal ball to predict that similar incidents would occur in Mongolia. Indeed, these sightings were reported swiftly and in jaw-droppingly large numbers, capturing the public's imagination. UFO reports became so frequent across all parts of Mongolia that, in the 1990s, a significant number of Mongols anticipated an imminent alien

---

59 Kull, *Burying Lenin*, 25-28.
60 Terbish, *State Ideology, Science, and Pseudoscience in Russia*, 79-110.

invasion from outer space, with their Motherland becoming 'ground zero'.

The generation of both Soviets and Mongols who grew up under socialism believed they were building a communist paradise in their respective countries. However, the collapse of the socialist system revealed that neither was a workers' heaven, and that the communist story was merely a myth invented by the Bolsheviks. Contrary to the expectations of Western liberal thinkers, the fall of communism did not lead these people to see reality as it was, nor did it turn them into blank slates on which to engrave liberal democratic principles. Instead, they reacted in a very human way, clinging to their old instinctive need for a grand communal story or national mythology that could both unite them and make them feel unique. In this climate of nostalgia and ideological soul-searching, long-suppressed myths—as well as newly invented or adopted ones—emerged openly to fill the void left by the collapse of the communist ideal. Hence, the proliferation of local variations of beliefs related to the occult, astrology, Christianity, Buddhism, shamanism, paganism, and extraterrestrial beings, alongside the myths of liberal democracy, in both countries.

Human culture thrives on enchantment and mystification. When certain dominant myths are dismantled and humans become disenchanted, we, as cultural beings, feel out of our depth and find creative ways to adopt new myths to re-enchant and mystify ourselves, returning to where we feel most comfortable and united. However, some myths are more toxic than others. In the case of communism, it was arguably one of the most damaging myths—not only for its suppression of freedoms but also for its role as one of the most oppressive and murderous ideologies in modern history.

While the collapse of state socialism left a vacuum that other myths and alternative beliefs rushed to fill, it's important to note that not all aspects of the socialist legacy were discarded. In socialist Mongolia, despite its foundational dogma, national education was based on the ideals of scientific research and secular knowledge, promoting rational thinking. Though state socialism failed to live up to these enlightened ideals, they stayed dangling in the minds of the people. Even after the collapse of the socialist system, respect for science remained unwavering, despite the resurgence of alternative ideas and movements that offered different solutions to the myriad problems, fears, and uncertainties that plagued a young democracy, one that had recently abandoned its aim of attaining communism and didn't know where it was headed.

This coexistence of rationality and alternative beliefs created a seeming paradox. Despite the persistence of respect for science, the post-socialist Mongolian society simultaneously experienced the flourishing of belief systems once considered antithetical to science. The reader may ask: How these two paradigms—the occult and pseudoscience on one hand, and mainstream science on the other—once considered opposites during the socialist era, could coexist?

One way to understand this paradox is by considering both human cognition and historical context. Humans are primates with a divided brain, capable of holding conflicting beliefs simultaneously. More importantly, these paradigms always coexisted under state socialism, albeit in an antagonistic relationship. The collapse of socialism only eased this conflict, and today, religious or alternative concepts comfortably coexist alongside mainstream science. Not only do they coexist, but pseudoscience and the occult derive their legitimacy from mainstream science. To provide an analogy from the animal kingdom, consider the relationship between barnacles (marine crustaceans) and whales. Barnacles (symbolizing pseudoscience, conspiracy theories, the occult, and their practitioners) attach themselves to the skin of whales (representing science), benefiting from the whale's movement through the ocean, thereby gaining access to nutrient-rich waters. The barnacles receive food for survival and growth, while the whales are generally unaffected by the presence of these adhesives.

Today, there is a pervasive tendency to explain everything by piggybacking on science, even concepts that lack proper scientific validation. Folk healing, in its quest for validation, is one of the practices seeking to cling to (pseudo)scientific terminology, embracing theories from diverse disciplines such as biochemistry, neuroscience, astronomy, and even quantum physics. As can be expected, the application of scientific theories in such a manner often involves a misinterpretation and twisting of scientific facts by folk healers, psychics, and seers.

Folk Healing Reinvented

The metaphor comparing folk healing and its practitioners to barnacles is particularly apt. Related to crabs and lobsters, barnacles are also quite curious creatures. In comparison to their multi-legged cousins, who scuttle sideways with a distinctive side-to-side motion resembling a dancer executing 'Sidestep' movements during Western dancing, barnacles have completely relinquished their mobility, opting instead for increased food security by evolving to permanently attach themselves to rocks, ships, or large marine mammals like whales. A more intriguing aspect of these legless crustaceans lies in their fluid reproduction. Lacking fixed sexes, each barnacle possesses both male and female reproductive organs, allowing them to fertilize and be fertilized. As they mature, barnacles can adjust their sexual systems in response to their surroundings, displaying a remarkable diversity ranging from hermaphrodite to separate sexes to a combination of both. To overcome the challenge of finding a mate, barnacles have devised an ingenious solution—a formidable penis, unparalleled in the animal kingdom as it extends several times their body length. In the absence of suitable mates within the reach of their penises, they resort to self-fertilization, leading to a form of 'virgin birth'.

In today's Mongolia, most folk healers, psychics, and seers employ fluid healing methods. They rely neither exclusively on traditional healing practices nor on modern medicinal techniques, often lacking proper knowledge of the latter. They hedge their bets by attaching themselves to the realm of pseudoscience. Their healing approaches are remarkably eclectic, incorporating cherry-picked ideas from ancient medicinal treatises, Tibetan and Chinese medical practices, religious books, folk wisdom, and modern sciences. In the absence of readily available sources of knowledge, these practitioners typically resort to self-generating medicinal insights. While they may not possess extravagantly elongated penises, they certainly wield long wagging tongues—the most crucial tool in their line of trade—to disseminate their idiosyncratic knowledge and healing methods to those seeking their guidance. Consider the healer featured at the beginning of this section that my family hosted in the early 1990s, seeking his magical healing powers.

However, he was not alone in claiming to have an eclectic range of supernatural powers and deep pseudoscientific knowledge. In fact, there was a growing demand for spiritual practitioners and faith healers, not only due to widespread mistrust in the bankrupt public healthcare system but also because of various previously unknown social problems that surfaced, including mass unemployment, widespread poverty, life uncertainties, heightened levels of alcohol abuse, and pervasive social conflicts. Additionally, there was a growing awareness of supernatural phenomena such as ghosts, spiritual pollution, and aliens. No wonder, politicians and business people, eager to harness new psychic powers to gain the upper hand, started patronizing seers, psychics, and folk healers, setting a new trend. It was in this hectic and surreal climate that President Ochirbat enlisted the services of Dashtseren. Ochirbat wasn't the only chump when it came to seeking astrological insights to help manage his country. His Russian counterpart, Boris Yeltsin, whose country was undergoing similarly dramatic changes, also received reports from psychics and clairvoyants employed by General Alexandr Korzhakov, the chief of the Presidential Guard.[61]

Amongst numerous famous psychics and healers to emerge in the 1990s, one woman, Önörmaa, stood out for her ability to produce fire from her body, reminiscent of a character called the Human Torch from Marvel Comics. Önörmaa gained public attention when she claimed to have unconsciously burned down her *ger* using her marvelous skill. The story took an even more comical turn when she was declared a national treasure. In acknowledgement of her unique psychokinetic abilities, the state awarded her a brand new flat and a monthly stipend. Scientists from the Mongolian Academy of Sciences, known for their outstanding expertise, verified the authenticity of her ability to produce fire using only the power of her mind and provided several watertight scientific explanations. They noted that on the day Önörmaa became overenergetic and burned her *ger* to the ground, a space launch took place at the Baikonur Cosmodrome in Kazakhstan. This event provided a lead for further scientific inquiry, including the burning question of whether her otherwise destructive energy could be harnessed and transformed into a force for healing. However, Önörmaa hardly gave

---

61   Soldatov and Borogan, *The New Nobility*, 14.

Mongolian scientists enough time to make any trailblazing discoveries and perhaps even earn a couple of Nobel prizes in Physics and Medicine, as she was soon caught red-handed attempting to set her new flat on fire. To be duped in this way must have felt like a kick in the balls for the Mongolian scientists. However, this and similar painfully embarrassing stories, publicized in the news and national TV, never deterred people from believing in the power of spiritual practitioners, seers, and folk healers. On the contrary, it only fueled interest in the supernatural and the mysterious.

Today, interest in pseudoscience and the occult is as high as ever before. The use of pseudoscientific terminology and concepts is not restricted to folk healers and their numerous copycats; it has become a growing trend among ordinary people, especially those living in Ulaanbaatar, a city hosting a significant number of self-proclaimed shamans and social media stars who inundate their followers with copious amount of pseudoscientific content. Even when indulging in potentially harmful foods like raw marmot parts, some city dwellers rationalize their choices with pseudoscientific explanations.

Consider the case of a woman called Tsetsegjargal, a self-appointed 'fire shamaness' and well-known social media personality with a substantial Facebook following, who also gives talks on TV and writes books on folk healing using pseudoscientific language. A fan of marmot meat and body parts, she advises her followers to wear marmot ankle bones. Specifically, women are instructed to wear them on their left legs and hands, while men are directed to wear them on their right limbs because ankle bones serve as protective talismans, guarding against injuries, broken bones, and angry nature spirits. Her advice extends to pregnant women, assuring them that wearing a marmot ankle bone guarantees a safe and sound delivery without the risk of abortion because 'marmots never abort'.[62] Furthermore, Tsetsegjargal asserts that the marmot is a miraculous panacea on four legs, with each of its body parts possessing medicinal properties. For instance, the

---

62   So, if you happen to have a number of unhealthy or risky habits, such as chain smoking, binge drinking, or hopping down the stairs instead of normally walking, don't worry about changing your habits when you get pregnant. You are guaranteed to have a safe pregnancy provided you wear a pair of marmot ankle bones.

animal's internal organs can supposedly heal corresponding human organs. A person experiencing kidney failure should consume raw marmot kidney for three consecutive years, while any ailment related to the cervical canal in women can be cured by ingesting a raw marmot cervical canal three times. Following this rationale, men grappling with impotence, possessing a modest manhood, or finding themselves in a hairy situation can deduce for themselves that they should snack on a raw marmot penis, perhaps in some combination of three.

If the fire shamaness' claims held any water, Mongolia, with its love for marmot meat, would have been the healthiest and most virile nation on the planet. People from all corners of the globe would be flocking to the country to receive treatment at marmot-meat-fueled hospitals and purchasing ankle bones as a health insurance policy. All assisted reproductive technology (ART) and Viagra pills would go extinct, replaced by the new global trend of chewing marmot scrotum and wearing marmot tails in underpants, causing human population growth to shoot through the roof. These transformations would have turned Mongolia into the Mecca of health tourism. Alas, public health indicators in Mongolia leave much to be desired, prompting many individuals who can afford it to seek medical treatment abroad.

In more esoteric cases, certain healers claim that raw marmot meat harbors unique energy with beneficial properties for humans, contingent on the consumer's faith in its efficacy. According to their advice, the healing potential of the meat gets unlocked—like Aladdin's cave of wonders—when it is consumed with strong faith and adherence to traditional customs and rituals. Undeterred, some healers venture even deeper into the realms of quantum physics to prove the health benefits of raw marmot meat. These justifications showcase a remarkable spectrum, ranging from mildly unconventional to moderately risky to outright dangerous.

In today's globalized world, where Mongols have the freedom to travel in and out of their homeland, pseudoscientific explanations aren't confined to the borders of Mongolia. In 2023, I attended a workshop at Cambridge University where guest speakers included a Mongol Buddhist doctor, a manager from a hospital in Ulaanbaatar specializing in folk medicine, and a few anthropologists and folk remedy enthusiasts. The Mongol man who managed the hospital delivered a rather typical presentation. With the demeanor and authority of a physics professor, he began reading his paper on experiments in quantum physics conducted in a laboratory in the United States. After a prolonged and monotonous reading on quantum entanglement, highlighting the interconnectedness of the universe, he wrapped up with an equally entangled conclusion, asserting that quantum physics proves the effectiveness of traditional Mongol medicine, which also adopts a super holistic approach to understanding the universe. This line of reasoning, or false analogy, is not much different from arguing that Vladimir Putin is as compassionate and pacifist as the Dalai Lama because both love sausages.

In contrast to the self-appointed quantum physics professors, healers, and shamans based in Ulaanbaatar, many well-regarded folk healers, bone setters, and herbalists in rural areas of Mongolia tend to be more conservative in both language and methods. These individuals typically avoid entangling themselves in discussions about science, energies, or quantum phenomena, focusing instead on traditional healing concepts and methods. While their claims of healing diseases considered unhealable by modern medicine should be taken with a pinch of salt, they are valued by their customers for their practical abilities in setting bones, readjusting displaced joints, performing head massages, or being a soothing presence. The difference between famous Ulaanbaatar-based healers and their rural counterparts may reflect the urban-rural divide, partly due to the fact that rural dwellers binge-watch television less and don't follow YouTube channels promoting pseudoscience to the same extent.

In popular perception, folk medicine is often seen as more resistant to change compared to modern medicine, given its deep-rooted connection with cultural traditions passed down through generations. While this generalization holds some merit, it is worth noting that many methods attributed to folk medicine by contemporary healers aren't ancient practices but rather innovations that have emerged amid shifts in societal beliefs, globalization, the popularization of traditional Chinese medicine, growing nationalism, religious revival, and a rise in toxic masculinity—all prevailing aspects in today's Mongolia. An illustrative example of 'invented' or 'borrowed' tradition can be witnessed in the use of animal testicles.

The consumption of boiled or barbequed testicles is a longstanding tradition in nomadic cuisine. Mongol nomads practice castration for all the livestock under their care, which includes bulls, stallions, lambs, goats, and camels. Castration is typically performed when these animals are still young and their vulnerable parts tender and delicious. The castrated testicles of young bulls and stallions are primarily barbequed by inserting them into burning dung. As for the testicles of lambs and young goats, they are commonly boiled in water with rice. Camel testicles are the only testicles not consumed. Seen as a variety of meat, these testicles are typically eaten by everyone, regardless of age, gender, or social status. In the past two decades or so, a novel method has emerged on the waves of nationalism and toxic masculinity under the guise of the revival of tradition. It is becoming increasingly popular to consume the raw reproductive edges of stallions or lambs immediately after they have been trimmed with a clean cut and are still warm and bloody. Testicle enthusiasts claim a wide range of alleged health benefits, from improving sexual prowess and building muscles to curing cancer and even rejuvenation. This mirrors the traditional practice in Chinese medicine of consuming testicles from animals such as sheep, goats, and other species, which is gaining popularity in diverse forms and disguises in Mongolia. Ultra-nationalists, patriotic bodybuilders, xenophobic wrestlers, self-appointed quantum physics professors, and playboys who suffer from fatigue are the primary consumers of this cutting-edge treatment.

Conclusion

The relationship between Mongols and marmots is a story of culinary love and vigilance. Mongols love consuming marmots, yet they approach this culinary preference with caution, mindful of the potential for these creatures to transmit deadly plague or provoke divine retribution.

The marmot in contemporary Mongolia is perceived through two distinct lenses. First and foremost, it is seen as a delicious biological species with the potential to harbor the plague bacterium. This perspective is meticulously constructed through scientific classifications by experts, including epidemiologists, zoologists, ecologists, and medical specialists.

Secondly, the marmot embodies a chimerical identity, existing as a creature intricately interwoven with taboos, spirits, and folk medicine rites. In this context, the marmot transcends its rodent classification; it becomes a spirit being, a mythical tiny person, and even a human-turned-burrow dwelling creature typically inhabiting spirit-protected places.

For individuals adhering to traditional beliefs, encountering a marmot, especially in spirit-protected places, can be a potentially unpredictable experience that requires caution, as it may manifest in various forms. However, during the socialist era, citizens were compelled to adopt scientific paradigms that viewed the marmot solely as a biological species. This shift also led to the perception of the marmot as a mere commodity, to be exploited for the financial benefit of the socialist Motherland.

After the demise of socialism and the revival of religion, some of the marmot's chimerical attributes have openly resurfaced and are being celebrated. Despite scientific explanations that attribute the plague to bacteria, many Mongols view the marmot not only as a potential host of the bacteria but as a spiritual being with cosmological significance. Many believe that certain parts of the marmot's body have powerful medicinal properties, a belief that keeps the tradition of eating raw marmot meat alive.

In July 2020, amidst the global grip of the COVID-19 pandemic, Mongolia faced its own battle against plague outbreaks in the Hovd Province of Western Mongolia—a crisis largely unnoticed by the international community. The concerted effort to combat these outbreaks was spearheaded by the National Center for Zoonotic Diseases (formerly the Marmot Plague Control Center). In the affected province, the state didn't seek the aid of religious specialists but instead implemented a series of scientifically-informed measures. Five regional centers were placed under internal lockdowns. Plague patients or those suspected of being infected were promptly isolated by medical staff, and the health of the local population was closely monitored by doctors and nurses. Additionally, household patrols were organized, and extensive disinfection efforts utilizing modern medicine were carried out.

Within the province, a man and a teenage boy were admitted to the hospital after contracting plague. Both individuals had fallen ill after consuming marmots but fortunately managed to recover, thanks to prompt medical intervention. However, in an unrelated incident in the neighboring Govi-Altai Province, a fifteen-year-old boy tragically lost his life after hunting and consuming marmot.[63]

This incident in 2020, like those in all other years, highlights Mongolia's resilience, adaptability, and the crucial importance of preparedness and swift action in managing health crises, even amidst global pandemics. Without the state's expertise and response, the number of infected people and deaths would certainly have been higher. However, the loss of even one life remains a profound tragedy, leaving behind grieving families. Despite this bittersweet success, a sense of cautious uncertainty permeates the air regarding the future. Despite past achievements, there is prevailing apprehension about the challenges tomorrow may bring, a concern linked to the accelerating climate change.

Previously in the chapter, we discussed that the last significant climate change event unfolded on the Mongolian Plateau in the first half of the thirteenth century. This period was characterized by abundant rainfall and mild temperatures, a departure from weather patterns unseen for over a millennium. This dramatic shift had far-reaching consequences for the ecosystem, reshaping the grasslands that supported diverse wildlife, including large herds of horses crucial to the rapid expansion of the Mongol Empire. Additionally, it coincided with the 'Big Bang' event that gave rise to several distinct branches of *Yersinia pestis* strains.

As the fourteenth century commenced, the region experienced a sudden cooling trend. This era of unprecedented climate fluctuations provided the backdrop for significant human events, including the unification of the Eurasian landmass by Mongol cavalrymen and the proliferation of plague outbreaks originating from the 'Big Bang' event. These outbreaks culminated in the devastating Black Death, the deadliest pandemic of the Middle Ages, and possibly in all of human history. Climate change, the unification of the Eurasian landmass, and shifts in the pathogenic situation proved to be deadly bedfellows.

Fast forward to the present day: Mongolia finds itself in a situation reminiscent of the Black Death era, but this time, the challenges are even more severe and unpredictable.

---

63 Guy, Jack, and Bilegdemberel Gansukh, 'Teenage boy dies from bubonic plague after eating marmot', *CNN*, July 15, 2020, https://edition.cnn.com/2020/07/15/asia/mongolia-plague-death-scli-intl/index.html

We live in an extraordinary era of unprecedented and rapid climate change. According to authoritative projections, if current trends persist, we could experience a four-degree Celsius increase, with truly catastrophic consequences, where vast areas in Africa, Australia, the Americas, and Asia might become uninhabitable due to desertification, by the end of this century, if not sooner.[64] Each year more or less breaks the previous year's temperature record, with 2024 marking the warmest year on record since systematic temperature data collection began in 1850. Furthermore, research indicates that 2024 was also the hottest year in the past 100,000 years.

While today's headlines have been dominated by natural disasters such as California's 'gigafires', frequent tsunamis along the American coastline, unprecedented wildfires in Siberia, and heatwaves striking European cities, numerous peripheral regions worldwide are experiencing extreme weather events in equally, if not more, dramatic ways. One such area is Mongolia. Presently, the country faces climate change on an unparalleled scale in its history. In recent decades, Mongolia's climate has been changing at an alarming rate, surpassing the global average of one degree Celsius. Certain regions have witnessed temperature spikes of up to two degrees Celsius. Mongolia has been plagued by severe summer droughts, followed by harsh winters (*dzud*). Research indicates that the severity of the 2002-9 drought, for example, rivals only the arid periods of the late 1100s. The unprecedented droughts and winter *dzud*s in combination have decimated livestock, devastating the livelihoods of thousands of herding families and creating what the Mongols call *Ih Nüüdel,* or 'the Great Migration', whereby impoverished nomads migrate en masse to the already overcrowded capital of Ulaanbaatar. With each passing year, the intensity and frequency of droughts and winter *dzud*s continues to escalate, transforming entire grassland regions into patches of expanding desertification and dust. This dire situation is poised to worsen, posing significant challenges for Mongolia's environment, biodiversity, and pathogenic situation.

We also inhabit a world where the transformative power of technology has turned the globe into a closely-knit village through advancements in communication, computation, and transportation. Just as fools can be

---

64 Wallace-Wells, *The Uninhabitable Earth*; Klein, *This Changes Everything.*

found in any settlement, our global village is not immune to misguided individuals and malevolent actors. In this era of escalating sectarianism, ultra-nationalism, and terrorism—coupled with the unprecedented empowerment of individuals through technologies—the actions of a single globally-oriented malefactor can wreak havoc on the entire international community. Until recently, the historical consensus, based on accounts by Gabriele de' Mussi, a non-eyewitness chronicler of the Black Death, suggested that the pandemic was transmitted to Europe from the Crimean port of Caffa, which endured a siege by the Golden Horde Mongols, allegedly using the plague as an early example of biological warfare. However, recent research has cast doubt on the veracity of de' Mussi's account, challenging the notion that the Black Death was a deliberate act of biological warfare. Nevertheless, this may become a reality in the context of emerging biological threats, set against the backdrop of increasing access to powerful technologies and biological elements among the general population.

After considering these variables, a question arises: With unprecedented climate change, globalization, the persistent consumption of marmot meat, and changes in the pathogenic situation that once led to the deadliest plague in the Middle Ages, could history repeat itself given these converging factors today?

4. The Cat

In the early 1980s, during the socialist era in Mongolia, a six-year-old boy named Tsolmon secretly accompanied his parents to visit an elderly Buddhist monk who lived alone in a *ger* near the Gandan Monastery in Ulaanbaatar. Despite Mongolia's official atheism, many citizens had a secret fondness for religion and spiritual rituals, and for the socialist state to attempt to control the religiosity of its citizens was like herding cats. Tsolmon's family visited the monk at dusk to have a ritual performed on him. Inside the dimly lit *ger*, filled with the scent of juniper incense, Tsolmon sat in terror, remaining motionless throughout the entire ceremony. As the flickering light of the ghee butter lamps illuminated bowls of silver and brass, and colorful *thangkas* of Buddhist gods and demons danced in the shadows, the ancient monk recited strange incantations while repeatedly spitting on Tsolmon's face and occasionally moaning. To heighten the sense of dread, the interior was teeming with a dozen pussycats, purring and cuddling the old monk and slipping in and out through the rooftop hole into the darkness of the night. In everyday life, Tsolmon and his friends hounded down stray cats with sticks and stones, as that was the norm for how felines were treated then. However, Tsolmon's father saw these cats as special, believing they protected the venerable monk. Tsolmon's mother, on the other hand, was less impressed, convinced that these 'evil cats' were holding the elderly monk hostage. This story was recounted to me by my friend, Tsolmon.

Fast forward forty years, and the land of Genghis Khan has shed its socialist cloak. Religion is flourishing once again, people are embracing capitalist consumerism and immersing themselves in pet-friendly culture. There is a daycare center for pets and a few shops in Ulaanbaatar where pet lovers can buy special food, treats, and accessories for their kitties. However, one thing that hasn't changed is the mix of emotions

 https://doi.org/10.11647/OBP.0450.04

people still hold toward cats. Many Mongols can still easily relate to the diverse and conflicting attitudes exemplified by the four individuals in this story: the old monk (representing a suppressed group practicing a forbidden worldview), Tsolmon's parents (communist citizens), and Tsolmon (a young boy learning to internalize the values of those around him).

This chapter discusses the world of Mongol cat, a subject no less controversial than that of dogs and marmots. We saw in previous chapters that the dog and the marmot underwent distinct treatments across different historical periods, their characteristics and images evolving with the changes in Mongol society itself. The cat is no different in this regard, embodying a unique fusion of images: it is like a good, bad, and ugly animal all rolled into one.

In a three-part analysis, this chapter explores the multifaceted image of cats. Part I recounts the image of cats in contemporary cosmology and their roles as protagonists in both ancient legends and modern *bolson yavdal* stories. Part II traces the chronology of the ever-shifting image of cats, spanning the pre-socialist, socialist, and post-socialist eras, each marked by diverse religious and political ideologies. The Conclusion summarizes and offers final thoughts on the topic.

To set the stage, let's make a brief tour, exploring how cats have been perceived across diverse cultures.

The Cat in Different Cultures

Similar to dogs, cats have been domesticated for millennia. Their story begins in a most exotic place: Cyprus, around 9500 BCE, known in Ancient Greek mythology as the realm of the goddess of love, Aphrodite, no less. A cat and a person were found buried side by side. Although we know almost nothing about the context and symbolism of this burial and the human-cat relationship in that society, Ancient Egypt provides the first clear glimpse of the cat's role and image. Here, cats take center stage with an entrance fit for a pharaoh's party. From around 2300 BCE, they started appearing as fancy amulets. Then, by 1950 BCE, felines were the celebrities of tomb walls, depicted alongside humans and doing everything from lounging like royalty to solo playing to indulging in some fine dining consisting of fish. But it didn't stop there. Cats went from being household companions to gods themselves. The male cats began to be worshipped as one of the manifestations of the sun god, Ra, while the female cats were associated with the goddesses Hathor and Bastet, representing sexual energy, fertility, and motherhood.[1]

Now, fast forward to the Romans who were probably responsible for introducing cats to their imperial outposts, including Northern Europe.[2] Afterwards, the story took a dark turn with the rise of Christianity in Europe, which went hand in hand with suppressing pagan gods and goddesses and promoting anti-sex doctrine. Having fingers pointed at, cats were now labelled as demons, witchy sidekicks, and overall troublemakers. There circulated stories in medieval and post-medieval Europe of witches turning into black cats, heretics throwing wild parties involving kissing the anuses of giant felines, and cats bewitching and subverting unsuspecting humans. That they became associated with evil was like the kiss of death to cats. Disgusted and horrified, clerics and their flocks subjected cats, especially black cats, to horrendous treatment by catching, torturing, and throwing them onto bonfires, sometimes along with female mistresses accused of witchcraft. The cat's transformation from a divine figure into an evil being evokes parallels with the movie *American Psycho*, where the protagonist Patrick (portrayed by Christian Bale), initially seen as a successful and charming figure in society, descends into madness and is perceived as sinister and evil. This feline horror show persisted until the birth of the Enlightenment in the seventeenth century, a period that championed respect for reason and humanism. It was during this time that the cat gradually shed its diabolical religious skin, becoming the cute puss of today, although many in Western societies continue to harbor negative attitudes toward felines, a legacy of ancient beliefs and superstitions.[3]

However, not all cats had a rough time across Christendom. Take Russia, for example, a country where Slavic folklore incorporates Orthodox Christian values and shamanic beliefs permeated with nature spirits and magical animals.[4] The Slavs believed in a cat named Bayun meaning 'talker', a real chatterbox who could put humans to sleep with its stories or songs and even heal illnesses with magical purring voice.

---

1   Turner and Bateson, *The Domestic Cat*, 86-92.
2   Faure and Kitchener, 'An archaeological and historical review of the relationships between felids and people'.
3   Turner and Bateson, *The Domestic Cat*, 94-99.
4   Rock, *Popular Religion in Russia*.

Unlike their Western counterparts, Russian cats had a bit of a Jekyll-and-Hyde personality, balancing between luck-bringers and mischief-makers. They have been regarded as harbingers of luck, as possessors of worldly wisdom, as helpers and protectors of the hearth, on the one hand, and capable of stealing, lying, behaving in cunning ways, and serving evil entities, on the other.[5]

Another region where cats have fared better than their fellow felines in medieval Europe are countries along the Silk Road, the historical cat-friendly highway, where the earliest mention of domestic cats originates from Persia and dates from the sixth century BCE. Thanks to Islamic culture, in which cats are tolerated and to some extent even revered,[6] ancient settlements in Persia, Khorasan, and Khorezm served as refuges for domestic cats that were valued as mouse-catchers, among other characteristics. Further to the east, in Central Asia, the oldest known cat skeleton was found in the early medieval city of Dzhankent, Kazakhstan, dating from between the eighth and the tenth centuries CE,[7] around the time when Central Asian peoples began to convert to Islam. There is evidence that the Dzhankent cat was well cared for by its human owners who nursed it back to health after it had been injured. China, at the far eastern end of the Silk Road, couldn't resist the charms of these mystical creatures either. While endowed with supernatural abilities of the dark forces to shape-shift and communicate with spirits, cats also became guardians against evil spirits,[8] mousers par excellence, and symbols of fertility, longevity, and wealth.[9] They were the royalty of the pet kingdom pampered by the Chinese nobility and officials, even getting poems and paintings dedicated to their fabulous selves.[10]

Geographically speaking, the Mongols, whose country is today sandwiched between Russia and China and who in the past culturally enhanced the Silk Road, are well positioned—one could argue—to be cat-tolerant. Plus, their traditional religions, shamanism and Buddhism, not only don't have teachings detrimental to felines but are in general

---

5   Bresheva, 'Obraz koshki v mifologii'; Gou and Korovina, 'Image of cats in Russian and Chinese omens'.
6   Campo, *Encyclopedia of Islam*, 131.
7   Haruda et al., 'The earliest domestic cate on the Silk Road'.
8   Laukner, 'Die Katze in der Religion'.
9   Gou and Korovina, 'Image of cats in Russian and Chinese omens', 89.
10   Idema, *Mouse vs. Cat in Chinese Literature*, 35-55.

protective of animals. Culturally speaking, as a nomadic people who deal with various animals on a daily basis, the Mongols are also not predisposed to show cruelty to living beings. While the proverbial bird's-eye view of Mongol history and culture, involving geographical, religious, and lifestyle explanations, has some merit, the situation on the ground, from a cat's-eye view, is slightly more complicated than it seems. Cat-keeping is mostly an urban phenomenon, and Mongolia wasn't exactly a cat's playground in its nomadic days when there were no settlements around. Cats became a part of people's life only recently, during the era of state socialism marked by urbanization and modernity. That means today's attitudes toward these species were mostly formed during a time of complicated relationships between religion and atheism, traditional culture and modernity, nomadism and urbanization.

Part I

The Cat in Cosmology, Modern Stories, and Ancient Legends

This *bolson yavdal* story is rumored to have occurred in post-socialist Ulaanbaatar. One day a cat mysteriously appears inside a man's family *ger* on the outskirts of the city. To the astonishment of witnesses who cannot fathom how it entered, the feline slowly paces back and forth as if asserting its territory. Disgusted and suspicious, the father of the family opens the door to expel the uninvited guest, only to witness the cat leap out and vanish into thin air. Tragically, the following day, a child from the family passes away. Grief-stricken, the family concludes that the cat must have been a messenger from Erlig, the Ruler of the Underworld.

In the previous chapters, we explored Mongol cosmology and the idea of spiritual animals that occupy 'liminal spaces'. Such species are often believed to have originated from humans, are able to manifest themselves in either human or animal form, or are seen as capable of being reincarnated as humans or vice-versa. Sometimes such species figure in pairs as opposites. In Mongol cosmology, the cat and the dog are two such animals.

The Cat in Cosmology

In contrast to the dog, the cat isn't believed to have karma to reincarnate into Mongols. By residing inside human dwellings, unlike dogs that stay outside, the cat is physically the closest animal to humans. However, its behavior is as enigmatic and distant from humans as that of wild beasts. The cat, being physically close yet behaviorally distant, emerges as a paradoxical figure in the eyes and cosmological imagination of Mongols. If the dog represents what Mongols love, the cat embodies what they fear. In a way, the cat is the dog's opposite, just as love is seen as the opposite of fear.

In today's cosmology, the cat symbolizes one of the most personal and intense fears humans experience—the fear of death and the underworld. This is why Mongols also refer to the cat as 'the dog of the Ruler of the Underworld' (*Erligiin nohoi*)[11] and 'the animal of bad omens'. As a result, the cat is seen as a blood-curdling and eerie creature, towards which Mongols feel an instantaneous sense of aversion and hatred. While cats are rarely encountered in Mongolia, there exists a prevailing fear and suspicion surrounding them, including beliefs that cats harm young children or sleeping men—two significant categories representing the family's future and the authoritative figure in a patriarchal society.

As an 'impure' and 'dangerous' animal, the cat possesses spiritual powers that include hovering in an ambiguous space between the world of the living and the dead, casting curses, seeing ghosts and death, and entering people's dreams to foretell diseases, disputes, and misfortunes. Conceptualized in this way, the cat's 'otherworldly, cold' behavior and its proximity to human bodies becomes clear, explainable, and even manageable.

Of course, a fear of death doesn't have to be paralyzing, and all societies have mechanisms to deal with death, which is, after all, an inextricable part of life. In Mongolia divination and rituals related to life preservation are not only the domain of religious specialists but are also performed by ordinary people in their daily lives. To comprehend life, one must confront and understand death. Despite being 'the dog of the

---

11   In the myths of Mongol and Turkic peoples, Erlig is the shamanic God of Death and the Underworld. In Mongolia it was later incorporated into Buddhism and perceived as the Ruler of the Underworld.

Ruler of the Underworld', the cat's spiritual powers can be managed and harnessed to extend life or bestow blessings.

In Mongolia today, a common belief is that the more one fears or despises cats, the more potent their dark powers become in relation to that person. Conversely, respecting and caring for cats is believed to extend a person's life by safeguarding them from malevolent spirits or simply by allowing them to continue living. Many religious specialists, including monks and shamans, not only keep cats but also teach the general population to be respectful to felines and provide for stray cats, thus transforming their potential harm into blessings.

From what I've described, the Mongol cat can be likened to a magical creature known as the Boggart, featured in the *Harry Potter and the Prisoner of Azkaban* series. The Boggart is a being that takes on the shape of the viewer's greatest fears. The more someone fears the Boggart, the more powerful and menacing it becomes. The only method of overcoming this creature is to think of something that turns the fear into laughter.

While the Boggart is an imaginary creature, its resemblance to the image of the Mongol cat, also a product of cosmological imagination, is noteworthy. Both creatures illustrate the idea of fear influencing the power of a magical entity. In a broader sense, even though the *Harry Porter* series is a work of fiction set in a magical realm, much like any other well-crafted work of fiction it contains various creatures and themes that often mirror our real-world cultural experiences. This is not only because writers project real-world situations into their literary creations but mainly because what we call the 'human world' or 'human culture' is nothing more than a product of our collective imagination, encompassing imagined social structures, hierarchies, rituals, gods, magical animals, symbols, and histories. Since we perceive the world around us through human-centric cultural lenses, we don't see animals—or anything else for that matter—as they really are but as what we imagine them to be.

This inclination to find reflections of ourselves in the animal kingdom dates back to the earliest human records manifested through anthropomorphized animal figurines, petroglyphs, ancient rituals, and inscriptions. In Europe, for example, the recording of this reflective practice extends to the Middle Ages when Europeans began writing down events and their thoughts in chronicles, charters, and manuscripts. The era also witnessed the flourishing of bestiaries—early compendiums of the animal kingdom embellished with earnest descriptions of magical creatures, some with half-human features, ranging from griffins to camel-leopards to dog-headed humans and mermaids. Compiled by the Church, these bestiaries aimed to serve as much as encyclopedias of the animal kingdom as moral guides, encouraging readers to seek human-centric characteristics and hidden moral values in the behavior and looks of animals. Blending folklore with heavy doses of religious morality and allegory, these bestiaries revealed more about the anxieties and concerns of their compilers than about animals, which frequently underwent transformations into unrecognizable creatures. For instance, beavers were portrayed as castrating themselves, serving as a cautionary tale for men about the importance of eliminating all vices if they desired to lead a life of peace and godliness. Mother pelicans were depicted as embodiments of self-sacrifice, believed to wound their breasts to nourish their chicks with their own blood, reminiscent of Christ's sacrifice for humanity. Even with the dawn of the Enlightenment, which marked a shift in natural history writing away from the shadows of the Church, the impulse to anthropomorphize animals and impose moral judgments persisted in Europe. Modern science and zoology didn't entirely eradicate these tendencies, as people continue to attribute anthropomorphic characteristics to animals.

As creatures imagined to be inherently tied to the underworld, cats in Mongol culture are thought not only to bite the hand that feeds them but also to harbor a wish for the death of their human caregivers. It is said that cats awaken three times during the night to check if their feeder has passed away, while dogs, in contrast, wake up three times during the night to ensure the safety and well-being of their owners.

To reiterate, all these negative characteristics ascribed to cats pertain to today's cosmology and are manifested in *bolson yavdal* stories that cover the socialist and post-socialist periods. This raises a question about the place and image of the cat in Mongol cosmology during the pre-socialist period. The answer is that the cat didn't feature much in pre-socialist cosmology. This was mainly due to the fact that felines were rare animals, primarily kept in Buddhist monasteries or Chinese dwellings, and they did not possess spiritual powers to play any prominent role in cosmology. Cats were perceived as good, neutral beings, or even unknown animals devoid of spiritual powers, as will be discussed in the example of Buddhist legends and other folk genres that are much older than *bolson yavdal* stories.

Now, let's compare the bad, spiritual cats of *bolson yavdal* stories with the good or neutral 'earthly' cats of Buddhist legends and pre-socialist folk genres.

The Cat in Bolson Yavdal Stories

This story, rumored to have taken place in a provincial center, is about a cat that developed a habit of frequenting the local hospital ward. Nurses soon observed that whenever it lingers beside a particular bed for an extended period, the patient passes away the following day. Alarmed by the increasing death toll, the hospital personnel decide to keep the cat away from the hospital. Following this wise decision, the patients stop succumbing to the mysterious deadly pattern.

In another related *bolson yavdal* story, a nomadic family that has kept a cat in their *ger* to manage rodent infestations decides they don't need its services anymore due to the cat's laziness and neglect of its duties. Reluctant to take the feline's life but unable to secure it a new home, the family's patriarch takes the cat and sets off to a remote location, where he leaves it behind. Confident that the cat could never find its way back home and pleased to have resolved the issue so swiftly, the man returns to his family, only to discover the cat patiently waiting for him. Consumed by vengeance for the man's actions, the cat strangles him that very night. The following morning, the lifeless body of the man is found, with his eyes gouged out.

It would, however, be wrong to convey the impression that fear and strong aversion toward cats are universal in Mongolia, based solely on these and similar *bolson yavdal* stories. While it is common for people to shoo away uninvited stray felines from their *gers*, Mongols don't necessarily always associate these cats with foreboding omens related to the well-being of their family members. Instead their primary concern often revolves around stray cats potentially carrying harmful microbes and diseases from the outside world.

Bolson yavdal stories tend to depict exceptional scenarios, serving various moralistic purposes. These include providing behavioral templates for individuals who possess sensitivity to supernatural beliefs and are particularly concerned about encounters with animals in spiritually dangerous places ('wrathful places', areas protected by exceptionally ill-tempered Buddhist deities, haunted locations), or animals behaving in unusual ways, or having unusual looks. In everyday life, it isn't uncommon for some families, who don't share beliefs in evil cats, to keep felines as cherished companions, while numerous temples have resident cats that serve as mouse-catchers, thus contributing to hygiene and protecting Buddhist scrolls and food supplies.

The Cat in Buddhist Legends

Unlike the laity who believe in *bolson yavdal* stories about evil and vengeful cats, monks tend to have a different attitude stemming from Buddhist teachings that accord equal value and respect to all living beings. Recall the story at the beginning of this chapter about an old monk who lived with a dozen of pussycats near the Gandan Monastery in socialist Mongolia. Hence the 'good cat' is the protagonist in Buddhist legends where it figures as a skillful mouse-catcher, or a naughty food thief, or an animal that just happens to live in human dwellings, which are essentially what cats do in temples. In comparison with modern *bolson yavdal* stories, in old Buddhist legends the cat is an ordinary animal without malevolence or dark spiritual powers. Let me provide several examples.

In the Mongol legend *The Gold Arab Belt*, the cat is portrayed as an intelligent animal, who learns from a parrot how to get monks bring meat into the temple to partake of it.[12] In this legend, the cat is akin to the archetype of a smart character in Western folklore such as the sly fox or the clever raven, both of which are often portrayed as using their intelligence to outwit others and achieve their goals.

In another legend, *Cat the Teacher*, which is widespread among various Mongol groups, the cat somewhat resembles Tartuffe, the fictional character from Molière's comedy *Tartuffe*. Like Tartuffe, who is a cunning imposter feigning religious piety to manipulate and exploit gullible individuals, the cat in this legend impersonates a holy Buddhist

---

12   Skorodumova, *Skazki i Mify Mongolii*, 95-96.

teacher in a monastery and enlists mice as its disciples, all while intending to exploit them. After each lesson, the cat keeps its focus on one unsuspecting disciple, and—hocus pocus—the disciple ends up on its dinner plate. This circus continued until one day, when the cat was caught red-pawed by the mice. Squeaking to each other, 'It is not a holy teacher but a monster!' the horrified mice dispersed in all directions, abandoning the monastery for good. The cat sometimes deceives not only mice but the monks as well. In another version of the legend *Cat the Teacher*, collected by the renowned Mongolist Boris Vladimirtsov,[13] the cat steals food from the monastery and consequently loses its tail. Hence deceitful people are referred to in Mongolia as 'a cat the teacher' (*muur bagsh*) or 'a cat the thief' (*hulgaich muur*).[14]

Acknowledging the place of cats and dogs in human settlements, the Buddhist legend *The Cat And the Dog*, which also has different versions among various groups in Mongolia, Inner Mongolia, Kalmykia, and Tuva,[15] explains why the cat inhabits a human dwelling, while the dog is always kept outside. According to the legend, the dog and the cat are sent by their human master to get hold of a precious object (a gold ring, a valuable casket, etc.). Whilst the skillful dog finds the object, it is the intelligent cat that delivers it to their master, thus earning a place inside the warm human dwelling. Misunderstood, the dog, by contrast, is left out in the cold, which fits the Mongol Buddhist tradition of keeping dogs outside the *ger*.

In the legend *Why Man Has No Hair*, which also has different versions, the Buddha creates humans and, before returning to heaven to fetch elixir, instructs a cat and a dog to protect the humans in his absence from the devil. While the Buddha is away, the devil distracts the two from their duty by giving a bowl of milk to the cat and a piece of meat to the dog and urinates on the humans and flees. Upon his return, the Buddha scolds the cat and the dog and commands the former to lick the hair off the bodies of the humans defiled by the devil. The cat licks the hair

---

13 Vladimirtsov, *Mongol'skii Sbornik Rasskazov iz Panchatantry*, 126-28.

14 Unlike in Mongolia, the Kalmyks in Russia, long exposed to Russian culture, have positive attitudes towards the cat. In Kalmyk folklore too, the cat is often imbued with even more positive characteristics than in Mongol legends. The Kalmyk cat protects babies, serves as God's dog, and protects precious sutras in monastic libraries. See Burykin, 'Koshka v fol'klore Kalmykov'.

15 Osor, 'Todaevan temdglsn "Noha mis hoyr" domgin tuskar'; Burykin, 'Koshka v fol'klore Kalmykov'.

everywhere except their heads, armpits, and genitals, which explains why humans have hair in these body parts.[16]

The Cat in Pre-Socialist Folklore

Apart from old Buddhist legends that depict the cat in a positive light (as a smart, naughty, and cunning animal), in Mongol folklore there is a special genre where animals are endowed with human language and are used as avatars to elaborate on human relations, values, and social issues. This genre includes the following sub-categories: legends concerning animals and hunters (*am'tny tuhai* ülger *domog*), short üge poems, and fairy tales about animals.

Mirroring values of the pre-Buddhist period, many legends concerning animals and hunters (*am'tny tuhai* ülger *domog*) can be described as animistic legends where there is no clear distinction between animals and humans. For example, in the legend *Seven Brothers*, collected by Grigory Potanin,[17] there are two groups of industrialists: the first group consists of a fox, a human, a dog, a marmot, a rabbit, a badger, and a cat; the second group consists of other animals. Whilst in Buddhist legends the cat figures as a good character, in animistic legends the cat is either a neutral animal or someone nobody really knows. Like in Buddhist legends, in this genre the cat is also an animal devoid of malevolence and spiritual powers. Thus, in the legend *Seven Brothers* the animals who are ignorant about the cat decide to invite it for a meeting in order to learn more about what kind of animal the cat really is. In this legend, the animals' ignorance of the cat stands for nomads' general ignorance of the feline.

Examples of short üge poems are given in Chapter 2 about the dog and in Chapter 5 about the camel, where dogs and camels are endowed with human language. To remind, üge poems feature animals, and occasionally inanimate objects, that adopt a human voice serving to allegorically depict the plight of commoners trapped in impoverishment or subjected to the indiscriminate power of their overlords. Moreover, as illustrated in the works of monks such as Agvang-Khaidub (1779-1838)

---

16   Hangin et al., 'Mongolian folklore', 73-74; Nassen-Bayer and Stuart, 'Mongol creation stories', 324-25.

17   Potanin, *Ocherki Severo-Zapadnoi Mongolii*, 178-79.

and Ishisambuu (1847-96), üge could be employed to chastise the hypocrisies prevalent among the servants of Buddha.

Animals also speak in various fairy tales composed by individuals seeking to address social issues and problems without explicitly naming the culprits. These fairy tales share similarities with üge poems, the main distinction being that the former are written in prose, whereas the latter are written in short poetic monologues. One such fairy tale is called *The Pekingese, the Cat, and the Mouse* composed by a man called Genden, who lived at the end of the nineteenth century and the beginning of the twentieth century and was from the banner of Hurts Vang of the Setsen Khan *aimag*. In his fairy tale, which became popular among the Mongols and was even printed in 1923 in the capital city, the three animals, all of whom live in a Buddhist temple and can speak human language, are used as avatars to criticize certain corrupt practices taking place within the monkish community in the Setsen Khan *aimag*.[18]

These genres—Buddhist legends, animistic legends, and poems and fairy tales about animals—mirror how cats were imagined, treated, and with whom they were associated in Mongolia before the advent of socialism. Broadly speaking, cats were kept as mouse-catchers in Mongol temples and Chinese warehouses and dining halls. By contrast, nomads who migrated seasonally by following their herd animals didn't keep cats, as they were impractical for the nomadic lifestyle. The cat's traditional image as a low-profile animal and its absence from daily nomadic life partly explain the small number of folk or animistic legends about cats. This contrasts with the manul, a native species of wild cat that plays roles in legends and holds a distinct place in cosmology.

The Manul

'Manul' or 'mani' is a species of wild cat native to Mongolia. Its scientific name is 'Pallas's cat', named after the German naturalist Peter Simon Pallas (1741-1811) who first described this species for Western audiences. The size of a domestic cat, the manul, however, isn't your average kitty. It has dense grey fur with recognizable patterns, short legs and claws, and ears set low and wide apart. It has a short face, giving it a flattened look.

---

18   Tsendiin, *Hav, Muur, Hulgana Gurvyn Ülger*.

Its pupils are circular rather than vertical as in domestic cats. Spread across Central Asia, the manul is a solitary and elusive animal that lives in caves, rock crevices, or marmot burrows. Mongols don't keep them as pets not least because they don't adapt well to captivity and die quickly. Whilst today normally not hunted, manuls often fall victim to inexperienced hunters who mistake them for marmots. They are also incidentally caught in traps meant for other critters like hares and foxes.

Despite its vulnerability to traps and human habitat, in cosmology the manul is a powerful animal in its own right. The term 'manul' or 'mani', according to Potanin, is related to Mani, or 'Mother Nature' in Altai legends; thus the word evokes the idea of 'the creation of the world and all us humans in it'. In legends, the manul has seven sons, including a cat, a badger, a wolverine, a leopard, a lynx, a pig, and a tiger. Among many peoples—including Yakuts and Buryats, who are historically and culturally related to Mongols—seven is a revered number and in legends is often associated with the origin of groups. So, the manul is a proud father in the legends and the progenitor of one wild family tree.

The manul's seemingly fearless and relaxed behavior has also become part of its legendary reputation. Hunters observed the manul's tendency to watch them without displaying fear, a behavior that baffled them and led to various interpretations. Legends suggested that a fleeing manul posed an ominous threat to the hunter, who might face death if he failed to kill it. This belief gave rise to ritual practices: after killing a fleeing manul, the hunter would skin it and recite an incantation, holding the skin with both hands and uttering, 'Give me some good fortune and health from the grey skin of the manul' (*manuulynhaa ereenees hurai, hurai, hurai*).

Being baffled by the behavior of someone who doesn't exhibit fear while attacking others who show fear and run away is a stereotypical chimp behavior, which once again reveals to whom Sapiens is closely related, especially on an individual level. What sets us apart from chimps, however, is human culture, which justifies this predatory instinct by creating a sugar-coated justification that by running away, the manul somehow poses a lethal threat to humans and therefore must be caught and killed. Like many other human activities, the act of killing becomes ritualized—in this case by marking the conclusion of the killing with chants offered to the supernatural who listen to human prayers and whims, and suspend natural and physical laws to accommodate these entreaties.

Part II

The Origins of Cats in Mongolia and the Evolution of Their Image

Here are excerpts from the dairy of a Mongol man who keeps a cat at home:

> We've recently welcomed our third feline companion into our home. My daughter arrived, hugging an adorable kitten with a coat that resembled tiny prickles. We named it Zaraa or 'Prickly'. This cherished member of our family tends to spend most of its day lounging around the house, but come the night, it eagerly seizes any opportunity to latch onto a protruding leg or arm under the blanket... Hedgehog requires no concern when it comes to outdoor excursions. Simply open the door, and it willingly heads out. Mongols will never approach a cat, let alone try to snatch it... However, there was one unfortunate incident when someone callously kicked Hedgehog like a ball. The distressed feline returned home, yowling and covered in dust, with blood droplets from its nose. Fearing the worst, we hastily placed Hedgehog in a bag and rushed to the vet, only to discover that it had three of its ribs broken... There are numerous benefits to having a pet cat. It is believed that their presence is beneficial for those with cardiovascular issues and high blood pressure, particularly when stroking their backs... Moreover, cats possess an innate ability to detect underground movements, making them the first to sense an impending earthquake. This instinct can be a valuable asset, potentially saving a household from disaster... Many Mongols are disgusted by the fact that cats never fully domesticate in the manner of livestock... Among the Felidae family, only cats exhibit an aversion to water. Attempting to give them a bath results in anxiety-induced urination. Nevertheless, cats meticulously groom themselves, cleaning their faces and paws regularly... Cats are weird creatures, neither entirely ignorable nor effortlessly lovable. Nowadays, some seek feline companionship in response to rumors of imminent earthquakes.[19]

This was penned by a journalist named Gangaa in his article titled 'The repulsive green cat runs across the road'. Published online on March 25, 2010, the article vividly captures the ways cats are perceived and treated in today's society.

---

19   Gangaa, 'The repulsive green cat runs across the road' *Baabar*, March 25, 2010, http://www.baabar.mn/article/1659.

In the previous part, we explored seemingly inconsistent images of cats held by various groups in Mongolia's recent history. This include modern lay Mongols' intolerance of cats (as attested to in modern *bolson yavdal* stories); monks' traditional tolerance of cats (as seen in old Buddhist legends); pre-socialist nomads' ignorance of cats (as attested to in ancient animistic legends about humans and animals); and some pre-revolutionary Mongols' use of cats in moral stories (as shown in moralistic fairy tales). This variety can be explained, as alluded to before, by the fact that the image of the cat has several layers constructed in different historical periods and has different—shamanic, Buddhist, folk, socialist, post-socialist—influences. Let's now dissect this complex image further and trace its evolution in different historical periods in Mongolia.

The Origins of Cats and Settlements in Mongolia

In contrast to manuls, domestic cats exhibit a diverse range of colors from black to grey to fawn, but modern Mongols collectively label them as *nogoon muur*, meaning 'green cats', due to the green hue of their eyes. Another notable distinction between cats and manuls is the former's unsuitability for thriving in Mongolia's harsh climate without the provision of human shelter. This raises questions about the origin and history of settlements in Mongolia and their potential role in sheltering cats.

Before the establishment of the Mongol Empire in 1206, the region that is now Mongolia was inhabited by various nomadic and semi-nomadic peoples. Archeological research indicates that some of these groups left behind settlements, with one of the best-known and last being Karabalgasun, believed to have been abandoned in the tenth century CE, that is three centuries before the rise of the Mongols.

The first settlement among the Mongols emerged only after the establishment of the Mongol Empire as a necessity of running a rapidly expanding empire. The foundation of the capital of Karakorum was laid around 1220 by Genghis Khan himself, but the city was primarily constructed during the reign of his son, Ögedei. As the Mongol territories expanded, Karakorum became a major site for world politics and a significant commercial hub along the Silk Road. The imperial capital was truly a melting pot of ideas, religions, peoples, goods, and more. It was surrounded by 'twelve heathen temples, two mosques, and one church', and was 'not as big as the village of Saint Denis', according to William of Rubruck, who visited the city in 1254. Unlike other cities along the Silk Road, Karakorum was not occupied permanently but was used by the Great Khan and his court on a seasonal basis because the Mongols still pursued their nomadic lifestyle. They moved between seasonal pasturelands and used the capital city to receive foreign emissaries, store goods and tributes, conduct commerce and diplomacy, and house the accompanying bureaucracy, servants, and artisans.

The central attraction and pride of the city was the Silver Tree, which decorated the courtyard of the opulent imperial palace. Designed by the enslaved Parisian goldsmith Guillaume Bouchier, the Tree was a large sculpture made of silver and other precious metals. Its branches were weighed down by silver fruit, and four golden serpents coiled around the trunk, while an angel holding a trumpet adorned the top. Upon the Great Khan's command, this automaton would spring to life: the angel would raise its trumpet to his lips and sound the horn, whereupon the mouths of the serpents would gush alcoholic beverages into the large silver basin at the base of the Tree for the guests' enjoyment. Although historical documents or archeological finds confirming their existence in Karakorum have yet to be discovered, three factors suggest that cats may have been present in the city to witness this spectacular sight as well:

1. Absence of religious obstacles: Mongol shamanism never contained negative rulings or taboos associated with cats. This means there were no religious obstacles to keeping cats in the city.

2. Attractiveness of cats as rodent controllers: Settlements like Karakorum, with their permanent structures such as homes, temples, and palaces, as well as grain store houses and gardens, would have been irresistible to rodents. Cats, being natural mousers, would have been invaluable for controlling these pests.

3. Historical encounters: During their military campaigns from Europe to China, the Mongols encountered cats in countless settlements. Many artisans, builders, and slaves brought to construct Karakorum and serve

there came from cities along the Silk Road, where cats were commonly used as mousers. As the Mongol Empire expanded, Karakorum became one of many cities under Mongol rule, suggesting that cultural exchanges between these cities could have included the sharing of cats and other useful animals. Given this historical context and the prevalence of cats in other Mongol-controlled cities, it is reasonable to assume that cats were also present in Karakorum.

Following Kubilai's rise to power who moved the imperial capital to Dadu (present-day Beijing), Karakorum was reduced to an administrative center of Mongolia, a province of the Yuan. Despite its downgrade, the city saw expansion eastwards in the first half of the fourteenth century. Following the fall of the Yuan, Karakorum served as the capital of the Northern Yuan until it was razed to the ground in 1388 by invading Ming troops. The consequent return of the Mongols to a full-time nomadic way of life following the destruction of the only settlement in the entire country likely led to the disappearance of domestic cats. As far as we know, cats didn't hold any companionship role or spiritual significance for the nomads, which would have been primary reasons for Mongols to keep these species in their *gers*, which apparently was not the case.

The first mention of cats in Mongolia in that period is associated with the spread of Buddhism. Cats made their appearance in Buddhist legends and literature that were translated from Tibetan into Mongolian. As discussed earlier, in the post-Yuan period the conversion of the Mongols into Buddhism began in the sixteenth century. By 1575, a Buddhist temple had been erected on Altan Khan's land (in today's Inner Mongolia). In 1640, the Halha Mongols and Oirats adopted Buddhism as the state religion and forged a political-military alliance.

This event was preceded by another noteworthy event a year earlier, when in 1639 Halha nobles elected Eshidorji, a four-year old son of a Mongol Tüsheet Khan of Genghis Khan's Golden Lineage, as the spiritual leader of the Halha Mongols. The boy was later recognized by the Dalai Lama as the reincarnation of the Buddhist scholar Taranatha and was bestowed the name of Zanabazar (in Sanskrit 'Jnanavajra'). In Mongolia's history, he is also known as the first Javzandamba Hutugtu. During the 1639 ceremony, Zanabazar was gifted 108 disciples (*shabi*) and several *gers*. With these, he established his nomadic palace-monastery, named Urga (Örgöö), meaning 'palatial *ger*', or Hüree, meaning 'a circle' (due to the arrangement of the *ger*s in circles). For several decades, this palatial *ger*-monastery on wheels roamed the Mongolian steppe, similar to how nomadic bands of magicians and circus performers traveled across Europe, setting up shows in different locations. However, in 1706, Urga settled permanently on the banks of the Tuul River, gradually evolving into the country's most significant religious and cultural center.

Nascent settlements in Mongolia received a boost following the country's incorporation into the Manchu Qing Empire in 1691. This watershed event opened the gates for waves of Chinese men to migrate to Mongolia. Given Urga's growing status as the epicenter of social and cultural life, it naturally attracted most of these men, who built Chinese-style mud houses and opened shops, warehouses, brothels, and dining halls that drew in rodent populations. While the exact timeline of cats' emergence in Urga and other smaller settlements around the country remains unknown, by the time the living god Javzandamba Hutugtu returned as his eighth reincarnation in the second half of the nineteenth century, Urga had already been sheltering cats.

The Bad Cat in the Socialist Period

While limited urbanization preceded the onset of socialism in Mongolia, the victory of the People's Revolution in 1921 marked a subsequent expansion of settlements. During this period, cats became associated with urban environments, their image shifting to that of a 'dirty animal' as they adapted to modern urban infrastructures such as sewage systems, heating pipes, and Soviet-type buildings with stinky basements. These places became the primary habitat for stray cats, not only in Ulaanbaatar (previously Urga), which experienced a construction boom after World War II, but also in the new industrial townships of Bor-Öndör, Darhan, Erdenet, and others that sprang up across the country.

As feline populations increased, their treatment and quality of life significantly worsened under state policies. Stray dog and cat-killing campaigns, implemented in the name of public hygiene, reflected broader anxieties about control, disease, and cleanliness in rapidly urbanizing spaces. These campaigns often inspired children and teenagers, who organized brutal pet pogroms in basements and on the streets. Recall Tsolmon's surprise at seeing cats peacefully living in an old monk's *ger* near the Gandan Monastery—a stark contrast to how Tsolmon and his friends typically treated felines.[20]

In addition to being viewed as filthy, cats came to be regarded—strange as it may sound in an atheist country—as 'spiritually dangerous' animals symbolizing death. This feline symbolism arose not from the industrial-scale extermination of cats during pest control campaigns but from the traumatic events when the murderous regime targeted its own citizens by the thousands in the name of cleansing society of counter-revolutionary 'human scum'. These brutal measures may have created order among the frightened populace, but they also led to the proliferation of incredible *bolson yavdal* stories about ghosts and evil cats that continue to circulate to this day.

The image of the evil cat, a messenger of the Ruler of the Underworld, emerged during the socialist period against the backdrop of state-sponsored violence and its lingering memory. This prompted people to seek explanations for the unexplainable and the hidden, trying to make sense of their lives under a new regime that had disrupted the old cosmological order. Historically, matters concerning death and misfortune fell under the purview of religious specialists. However, their near extinction as a social class under socialism necessitated that a new explanatory framework be found to link life, death, and the afterlife within the context of state violence.

In the anthropology of memory and traumatic events resulting in mass deaths, ghostly manifestations have been explained in post-socialist Mongolia[21] and elsewhere[22] as materializations of traumatizing events or disrupted memories. In a society like Mongolia, with a long tradition of anthropomorphizing animals to express human emotions,

---

20   In the late 1930s, nearly all monasteries across Mongolia were destroyed, with only a few religious structures spared. However, in 1944, there was a partial revival of Buddhism when the state reopened the Gandan Monastery, or what remained of it, as a 'life museum' in Ulaanbaatar, staffed by five dozen monks. This reopening aimed to showcase socialist Mongolia as a democratic nation where individuals had the freedom to choose their religious beliefs, among other liberties. Placed under the watchful eye of the secret police, monks were allowed to preserve some aspects of their monastic lifestyle. Some mostly elderly monks continued to care for cats, offering them shelter from the harsh realities of a socialist world hostile to stray animals.

21   Delaplace, 'Chinese ghosts in Mongolia'; Delaplace, 'Parasitic Chinese, vengeful Russians'; Solovyeva, 'Faces of Mongolian fear'.

22   Carsten, *Ghosts of Memory*; Kwon, *Ghosts of War in Vietnam*.

anxieties, and social issues, it was no coincidence that an animal would emerge to mirror a new form of socialist violence, much like the mass appearance of ghosts did. That this role fell on the cat was not surprising for the following interrelated reasons.

First, the cat was historically associated with monasteries, that is, spiritual realm. Second, the manul has been associated in legends with (the lack of) fear, omens, and death (hunters had to kill a fleeing manul, on pain of death). Cosmologically speaking, the domestic cat, the wild manul's legendary 'son', was best placed to inherit some of its 'father's' characteristics during a time of cosmological disruption and be reimagined as a being which causes fear and brings about death. Third, a belief in omens (*yor, beleg*) as reflecting anomalies in cosmological order, which does not necessarily require the involvement of gods, makes it possible to think about abnormal changes in society as omens. The emergence of the cat as an exceptionally 'ominous animal' in socialist Mongolia, where religion was officially banned but omens tolerated, also fits this way of thinking. Fourth, according to lay Mongols, the cat is a paradoxical animal which is both close to and distant from humans; this potentially allows the cat to be used as a conceptual tool to think about death as something that is both an inseparable part of life and so different from life. Fifth, in Buddhist legends the cat and the dog are perceived as opposites (the former lives indoors, the latter outdoors; the former is cunning, the latter is gullible). Since the dog signifies life's joys such as prosperity, love, loyalty, and kinship (as when deceased relatives are believed to return to their family as dogs), it did not require a great leap of imagination to label the cat, when it acquired negative spiritual associations, as 'the dog of the Ruler of the Underworld' and see this species as embodying the opposite values.

These five interrelated reasons, in my view, help explain how the cat— originally an 'earthly' creature with a great talent for 'mouse-catching deeds' and devoid of any spiritual powers—acquired paranormal powers in modern *bolson yavdal* stories, where it is associated with death.

Here, I wish to make one point clear: in all the cat-related *bolson yavdal* stories that I came across, the cat does not represent the cannibalistic socialist state, the murderous secret police, or the executed monks. Rather, the cat, as a messenger of the underworld, embodies a particular concept or fear—the horror of the suddenness and dark mystery of death, a grim reality under state socialism. To remind, the cat in this role emerged alongside a multitude of ghosts[23] against the backdrop of a cosmological order turned upside down by mass traumatic events perpetrated by the atheist state.

Aside from the Buddhist establishment, another group historically associated with cats was the Chinese, who during the socialist period came to be viewed by Mongols with suspicion, fear, and incomprehension (see Chapter 2). One *bolson yavdal* story, which recounts a case that allegedly occurred around the 1920s, is representative. In the story, a Chinese man lives alone with a cat who happens to be the reincarnation of his deceased father. The man's usual meal is 'Three Squeaks', a Chinese dish that involves live baby mice. The name comes from the sounds the mice make during the eating process. The first squeak occurs when the diner picks up the baby mouse with chopsticks, the second when it is dipped into a vinegar, and the third when it is bitten and chewed. One day, the 'Three Squeaks' enthusiast hears from his friends about Mongolia and decides to try his luck in the new place. In Urga, he finds employment in a Chinese dining hall where he lives in a back room. His hard work and the cat's ability to keep the kitchen free of mice make him a valued employee, and for a time, the man and the cat enjoy a peaceful life. Both are well-fed and sheltered, and their bond remains strong. However, this happy life was not to last. One day, the Chinese man brings home a Mongol woman (a person who belongs to a people who reincarnate into and from dogs) to live with him. The cat is angry with the foolish choice of his 'son'. Unable to contain its anger, the cat one day attacks the man, scratching his face. In the chaos, a cook from the dining hall rushes to the man's aid and kills the cat, unaware that it was the reincarnated father of his colleague. Stricken with grief, the Chinese man blames himself for not revealing the cat's true identity to his co-workers.

What is interesting about this and similar *bolson yavdal* stories is that they are set within a relatively recent past and describe fears that today's Mongols can understand and identify with. To the best of my knowledge, there are no ancient legends of this kind in Mongolia, which suggests

---

23   In Mongol worldview, ghosts (*bug, chötgör*) are believed to be the souls of deceased people who stayed on earth, unable to transition to the afterlife or get reincarnated. The reasons for souls getting stuck on earth are many, including a tragic or violent death.

that stories about the Chinese reincarnating into felines and vice versa were likely invented during the socialist period when Mongolia, under Soviet pressure, promoted Sinophobia.

In socialist Mongolia, the image of the evil cat with supernatural powers was, of course, not an official view. Officially, the cat was just a biological species in the same way as death was taught to be a biological termination of one's life with nothing waiting beyond it. In kindergartens and secondary school curriculum, as I can attest from my own childhood experience, the cat appeared as a character from fairy tales and legends. Many people who grew up in socialist times remember two such popular legends, namely *Cat the Teacher* (*Muur bagsh*) and *The Wealthy Cat* (*Bayan muur*). As the names suggest, the former depicts a monastic cat and the latter a fat cat. Owing to the politicization of every aspect of life, including education and literature, these legends were supposed to be taught to children as a critique of pre-socialist society in which the monks (cats in temples) exploited and tricked the people (mice) while the wealthy enjoyed life at the expense of the poor. No wonder, many *dacha*s on the outskirts of Ulaanbaatar that stood out by their size and expensive exteriors, typically owned by corrupt apparatchiks and party functionaries, were euphemistically referred to as 'cat houses' and were suspected of being hideouts where their owners engaged in debauchery and other anti-ideological activities.

The Good Cat Under Socialism

The cat in socialist Mongolia was an ambivalent animal reflecting social tensions, people's innermost fears, prejudices, and sometimes even aspirations. Among various groups, it evoked a host of feelings, mostly negative. That said, whilst historically, tolerance and affection towards cats were expected on the part of Buddhist monks, in the socialist period such tolerance characterized Soviet specialists who arrived in Mongolia in their thousands accompanied by their pets.

The lion's share of cats, both feral and domestic, lived in Soviet neighborhoods in Ulaanbaatar and other settlements built by Soviets across the country. From their Soviet colleagues, some Russophile Mongols not only learnt to tolerate cats but also welcomed felines into their flats, similar to how they opened their doors to dogs (see Chapter

2). Mongols openly began keeping cats in small numbers, not only in Ulaanbaatar, but occasionally cats could be seen in nomadic camps in the countryside. Nomads who led a semi-sedentary lifestyle, such as those working as guards in collective farms or those who migrated less and spent more time in a single pastureland, as well as some elderly individuals without children, were known to keep cats as mousers and companions.

As previously noted, Russians have traditionally viewed cats as both bringers of luck and mischief-makers, capable of cunning behavior and serving malevolent entities. During the socialist period, Mongols also adopted various Russian superstitions, including the belief that a black cat crossing a road is a bad omen. Hence the modern expression *har muur güilgeh* ('to make a black cat run across'), which means 'to spoil one's day or business'.

My Childhood and Teenage Years

I'd like to share a childhood and teenage memory from the years 1985 to 1993. Our family lived in a small settlement called Bor-Öndör, located in Hentii Province, for five years. After that, we relocated back to Ulaanbaatar, where I attended school for the remaining three years before completing my secondary education.

Constructed by the Soviets, Bor-Öndör was home to Soviet and Mongol miners and specialists, along with their families, most of whom were employed by the newly established fluorspar mines on the outskirts. The mining company founded in 1973, had forty-nine percent of its shares owned by the Soviet government and fifty-one percent by the Mongolian government. My father served as the representative of the Mongolian government in this joint venture.

Bor-Öndör comprised two distinct districts: a cluster of five-storey Soviet-style houses and a *ger* district. The modern houses were occupied by Soviets and a small number of Mongols, while the majority of Mongol toilers lived in the traditional *ger* district. Nestled in the middle of the settlement was a Soviet military garrison, like a bear camping in a marmot colony. As my father held a position of authority, our family lived in a modern building and my siblings and I attended the local Soviet secondary school while taking occasional classes in the

Mongolian language and literature at the Mongolian secondary school. This circumstance allowed me to bridge both Soviet and Mongol worlds, gaining insights to compare these two distinct social environments.

Soviet imperial ideology was supposed to be inclusive of all socialist peoples, fostering a sense of unity under the shield of communism in opposition to the capitalist world. This ideology also had a missionary quality, aiming to spread the 'religion' of communism and was framed through the metaphor of familial ties. The Soviet Union was portrayed as the wise 'elder brother', responsible for the protection, cultural development, and well-being of its socialist 'younger siblings'—the other nations within its sphere of influence. Nothing symbolized this Soviet position better than the iconic fraternal kiss, epitomized by Soviet leader Leonid Brezhnev. Instantly recognizable for his thick eyebrows, Brezhnev would greet leaders of fraternal countries with a long kiss on the mouth—especially those with whom he felt a close connection or those whom he wished to impress. This imperial missionary position, sealed with a kiss, served as a justification for the Soviet Union's domination of countries like Mongolia—a relationship symbolically affirmed by Brezhnev exchanging mouth kisses with Mongolia's leader, Tsedenbal, during his visit to Mongolia. The propaganda kiss was every bit as passionate as a 'French kiss'—or, some may argue, a 'bonobo kiss'—the only obvious difference being the absence of active engagement of the leaders' tongues. Not that Brezhnev needed to win Tsedenbal over with his passionate embrace, as Tsedenbal was already enchanted by his Russian wife, Anastasia Filatova, widely regarded as the *de facto* co-ruler of Mongolia and a KGB agent.[24]

Despite the romantic intertwining at the highest echelons and official propaganda singing an ode to the eternal love and loyalty between the two brotherly nations, the Soviet Union behaved like a disciplinarian empire builder ready to chastise and browbeat Mongolia for every transgression, whether real or imagined. This relationship, rooted in hierarchy and power disparity, resulted in Soviets and Mongols in Mongolia inhabiting separate worlds that temporarily intersected in the workplace through

---

24 Initially praised by the People's Revolutionary Party as a stable genius, Tsedenbal later became a liability for the Soviet leadership when he revealed his sharp tongue and erratic behavior, criticizing the Soviet Union. This ultimately led to his downfall in 1984.

formal interactions. This was particularly evident among members of the respective proletariat. Beyond the confines of work, the two groups seldom socialized, and this segregation was reinforced by distinct institutions and infrastructures, including separate living arrangements, schools, shops, transportation, social clubs, and so on.

Let's take the school as an example. The Soviet school in Bor-Öndör was typically off-limits to Mongol children, and I only knew a few other Mongol kids who attended, mainly those with high-ranking officials as parents. Two of such kids were the offspring of the Mines Director, the most obese man in the settlement. Strutting around like North Korea's leader Kim Jong Un, he was known for his authoritarian leadership, gluttony, and a penchant for surrounding himself with minions ready to construct a mini-cult of personality around him. His nickname was 'The Piglet', underscoring his potential for further growth, both physically and politically, given his ambitions and marital status. In socialist Mongolia, there was a joke about securing a successful career by marrying a Russian woman. The Mines Director, who happened to have a Russian wife, was a walking embodiment of this joke, prompting many to speculate that his appointment to the post was not due to his working his butt off but influenced by his auspicious marriage.

Speaking of Kim Jong Un, whenever I watch short videos or documentaries about North Korea these days—where half-starving people enthusiastically cheer, jump, clap, and otherwise display child-like, exaggerated loyalty to their morbidly obese leader—it brings back memories of socialist Mongolia, a mirror image of the Soviet Union. In Mongolia, leaders were similarly welcomed by the toilers in choreographed fashion, though not to the same extreme as in the Hermit Kingdom. During public meetings, the Mongol toilers rejoiced at the sight of their leaders like Pavlovian dogs salivating at the sound of a bell. When North Koreans excitedly express, in front of cameras, that they believe their impoverished Fatherland is the best country in the world, or that their totalitarian dictator is their national treasure, I don't see it as mere pretense because saying otherwise may have lethal consequences. I know that many North Koreans mean what they say, as many *Homo Sovieticus Mongolicus* felt the same way about their country and leadership during the socialist period. Despite enduring an erratic authoritarian leader like Tsedenbal and facing low living standards, many Mongols praised him as 'the best leader of the Party and state' and genuinely believed their country to be the second-best in the world, only behind the Soviet Union. These examples illustrate the power of state propaganda and storytelling in authoritarian states.

If we are to return to Bor-Öndör, the segregation between the Mongol and Soviet worlds extended to two sets of shops, each catering to their respective groups. Besides the Soviet military shop exclusively serving Soviet military personnel, there were three Soviet civilian shops, brimming with an array of goods imported directly from the Soviet Union, that stood as emporiums of plenty, tantalizingly out of reach for ordinary Mongols. The only locals who could shop at these revered Soviet institutions were holders of special IDs, typically senior management or workers in strategic industries, such as chefs employed in the local sanatorium. Both my father, serving as Mongolia's representative, and my mother, a chef at the sanatorium, were proud holders of these coveted IDs. In contrast, there was a single Mongol shop that displayed a mere selection of essentials (meat, milk, millet, etc.), echoing the simplicity of daily necessities against the backdrop of the Soviet extravagance. It was a common sight to witness Mongol workers politely beseeching Soviets or their influential compatriots in front of these Soviet shops to purchase items unavailable in the Mongol shop.

Transportation further accentuated the segregation and power disparity. Soviets had their own buses, separate from those used by Mongols. Soviet buses were more comfortable and less crowded, in stark contrast to the overcrowded conditions endured by Mongol commuters, who, particularly during rush hours, resembled sardines packed in a tin.

Whilst Soviets could go into and use any Mongol facility at any time, rarely doing so except out of curiosity, the reverse was prohibited for ordinary Mongols. Soviets generally enjoyed better facilities, more food variety, better clothing, higher salaries, and better living standards compared to Mongols. After all, as bringers of superior socialist culture to Mongolia, the Soviets were 'givers' and the Mongols were 'recipients' and were supposed to behave accordingly. This cultural and social segregation between the Mongols and Soviets, with all its ensuing consequences, was not unique to Bor-Öndör but was replicated across the toilers' and herders' paradise on the steppes.

Humans are xenophobic beings who instinctively categorize humanity into 'us' and 'others'. The former comprises individuals who share common language, customs, norms, and history. The latter refers to everyone else. 'Us' is often associated with the notion of superiority, while 'other' is usually perceived as inferior and avoided. The reinforcement of this division—'us'/'superior' versus 'other'/'inferior'—by political, social, cultural, and other arrangements only tend to amplify xenophobia. No wonder, given the situation in socialist Mongolia, many Soviets, instead of embracing Mongols with a bear hug, viewed Mongols as 'others' and considered themselves socially superior, smarter, more hygienic, and fashion trendsetters. These sentiments were often sheepishly acknowledged by Mongols themselves. Holding a condescending view of the Mongols, many Soviets also saw Mongolia as a second-rate country, enduring their time there only because it allowed them to earn more money than in the Soviet Union. In other words, despite the beautiful ideology of enlightening the Mongols and helping them build communism on the steppes, ordinary Soviets were interested in little except enriching themselves.

In Bor-Öndör in the apartment block where our family lived, the basements served as a refuge for cats and even housed a pregnant dog who soon delivered a noisy litter of eight puppies. Amongst these furballs, I discovered my Sharik, who stood out among his dark-furred siblings as the only one with a gold-hued coat. My elder sister named him Sharik, and we embraced him as our 'pet'. My sister and I spent our days playing with Sharik and ensuring he had enough to eat. During a distressing dog-killing campaign, we provided refuge for the entire canine family in our kitchen, protecting them from harm until the campaign's conclusion. I actually knew Sharik's grandmother, a dog called Tsyganka, meaning 'Gypsy' in Russian, who lived in the basement and was fed by the dwellers of our apartment block. Tsyganka gave birth to several litters, but only two of her daughters from the same litter stayed with their mother. One was Berta and the other Linda, names given by local Russian children. Berta was Sharik's mother.

Just like any other apartment block, ours had its share of feline residents. Most Russian children knew the local cats' genealogies well just as they knew those of yard dogs. Whilst most of these cats called the stinky basement home, some lucky cats found a place inside the cozy flats, cared for by Soviet puss lovers. One of our neighbors even had a chubby pet marmot that spent most of its time in a small, dark box throughout the year. Another neighbor kept guinea pigs, which became the main attraction for the local cats whenever they were taken out for a stroll around the playground. Most residents in our apartment were fond of cats, regularly providing them with milk and spoiling with delicacies, exclusively found in the Soviet shops. This included slices of sausage—a source of joy and delight cherished by all carnivorous Mongols. When Soviet specialists who kept cats returned to the Soviet Union, they often left their feline friends behind, contributing to the growing population of stray cats.

In comparison, the Mongols, both young and old, held a negative attitude towards cats, to put it mildly. Except for a few Mongols who were puss lovers, most adults openly avoided felines, while children chased them with sticks and stones, much to the horror of the Soviet onlookers. Pussycats and stray dogs sought shelter not only in apartment basements but also in various buildings under construction, frequently used by teenagers, toilers, and Soviet soldiers as romantic rendezvous spots with girls. These unfinished structures were often littered with mattresses and the walls were invariably marked by graffiti depicting oversized genitalia. This choice of location was driven by an acute housing shortage, where entire families, sometimes consisting of three generations, shared a single flat or lived in cramped *gers*. With no hotels or other places to meet up with their girlfriends, such buildings were also the only available option for testosterone-fueled Soviet soldiery.

During the summer holidays, Soviet children usually travelled to the Soviet Union and returned in autumn for the beginning of the school year with stories about their mind-blowing experiences in their home country—the best place in the entire world, no less. These stories often left me envious in much the same way that Facebook photos of perfect holidays posted by acquaintances leave many people feeling jealous these days. In contrast, my summers were spent in Dundgobi Province with my paternal aunt's family, where I was exposed to the harsh realities of rural life—an experience I thoroughly enjoyed, even as the stories of my schoolmates sounded captivating. In moments of conflicting emotions, I instinctively knew that the comfortable lives or holidays of Mongol bureaucrats or Soviet specialists could never compare to the exhilarating thrill of galloping on horseback across an endless semi-desert, or the moments of a bond with nature, or the serenity and peace of nomadic dinners around a flickering fire.

While originally absent in the semi-desert, cats managed to find their way into the administrative center of Dundgobi Province, notwithstanding the prevailing disdain for them among the local population. My aunt's *ger* there was occasionally raided by feline thieves who stole dried meat and other provisions from the wooden shed used as a storage facility. Following such incidents, my aunt had little to say but to mutter, 'These thieving cats, these feline teachers!' alluding to the legends *Cat the Thief* and *Cat the Teacher*, which were popular among Mongols of all ages. The feline population must have been small, as I never personally saw one, but I heard stories from others who had. However, after Sharik arrived to live with my aunt, the feline visits to her wooden shed came to an end, bringing great joy to my aunt.

In the summer of 1990, our family returned to Ulaanbaatar, where it became evident that being born as a cat in the capital city, especially in a Mongol neighborhood without the mitigating influences of Soviet puss lovers, was one terribly unlucky fate. In our neighborhood, cats never dared to venture outside during the daytime because the mere sight of a cat would prompt children and teenagers alike to assault them with whatever happened to lie around on the ground—iron bars, bottles, pavement stones. Occasionally, I would come across dead cats sent to the afterlife in the most gruesome way. Although many hated and feared cats, there was one particular sadistic teenager in our apartment block who derived pleasure from torturing felines or any other living beings. Last time I heard of him, he was said to be running an illegal brothel and mistreating prostitutes. To compensate for his sickly-looking stature, he resorted to filling his penis with Vaseline to enlarge it, which often leads to complications and can eventually result in the need for prosthetic testicles. This practice of penile augmentation, which became popular in Mongolian national prisons, is said to have been adopted from the Soviet penal system. Next time you come across a Mongol thug flaunting his pumped-up manhood in a sauna or a public bath, you'll know that the marketed appearance doesn't necessarily reflect the product's quality.

In Ulaanbaatar, along with one of my siblings, I attended Mongolian Secondary School No. 23 located in the city center. My other siblings went to typical Soviet schools. In just three or four years, some of my siblings had to change their Soviet schools three times due to the exodus of Soviet specialists, who, having failed to build a communist paradise in Mongolia, were returning home in large numbers. Consequently, schools that their children attended had to close and merge, reflecting this political-demographic change.

Initially established to cater to the children of residents in the neighborhood, many of whom were high-ranking bureaucrats, Secondary School No. 23 gradually transformed into a quasi-elite institution and was designated as a 'special school'. Despite our family living on the outskirts of the city—due to our father's insistence, who had a sentimental attachment to our apartment block—these secondary schools situated in the city center accepted my siblings and me. Our father's ability to pull strings made it possible. During the socialist era, a significant number of teachers at my secondary school were Soviets instructing Mongol children. However, by 1990, the majority of the teaching staff were already Mongols. Eventually, the remaining few Soviet teachers also left the school for good to return to their home country, which was in existential turmoil. Many of my classmates were from privileged backgrounds, with parents serving as directors of institutes, Mongolian ambassadors, Party functionaries, university lecturers, and suchlike. This starkly contrasted with the children in my proletarian neighborhood. Some of my classmates had domestic cats, highlighting the disparities in lifestyles, hobbies, and values among different social classes.

The Cat Today

The two preceding chapters discussed how the dog and the marmot, both of whom had their spiritual significance denied during the socialist period, reemerged from the ruins of state socialism with their powers reinstated. These two species did not merely regain their powers and revert to their pre-revolutionary forms or images; they met the post-socialist challenges equipped with new supernatural characteristics. In contrast, the pre-revolutionary cat had never been associated with spiritual powers, but ironically gained them during the socialist period. Today, the cat is a multifaceted creature and remains a controversial species, evoking fear, suspicion, disgust, love, and even veneration. People either love or hate the feline, choosing to keep it as a companion or seeking to avoid it for a variety of reasons, some of which would not have crossed the minds of citizens during the socialist period.

Many modern Mongols dislike cats for various reasons. One is the cat's famously indifferent attitude, nicely captured in the English nursery rhyme 'Pussycat, Pussycat', about a cat who visits the grand Queen's palace but, instead of being impressed, goes about its usual business—chasing a mouse. Unlike dogs, who happily cozy up to important humans, cats are seen as individualistic animals that often give people the cold shoulder. For Mongols who love their loyal dogs and value hierarchy and obedience, cats come across as too aloof and not very dog-like.

In pre-revolutionary times, cats were cared for by Buddhist monks, who were expected to feel compassion toward all living beings, regardless of whether they cozied up to humans. During the socialist period, some Mongols welcomed cats into their homes by emulating the Soviets. In post-socialist Mongolia, many cat enthusiasts have embraced felines with a previously unfamiliar neoliberal mindset, influenced by an ideology that champions individualism, self-reliance, consumerism, and skepticism toward traditional institutions and conventions. Neoliberalism also encourages its adherents to form their own opinions on various matters.

Despite these lofty ideals, humans, as social beings, are never isolated in their worldview formation but are influenced by their environment, which today is shaped by social media, the advertising industry, and multinational corporations, among others. What neoliberal consumers really need to do is make up their minds about whom they choose to follow.

In this neoliberal context, consumerism and the practice of keeping specific pets serve as a means of self-expression and identity construction for many Mongols aspiring to be perceived as 'modern', 'unique', and 'sophisticated'. Brands like Hello Kitty and pet food producers, symbolizing modern Western values that equate pets with family members, exert influence on Mongol cat lovers, many of whom subscribe to the online culture of following both domestic and foreign influencers like pop stars, talk show presenters, top models, and famous academics. For example, one of Mongolia's most prominent superstars and national treasures, singer Bold—known for his signature move of covering his private area with his left hand when dancing in public or in front of cameras—is famous for keeping pussycats at home and sharing their pictures on social media, garnering thousands of 'likes'.

Over recent years in Mongolia, distinct consumer tribes have emerged based on shared consumption habits and interests, providing a sense of belonging to an 'imagined community' and defining their identity accordingly. An example of such a consumer tribe is the fanbase of popstar Bold. Another example is cat lovers.

Corporations, brands, social media influencers, NGOs, and news outlets play a significant role in shaping public opinion on cats and various other topics. They do this by disseminating information, framing narratives, and influencing discourse. This creates a platform that both promotes and counters anti-feline sentiments, encouraging certain lifestyles, such as cat rejection or cat ownership.

Notwithstanding, the cat-loving movement has made considerable progress, leading to the establishment of the Mongolian Cat Federation (MCF). In 2016, the MCF organized the first cat show, *The Cat is Beautiful*, in Ulaanbaatar. At this event, attendees had the opportunity to marvel at fifty breeds of pussycats and receive professional advice from veterinarians. Additionally, they were given the chance to spend their money on luxurious toys and accessories to spoil their four-legged, purring sweethearts—something that would have made Christian Grey, the main character of *Fifty Shades of Grey*, green with envy.

Shifts in social attitudes towards cats have also manifested in the way cats are being named and the cosmological role they occupy. Traditionally, cats were not bestowed with personal names and were not considered beings closely connected to Mongols in the cycle of reincarnation. However, in the present day, domestic cats not only bear names like Yagaan ('Pink'), Tazhii ('Fatty'), Tom ('Big'), Zaraa ('Prickly'), or foreign names such as Emma, Lucy, Lily, but many cats also carry distinctly Mongol human names, both male and female, including

Dulmaa, Sambuu, Jonon, Galsan, and others. This reflects a new belief that cats have the ability to reincarnate into and from Mongols. In this regard, the modern cat mirrors the traditional dog by adopting more canine-like and, therefore, human-like qualities in the eyes of Mongols.

That said, due to an overwhelmingly negative image ascribed to the cat in the socialist period, and because the cat is still a rare animal in Mongolia (the implication being that the majority of the population learn about the cat's characteristics from moralistic *bolson yavdal* stories or hearsays rather than from firsthand experience), today the cat is predominantly perceived as a dodgy animal than a docile and friendly species. Even individuals, particularly those of middle age or older generations, who keep felines at home for companionship, describe the cat, as articulated by journalist Gangaa, whose dairy opens this section of the chapter, as a 'weird animal that you can neither hate nor love'. The following comments on Gangaa's article exemplify the prevailing attitudes towards felines in contemporary Mongolia:

Comments:

It is cute only when it is a kitten, but when it grows up it is really ugly.

When foreigners see a green cat cross the road, they all go like 'wow what a cutie!' But when Mongols see one, we go like 'what an abominable green cat! Look at how it looks scornfully with its wolf-like eyes!'

Once a cat was lying across the entrance to our house. The local kids could not get in because they were afraid of it.

My fellow Mongols, we should love cats. That it is a bad omen when a cat crosses a road is just unsubstantiated gossip. Animals that come to your home can be a reincarnation of your deceased relatives. They long for their families and try to come back even if it means they turn into cats.

I used to be afraid of cats so much that I always went around them if I saw one. But now (that I have read this article) I won't be afraid anymore.

Broadly speaking, today the cat embodies oppositional qualities: it both curses people and heals people (from cardiovascular diseases and hypertension); it brings death to humans and protects people from malevolent spirits and ghosts; it is a polluting animal and a pure animal which provides emotional companionship; it brings misfortune and good luck; and it is both an ugly animal and a cute being. All these ideas, as we have seen, derived from pre-socialist, socialist, and post-socialist periods.

Conclusion

Mongols believe that a negative attitude towards the cat has been part of 'Mongol tradition and culture'. Those who hold this view find wisdom in 'traditional knowledge', and those who love cats tend to lament this view as outdated. Despite what many people think, the evil cat isn't an ancient image but was created as recently as the socialist period.

The cat's image is multifaceted. In pre-socialist society, the cat was a good and powerless animal (for the monks, as attested to in Buddhist legends), a human avatar in political fairy tales based on Buddhist legends, but mainly an unknown animal (for the nomads, as described in animistic legends). In the socialist period, it turned into a bad and ugly spiritual being (as recounted in *bolson yavdal* stories). Today it is a good, a bad, an ugly animal or a mix of all, mirroring the post-socialist liberal consumerist society with its multiplicity of choices, opinions, memories, and values that people have the freedom to choose, share, promote, or decline.

The cat also serves as a compelling example of how an animal can rapidly transform from an obscure and unfamiliar creature to a recognized and integral part, if not of daily life, then of cosmological imagination. Today, the cat is intertwined with beliefs in reincarnation concerning the Mongols.

The cat's multifaceted image also reflects a broader historical process. In the annals of Mongolia's history, momentous social and cultural transformations stand out as exceptional occurrences. Examples include the establishment of the Mongol Empire in 1206, the fall of the Yuan dynasty in 1368, the official conversion of the Mongols to Buddhism in 1640, the submission of the Halha Mongols to the Manchu Qing in 1691, and the People's Revolution in 1921. Between these historical milestones, social and cultural change unfolded gradually over centuries, meaning that ideas about animals, much like anything else, remained fixed for long periods. However, in the last century, the pace of change has accelerated to the point where social order has become dynamic and flexible. For example, a woman born in 1910 during the last days of the Manchu Qing Empire would have spent her childhood in the independent Mongolian theocracy under the Javzandamba Hutugtu (1911-24) and witnessed transformative changes during her working life under socialism (1924-90), unparalleled in previous generations. Had she lived longer, as is common today, she would have seen the collapse of socialism in 1990, marking the onset of a new liberal democratic era in Mongolia's history. In other words, during her lifetime, she would have witnessed four different regimes.

These socio-political transformations were made possible by the emergence of modern technologies in communication and transportation such as the telegraph, radio, telephone, television, trains, cars, and airplanes. Our imaginary woman would have been born into a world where the only modes of transportation were horses or camels and family life revolved around candles. She would then have spent her adulthood riding public buses and using electricity to watch television as it transmitted news about a Mongol cosmonaut's historic flight aboard the Soviet Soyuz rocket into the cosmos for the glory of the socialist Motherland.

These new technologies not only caused cultural disorientation and dislocation and undermined social structures, creating revolutionary situations, but also made mass surveillance, social control, connectivity, mass education, and propaganda more effective. The twentieth-century totalitarian regimes and liberal democracies would not have been possible without these technologies.

Generation Z (individuals born from mid-1990s to the early 2010s) has encountered changes even more radical and swift than the generation of their parents. Just think of ground-breaking developments since the mid-1990s that have transformed our daily lives—the advent of internet, portable gadgets such as smart phones, social media, E-commerce, advances in genomics and biotechnology, blockchain technology, self-driving vehicles, and AI. Still in their infancy, these new twenty-first century technologies have already seamlessly woven themselves into the fabric of our cultural existence, reshaping the way we think, communicate, work, relax, envision the future, and interact with the world. As they become more complex and integrated into our daily lives, these technologies are bound to make social structures even more flexible and create even deeper cultural disruptions.

In the past, life was much more predictable and settled, taking centuries to witness any discernible social or cultural change or technological breakthrough. The further we go back in time, the longer it took for changes to occur, spanning millennia and tens of thousands of years. In contemporary times, by contrast, each passing year is transformative, making any attempt to define the characteristics of modern Mongol society, or any society for that matter, akin to describing the ever-changing color and texture of an octopus seamlessly adapting to its surroundings as it swims through the ocean. Given the fluidity of the modern era, it is unsurprising that the cat symbolizes a multitude of qualities and ideas simultaneously for a variety of audiences. Throughout history, time has been a crucial factor in allowing ideas, such as those about animals, and norms to settle. Yet, in today's world, the relentless pace of change prevents any possibility for ideas, norms, and identities to solidify and ossify as a tradition. This dynamic churns out a multitude of lifestyles, value systems, knowledge systems, belief systems, identities, and more, colliding with each other and with those from the Cold War era and preceding periods. It is not only the cat that has been attributed a multitude of qualities. As shown in the previous chapters, dogs and marmots also exhibit multifaceted characteristics.

5. The Camel

During the spring season, a family of nomads in the Gobi Desert assists the births of their camel herd. The last camel to calve experiences a difficult labor, lasting for two days. With the devoted assistance and intervention of the family, a rare albino calf finally enters the world. However, the joy is overshadowed when the mother camel rejects the newborn, withholding her vital milk—a refusal that places the calf's life in jeopardy.

In a determined effort to restore the crucial bond between the mother and the calf and ensure the survival of the latter, the nomadic family seeks the spiritual assistance of a group of monks who conduct a special ritual. Perhaps unsurprisingly, the compassionate Buddhist gods stay deaf to the solemn chants of their devoted servants whose efforts fall short of establishing the desired bond. Undeterred, the family turns to a musician, asking him to perform a special melody designed for such occasions using a horse-head fiddle. Upon arriving at the nomadic camp, the musician initiates the ritual by carefully placing the horse-head fiddle on the front hump of the mother camel, establishing a cosmic connection between the instrument and the beast. Then he proceeds to play a melancholic melody, accompanied by a female member of the nomadic family who recites a soothing song known as 'hoos'. As the weeping sounds of the horse-head fiddle and the ethereal song fill the air, as it happened for so many times in the annals of Mongolia, nothing short of a miracle takes place—the mother camel begins to shed tears, the liquid grace of compassion, streaming from her eyes. Immediately following the completion of the musical rite, the mother camel allows her calf suckle life-granting nourishment from her teat, confirming the restoration of the maternal bond.

This is a scene from a 2003 documentary film titled *The Story of the Weeping Camel*, directed by Mongol and German filmmakers. The film captures the daily life of a nomadic family in the region, providing

©2025 Baasanjav Terbish, CC BY-NC 4.0   https://doi.org/10.11647/OBP.0450.05

a glimpse into the deep connection not only between nomads and animals but also between mother and offspring. In Mongol culture, the bond between a mother camel and her calf symbolizes the cosmic love between a human mother and her offspring.

Mongols have traditionally herded animals, collectively known as *tavan hoshuu mal* or the 'five types of livestock', which include camels, horses, sheep, goats, and cattle. Among these, the camel holds a unique significance, especially for camel herders. While not all herders across Mongolia keep camels, and those who do not tend to have only a general understanding of them, my extended paternal family had deeper than usual knowledge of them due to one of my uncle's occupation as a camel herder. His work provided our family with a closer connection to and understanding of camels. For many camel herders, the camel is one of the most anthropomorphized animals among the 'five types of livestock'. However, families that do not keep camels often view horses as the animals closest to humans. These differing perspectives highlight how herding families across Mongolia have varied experiences with and attitudes toward the animals they raise.

This final chapter discusses the treatment of camels by Mongol camel herders, highlighting the cultural and economic significance of this species, which broadly represents how other types of livestock are managed. It consists of three parts: Part I explores the role of camels in culture, while Part II examines camels as a biological species. The Conclusion briefly touches on broader themes, including how herders use animals, among other things, as a lens to reflect on existential questions such as the meaning of life.

Part I

The Camel in Culture

In autumn, a nomadic camp comes alive with the sounds of camels— some grumbling, others growling, and a few emitting their distinctive grunts. Amidst this lively scene, the gaze of an onlooker can be easily captivated by a particularly large and well-groomed camel. This majestic creature, with two humps adorning its back, stands proudly on a white felt in front of the *ger*, its head immersed in the nomadic dwelling.

Inside the *ger*, a festive atmosphere unfolds. Against a high wooden chest displaying a row of colorful thangkas depicting multi-limbed gods, fierce-looking bodhisattvas, and portraits of benign ancestors gazing down at the mortals, a table is laid with a spread of food and dairy products, signaling a joyous occasion. The camel, seemingly accustomed to such an ambiance and treatment, remains composed and motionless, its soulful brown eyes calmly acknowledging the moment. While partaking in the celebratory food, the nomadic family performs a series of rituals, beginning with the purification of the camel using juniper incense. The smoke envelopes the camel's head, drifting through the *ger*, and floats out the door into the morning light. Next, a *hadag* scarf, the color of the blue sky, is tied around the camel's neck. Then, the hosts embark on a ceremony, reciting a poetic tribute to their two-humped guest. With reverence, they extol the camel through formulaic lines that praise its unique physical characteristics:

> The camel possesses the ears of a mouse
> The gait of a cow
> The knees of a tiger
> The lips of a hare
> The neck of a dragon
> The eyes of a snake
> The head of a horse
> The wool of a newly shorn sheep
> The hump of a monkey
> The hair of a rooster
> The teeth of a dog
> And the tail of a pig.

In this praise, the camel embodies the qualities of all twelve animals in the traditional calendar. Despite this, the camel doesn't have a month named after it. This omission is explained in the following legend: Once upon a time, the Buddha allocated each month in the year to an animal, yet he left the slot for the first month unassigned. This turned into a bone of contention, attracting two contenders who couldn't be more different from one another: the mouse and the camel, each presenting compelling reasons for the first month to be named after them. The Buddha, in his boundless wisdom, decides to settle the matter through a competition. He informs the mouse and the camel that the winner would be the one who first glimpses the morning light. Eager to secure the honor, the camel ascends to the top of the highest hill, ready to welcome the first rays of morning light. The mouse, miniscule in size, positions itself at the camel's feet, aspiring to achieve the same feat. Observing the mouse from above, the camel, confident in its victory, relaxes, contemplating, 'How can this diminutive creature aspire to witness the dawn before me, the tallest among all animals?' As the first light breaks, the camel gracefully stretches its long neck and closes its eyes in blissful anticipation of the warm sunlight gently touching its muzzle. Seizing the moment, the mouse swiftly ascends the camel's neck, leaps onto its head, and joyously squeaks, capturing the first ray of light. Henceforth, the first month of the year has been named after the resourceful mouse.

After the purification ritual performed inside the *ger*, the camel is granted the freedom to join its herd awaiting nearby. The purpose of the ritual is to show respect to the camel herd and convey wishes for its prosperity.

Such scenes are a common sight across Mongolia, where nomads herd camels. This praise, which has many versions but is similar in content, accompanied by the legend about the absence of the camel in the twelve-year animal calendar, can be heard during various camel-related celebrations as well. These celebrations range from annual festivities dedicated to camels (as seen in this example) to consecrating a camel, camel races, castration, and releasing a bull camel among female camels. To grasp the role of camels in rituals, one must delve into cosmology, an imaginary realm with real-world effects.

The Camel in Cosmology

The camel stands out among livestock with its remarkable combination of diverse traits drawn from across the animal kingdom. For camel herders, the camel is, as mentioned, the most anthropomorphized of the 'five types of livestock'. Several popular sayings emphasize this deep cosmological connection, such as 'humans and camels have bodies that are related' (*hün temee hoyor mahbodyn töröltei*), 'only humans and camels are afraid of their dead' (*temee hün hoyor* ühseneesee *aina*), and 'the most adorable beings in the universe are a human baby, a puppy, and a camel calf' (*yörtöntsiin gurvan höörhön: hüühed, gölög, botgo*).

Despite its chimeric beauty and human-like characteristics, the camel is not considered close to humans in the Buddhist reincarnation cycle, nor is it believed to possess spiritual powers. Although the camel may hold an elevated place among livestock, it is still classified as one of the 'five types', signifying it as an indisputable possession of humans. This implies that camels, like all other livestock, are beyond the interest of nature spirits, shamanic gods, or Buddhist deities, who neither attempt to steal the camels from rightful human owners nor offer them protection voluntarily. Consequently, when any livestock crosses into sacred spaces, especially the so-called 'wrathful places', nomads become anxious, fearing that their animals might provoke these sacred locations and suffer as a result.

In the animal kingdom, creatures instinctively safeguard their 'possessions', such as a kill, by themselves. However, Sapiens are different. Instead of personally safeguarding their valuables, humans employ an array of technologies and entrust the protection task to various beings and entities, including family, friends, community members, the state, and the supernatural.

Supernatural protective technologies include rituals of consecration, affixing amulets to individual camels, and seeking the intercession of a Buddhist deity called Günjinlham. In Buddhist iconography, Günjinlham takes the form of a wrathful female deity with badass looks and formidable weaponry enough to scare the light out of predatory wolves or spirits that spread diseases and bring misfortune. She is depicted topless, with dangling teats, wielding a razor-sharp sword in her right hand, and cradling a cup made from a human skull in her left hand. Mounted on a wild yellow camel, she exudes a fierce presence that would make even the villains from a post-apocalyptic *Mad Max* world seem angelic by comparison.

The idea of animals or livestock being safeguarded by supernatural forces is not unique to Mongol culture but is prevalent in many societies worldwide. In Christianity, for instance, St. Anthony the Abbot is venerated as the patron saint of animals, and his intercession is traditionally sought for the protection of livestock. Similarly, rituals such as the blessing of animals on St. Francis's feast day underscore the enduring presence of such practices in European societies.

To add an extra layer of supernatural protection for their camels, Mongol herders perform a ritual called *seterleh*. This ritual is intended to transfer ownership of the animals from humans to the supernatural realm.

Seterleh, the Ritual of Consecration

In Chapter 2 about the dog, I pointed out that the *seterleh* ritual has traditionally been performed as part of a medicinal rite aimed at healing the sick. During this ritual, an animal is consecrated and dedicated to the gods. Once under the protection of the supernatural, the consecrated animal is emancipated from human control and must be treated with reverence. It is to be fed well, allowed to roam freely, and expected to die a natural death as a possession of the supernatural. In this sense, consecrated animals in Mongolia are similar to cows in Hinduism, which are holy creatures associated with the gods. The ritual of *seterleh*, however, extends beyond dogs and can involve any of the 'five types of livestock'.

The *seterleh* ritual may also serve more practical purposes beyond the healing of sick humans. It may be performed to improve the quality of the livestock. It is usually healthy and virile male animals who can sire superior offspring that get consecrated in this way. For example, a ram with good physical characteristics and impressive testicles can be consecrated with the hope that it will sire as many lambs as it could and simultaneously protect the whole flock through acquiring a divine patronage.

Another motive for performing this ritual is to acknowledge and reward the exceptional services rendered by a particular animal, which may be old, castrated, or female. In such cases, the fortunate animal is released from human service and provided with compassionate care for the remainder of its life.

These three functions of the *seterleh* ritual could be considered independently and pursued separately. However, more often than not, nomads perform the ritual with these three functions overlapping. For example, a ram might be released with the hope of curing a sick person, siring as many lambs as possible to improve the quality of the flock, and as a reward for being an exemplary specimen.

The *seterleh* ritual for camels is performed as follows, which gives an idea to the reader of how it is performed for other livestock animals. The chosen camel is typically an uncastrated male camel, exhibiting docility in riding, possessing a calm disposition, and at the pinnacle of virility and strength, bringing joy to the eyes of its human owners. The initiation of the ritual takes place outside the family *ger*, amid a festive ambiance, officiated by a knowledgeable person well-versed in its execution.

This person recites a special Buddhist text dedicated to camels, accompanied by a traditional praise and well-wishes to the camel. Incense is ignited, and the ritual performer circumambulates the camel in a clockwise manner, enveloping it in the purifying juniper smoke. A *hadag* scarf is tied around the camel's neck, while its leg, sole, nose, and mouth are anointed with ghee butter. Then a special scroll containing well-wishes or mantras is placed in a small bag and securely fastened around the camel's neck.

The underlying concept behind dedicating a camel to a deity is to designate the camel as the deity's riding companion. In return, the deity is expected to protect the camel and, by extension, the entire herd to which the camel belongs. Consequently, it is typically forbidden for mortals to ride such a camel. While the consecrated camel can be dedicated to various deities, primarily Buddhist ones, there are instances when it is also devoted to the shamanic Tengri. In such cases, a shaman typically officiates the ritual.

Post-ceremony, the consecrated camel cannot be sold on the market, slaughtered for meat, or employed in transportation and other customary camel activities, lest one wishes to incur the wrath of the gods. The Buddhist scroll tied to its neck is periodically examined for signs of wear and tear.[1]

Taboos

All societies have prohibitions or restrictions against certain practices, objects, substances, and places. The strongest expressions of such restrictions are commonly known as taboos. The word 'taboo' derives from the Polynesian 'tapu', meaning something sacred, prohibited, or set apart. Violating a taboo can lead not only to social consequences, ranging from ostracism to more physical forms of punishment, but

---

1   Traditionally, the only other scenario in which a camel was exempt from human use was when it was chosen to carry one's parent's corpse for an open-air funeral. Adorned with a *hadag* scarf and carrying two empty baskets turned downwards on either side of its body, the camel symbolized the inverted world for both the deceased and the survivors. After the funeral, the cart that transported the corpse was left outside with its wheels facing skyward for three days.

also to supernatural repercussions. However, what is considered taboo can vary from one culture to another. In some societies, consuming the brains of another person, for example, would be taboo; in others, not eating them during cannibalistic rituals would be considered socially unacceptable. In some, marrying a close relative is taboo; in others, such marriages are the norm.

The nomadic way of life in Mongolia is abundant with taboos. Many of these taboos are manifestations of cultural prejudices and biases regarding specific groups of people, animals, substances, practices, or places. Sanctioned by the supernatural, these taboos serve as mechanisms that enforce and perpetuate structures based on notions of purity and pollution, sacred and profane, social hierarchy, unequal power dynamics, and the delineation between 'us' and 'them'—topics we have explored.

Let's examine several taboos connected with livestock, focusing on camels. Camels hold a unique status as the only livestock whose young are prohibited from entering the *ger*. As readers may recall, Mongols extend a similar ban to dogs (see Chapter 2). This restriction doesn't rise from deeming camel calves impure, but rather stems from perceiving them as ambiguous beings—neither true beasts nor human infants. This example highlights the human tendency to fear the ambiguous or the unknown and to keep it at bay. In the case of the camel calf, this fear, however, is a product of the rich human imagination, where what is unequivocally a camel's young is imagined as an ambiguous entity—half-animal, half-human—in the cosmological domain. As a consequence, the camel calf is denied entry into the human habitat. Typical of *Homo sapiens*, what nomads deny in one instance, they accept as valid in another instance. Thus, to underscore the significance of camel calves, nomads ceremoniously hang camel calf placenta above human heads inside the *ger* at the roof opening, one of the most sacred parts of the *ger*. In Christian terms, this practice is somewhat akin to placing a placenta on the altar in a church. As discussed, during an annual ceremony to honor camels and wish for their health and multiplication, a camel is invited to place its head inside the *ger* to undergo purification and receive a *hadag* scarf.

In contrast to camel calves, the young of sheep, goats, cows, and horses, considered unambiguously proper beasts, are warmly welcomed on all fours inside the *ger*, particularly during freezing temperatures when protection within the warmth of human shelter becomes essential. However, if the need arises to bring a camel calf inside the *ger*, it is permissible only after putting a special hat (*zulai*) on its head. In the eyes of the nomads, this ritual signifies a symbolic transformation of the camel calf into an entity of the same status as a human baby, thus allowing it entry.

Such symbolic transformations can also be found in various cultures and traditions. For instance, in shamanism, animals can shapeshift into humans. Similarly, in numerous ancient religious practices worldwide, sacrificial rituals involved animals, which were often perceived as representing humans.

If animals can shapeshift or become symbolic representations of humans, the reverse is also possible in Sapiens' imagination, as seen when humans are symbolically imagined as animals. One well-known example in Christianity involves biblical symbolism, where, in the eyes of God, the congregation is likened to a sheep flock, and Christ is represented by a sacrificial lamb. So the Mongol practice of symbolically imagining a camel calf as an entity akin to a human baby, achieved by placing a hat on its head, shouldn't be deemed exotic or unusual in the broader context of human cultures.

Given the close symbolic association of camels with humans, the consumption of camel meat is often veiled under alternative names such as 'the meat of the long-legged one' or 'the meat of the tall one'. It is also prohibited to gather other livestock in a location where a camel was slaughtered, echoing a ban reminiscent of that observed in a human cemetery.

Many taboos have complex explanations that can be challenging to untangle. A case in point is the prohibition imposed on pregnant women, forbidding them from consuming camel meat and relieving themselves in the presence of camels. This taboo stems from the belief that such actions might result in the baby being born with a cleft lip, resembling the split appearance of a camel's upper lip. The rationale behind this taboo can be approached from different angles. Firstly, it may be linked to traditional anxieties surrounding pregnancies in the past when child mortality rates were high, and nomads had limited means to address birth-related deformities and conditions like cleft lip. Communities sought to protect pregnant women and ensure healthy deliveries, contributing to the establishment of such taboos. Secondly, this particular taboo could have been rooted in gender hierarchy, intertwined with concepts of purity and pollution. Prohibiting certain practices for women while allowing them for men suggests a potential patriarchal power dynamic, where women were traditionally perceived not only inferior to men but also polluted or susceptible to pollution. Hence, despite pregnant women being banned from eating camel meat and relieving themselves in front of camels, expectant fathers were, technically speaking, always able to expose their private parts to whatever livestock they wanted to and eat as much camel meat as they desired, without repercussions for themselves and their unborn babies. Some Mongols attribute the taboo against women relieving themselves in front of camels as a tradition rooted in showing respect to these amazing animals. While this explanation holds some cultural validity, what is notable is the absence of a similar prohibition for men, suggesting that camels, supposedly, don't take offense when men urinate in their direction.

Pregnant women in Mongolia face another taboo: riding camels during pregnancy, even though riding horses is deemed acceptable. The rationale behind this prohibition is the belief that if a pregnant woman rides a camel, her gestation period will extend to twelve months, contrary to the biological reality of nine months. As readers might have already guessed, this taboo doesn't extend to expectant fathers. However, as with many taboos, there exists a workaround: a pregnant woman can lift the potential negative consequences of this taboo by crawling underneath a camel. If you chance upon the sight of a pregnant woman maneuvering beneath a camel in the vast expanses of Mongolia, don't assume she's searching for a lost wedding ring. You now know the cultural context behind such an act.

To better comprehend the essence of these camel-related prohibitions, consider a fictional taboo in America: Pregnant women are strongly advised against driving a Ford Explorer SUV and, specifically, from urinating nearby. Ignoring these prohibitions may result in the child remaining in the womb for up to twelve months and experiencing issues with movement coordination upon birth—mirroring the reported transmission problems in Ford SUVs, such as rough shifting, slipping, or occasional malfunctions. In cases where a Ford Explorer is the only family ride, pregnant women are recommended to perform a purification ritual to counteract potential taboo effects. This involves opening and closing the SUV's hood seven times before hitting the road. This taboo, of course, doesn't apply to their husbands or any other man because they have superior penises.

Real taboos are often rooted in historical or traditional practices that might be biased or discriminatory. Over time, these practices become ingrained in culture, particularly within religions, and the associated taboos persist as a means of preserving tradition or as integral components of religious belief systems.

Mother-Offspring Bond in Biology, Culture, and Folklore

Female animals are often associated with motherhood, symbolizing nurture and self-sacrifice. However, contemporary animal studies, as demonstrated by Lucy Cooke, an authority on the subject, challenge this age-old notion, revealing a world far more complex and interesting.[2] One prevalent myth is that all females possess an inherent, almost mystical maternal instinct that effortlessly guides them to understand every need of their offspring and be devoted to them. In reality, across the animal kingdom, many male animals demonstrate remarkable commitment to parenting. In various bird, amphibian, and fish species, single fathers often shoulder the entire burden of raising the young, while mothers may simply leave for good after laying eggs.

Recent scientific evidence suggests that caregiving isn't the exclusive domain of one sex; both males and females possess the same neural architecture associated with caregiving instincts, which can be activated or deactivated like a light switch. This phenomenon also holds true for mammals, including the ever-so-popular laboratory mice. While mice exhibit nurturing behaviors toward their young, they also harbor a darker side, with both males and females sometimes engaging in infanticide. The galanin neurons in their brains play a crucial role, either activating parenting instincts or, conversely, triggering infanticidal tendencies.

In the animal kingdom, the goal of motherhood, however harsh it may sound, isn't about indiscriminate nurturing. Rather, it's about strategic investment. A female's limited energy is carefully allocated to maximize the number of offspring that survive and eventually reproduce. At its core, motherhood is fundamentally a selfish endeavor, driven by a simple evolutionary imperative: for reproduction to succeed, a female must

---

2   Cooke, *Bitch*.

first ensure her own survival in a dog-eat-dog world where she is either finding her next meal or trying not to become one. A 'good mother' instinctively knows when to make sacrifices for her offspring and when to prioritize her own survival. Despite the powerful drive to nurture and protect, and the undeniable strength of the mother-infant bond, the evolutionary perspective presents mothers as multidimensional and nuanced figures.

In contrast to the animal world, the mother-infant bond in humans operates on two levels: biological and cultural. Biologically, as in other mammals, this bond is forged through tangible and measurable physical and hormonal changes during pregnancy and childbirth. A key player in this process is oxytocin, a hormone that not only facilitates the physiological aspects of motherhood but also helps establish an immediate bond between the mother and her newborn. Often dubbed the 'love hormone', oxytocin is instrumental during birth and primes the new mother to form a deep connection with her newborn. Activities like breastfeeding further immerse the mother in oxytocin, effectively creating an addiction to caring for her baby. This surge of oxytocin rewires the mother's brain, making it exquisitely sensitive to her infant's cries, scents, and visual cues, which explains the well-known phenomenon of mothers exhibiting remarkable fearlessness in defending their young.

While oxytocin plays a starring role in early caregiving, the biology of maternal bonding in complex social creatures like humans goes beyond this initial rush—or the lack of thereof. Evolution has provided alternative, more stable pathways to attachment. This more enduring form of caregiving attachment develops through social interactions, where repeated exposure to babies has been shown to stimulate the production of other neuropeptides in those who interact with the babies. This extends the circle of caring attachment not only to biological mothers and fathers but also to more distant relatives and even foster parents.[3]

In human societies, the cultural aspect of the mother-child bond often takes precedence over its biological foundation. Across various societies, this bond serves as a cornerstone for familial relationships and social structures. Since the primary function of human cultures isn't to mirror reality faithfully but to ensure cooperation and social order,

---

3   Ibid., 122-54.

cultures create myths and ideals, including those about motherhood. In many societies, maternal love is exalted to a near-sacred status, praised as an enduring force that transcends challenges, adversity, and even space and time. This idealization strengthens the sanctity of the bond, embedding its significance into social norms, rituals, and myths.

As one might expect, this idealization overlooks the messier realities of daily life and the complexities of human psychology. Just as in the animal kingdom, not all human mothers naturally bond with their babies, and not all women experience maternal love. Many of us know mothers with depression who struggle to connect with their infants, or women who simply do not like children. Conversely, we see fathers and even unrelated men with a strong nurturing instinct, with many primary caregivers being fathers rather than mothers. Behaviors that deviate from idealized cultural norms are often dismissed or stigmatized as 'unnatural' or 'abnormal', implying that women who struggle to love children are frequently labeled as 'unnatural' or 'unfeminine'.

In Mongolia, where animals are frequently anthropomorphized and serve as human avatars in stories and rituals, the idealized love between a human mother and her offspring is often expressed through stories involving camel mothers and calves. In folklore, one particularly touching example of this bond is found in a popular üge poem composed at the end of the nineteenth century and the beginning of the twentieth century by Sangdag the Storyteller. This üge poem conveys the lamentations of a mother camel taken away on a caravan journey and her calf left behind in the pastureland. Through their expressions of longing and sorrow, both the mother and calf reveal their deep emotional connection, with their separation only intensifying the anticipation of their reunion.

Lamentation of the mother camel separated from her calf and hired in a caravan

> I bore him as fate had planned long ago,
> After conceiving, my love did grow,
> I brought him forth at the destined hour,
> As ancient destiny showed its power.
>
> While I raised him tender, from youth to this day,
> By my human master's will, we parted our way.
> I let him suckle my first milk, so tender and fair,

Raised him with love, with utmost care.
Why this abrupt parting, what did I do
To deserve such sorrow? I haven't a clue.
What did my little one think, as I left for distant lands,
With heavy burdens to bear, in harsh, unforgiving sands?

Resting his dark eyes on the vast plain's view,
Straining to recognize shadows dancing, they seem so true,
Will my little one, mistaking them for me, leap and run,
Dashing forward, under the scorching sun?

When grazing with his friends on the open plain,
In joyful reunion with mothers, they gain,
Will my little one run with excitement, but after finding I'm not
　　around,
Lie down, four limbs trembling, in sorrow, on the ground?

Hearing his mother's voice from afar, so keen,
Will my little one roll like tumbleweed in the wind?

Upon hearing calls from hidden place,
Mistaking them for his mother's vocal embrace,
Will my little one look around, seeking me in air
Longing for my presence, in deep despair?

Since he first saw the sun's soft golden light,
By my side, he grew up, day and night.
Will my little one, with sorrow etched on his face,
Run, his muzzle drooping, in the vast, empty space?
Unaware of his littleness and left to himself too soon
Will my little one fall into the traps of the ground?

If fate permits, I'll safely return from this caravan ride,
Meet my dear little one, joyfully by my side.
Protector spirit of my human master, as suffering's course is run,
Grant me safe return to my dear little one.[4]

Lamentation of the young camel separated from his mother

She who gave birth to me, so dear,
She who raised me, oh so near,

4　　Damdin, B. et al., 'The camel', 36-38.

My loving mother, gone from sight,
Left, vanished in the fading light.

Her return from far, lowing in quest of me,
Would lift my spirit before her shape I'd see;
I was happy then, oh dear poor mother mine,
Suckling endlessly, feeling so fine!

Her swift approach from pastures wide,
With melodious grunt as her guide,
Would cheer me up, oh mother dear,
Before I'd even see you near!

When I see other mothers' gazes,
Their eyes may resemble yours, but in different ways,
How heart-warming to rest beneath their cover,
Where I discover solace, just like with you, dear mother.

If only this parting from my dear mother
Had happened in my second year, when I am a bit more mature!
When I meet my loving, deserving mother,
As ancient destiny's virtue we uncover,
I'll be freed from the cruel separation's tether,
And be happy with her forever and ever.[5]

Stories such as these 'lamentations' undoubtedly humanize camels. They also influence human empathy for camels, particularly because, to the best of my knowledge, no comparably evocative stories exist in modern Mongol literature or folklore regarding other female animals and their offspring.

In fact, the idealized mother-child bond is a central theme in Mongol folklore and literature, dating back to the foundational texts of *The Secret History of the Mongols*, when oral traditions were first recorded in writing. Among the unique works from this period, known for their portrayals of khans and notable figures, is a poem that captures the mutual longing between an ordinary mother and her son, a cavalryman serving in a distant part of the expanding Mongol Empire. Written on parchment

---

5   Ibid., 38-39.

and believed to date back to the 1240s, this poem originates from the Golden Horde, a state founded by Genghis Khan's grandson, Batu.[6]

The idealization of the mother-offspring bond among camels mirrors that among humans, and this bond is even enshrined in an ancient legend recounting the burial of Genghis Khan. According to the legend, following the interment of Genghis Khan's grave, a special ritual was carried out—a camel calf was sacrificially laid to rest in the presence of its grieving mother. The purpose was to enlist the camel, as the only creature cognizant of the Great Khan's burial site, to guide his kin to the tomb when necessary. This genre is still popular in the folklore of Southern Mongolia, particularly in *bolson yavdal* stories that narrate events from the early twentieth century. Such stories often revolve around thieves who, in their quest to safeguard stolen goods buried underground, resort to killing camel calves with the intention of making their bereaved mothers etch these locations into memory, thus enabling the thieves to be led back to retrieve their ill-gotten gains at a later time.

These stories about the powerful bond between mother camels and their calves, however, are not mere baseless myths. Instead, they likely originated from observations that became idealized in culture and folklore. Among all livestock, when a camel calf dies, most mothers linger around the lifeless body for many days without food or water. This endurance is facilitated by the remarkable hardiness of camels, which can survive without sustenance for extended periods. While other livestock, like cattle, also exhibit grief when losing their offspring, their physiology prevents them from displaying the Spartan-level mourning seen in camels. The fact that the mother camel sheds tears and vocalizes her distress with high-pitched cries adds a human-like dimension. Witnessing such scenes is genuinely heart-breaking for any observer.

The maternal bond, however, may not materialize initially or may break later on for various reasons. In the case of camels, Mongols use a method to mend the relationship or establish a new bond, which consists of a ritual known as 'the song to encourage a mother camel to suckle her calf by uttering *hoos, hoos, hoos*'.

---

6   Poppe, 'Zolotoordynskaia rukopis' na bereste'.

Mother-Offspring Bonding Ritual

The opening scene in this chapter illustrates a popular ritual used by nomads to help mother livestock accept rejected offspring. This ritual is performed on all female livestock, including ewes, goats, cows, and mares, not just camels. The main difference when performing the ritual on various animals is the variation in song lyrics.

In the case of camels, nomads perform a ritual when a young calf is either rejected by its mother or faces starvation due to its mother's inability to produce milk. If the mother camel has milk but refuses to feed her calf, nomads encourage her to accept her offspring. When the mother cannot produce milk, or is sick or dead, the objective shifts to finding another lactating camel and persuading her to adopt the additional calf.

When a nomadic family decides to perform this ritual, both the head of the family and his wife actively participate. The husband is responsible for handling the mother camel by capturing, securing, and immobilizing her. Meanwhile, his wife ensures that the calf, typically tethered to a rope pegged to the ground, successfully suckles from the camel's teat.

Occasionally, during this ritual, someone plays a horse-head fiddle. Whether accompanied by an instrument or not, when the melody begins, both the husband and his wife start reciting a melancholic song, punctuating the verses with the repeated utterance 'hoos, hoos, hoos'. Although devoid of specific meaning, this repetition sounds sorrowful to Mongol ears and supposedly to Mongol camels as well. While many versions of this song exist, here is one to give an idea:

> Why are you squeamish
> About your young calf
> That became your offspring by suckling your milk?
> Your calf is waiting for you, hungry;
> Let it suckle your nutritious milk.
> Hoos, hoos, hoos.
>
> Why did you drive away
> Your beautiful young calf
> That became your offspring by partaking your white milk?
> Your calf is grunting under the midday sun;
> Let it suckle the maternal milk.
> Hoos, hoos, hoos.

> Why did you leave alone
> Your tiny calf
> That became your offspring by drinking your filling milk?
> Your calf is grunting in the evening;
> Let it suckle your warm milk.
> Hoos, hoos, hoos.

The melody varies across Mongolia, highlighting the diversity of Mongol culture. In some regions, the melody mimics the distressed cries of a young calf or a mother camel hurrying back to her calf. In Western Mongolia, among some Oirat groups, nomads may perform pieces from heroic epics such as *Jangar* for this purpose. In other places, nomads may simply sing beautiful melodies akin to love songs. The prolonged lyrics and soothing tone of the music—coupled with the fact that the mother camel is compelled to suckle the calf—typically influence the camel, softening her heart, reviving her maternal instincts, and guiding her to adopt her calf or a second calf. Legend has it that camel mothers who initially rejected their calves but later accepted them back develop an even deeper affection for their offspring.

In addition to the horse-head fiddle, nomads occasionally use the flute. When the nomadic family decides to enlist a skilled musician for this ritual, they extend an invitation, prepare a small feast, and show great respect to the guest. The musician begins by hanging his instrument on the hump of the mother camel, allowing the wind to generate a natural sound. As the musician plays the instrument, the *hoos* song gradually accompanies the melody. This ritual extends beyond the mother camel and calf; the audience also includes the gods and nature spirits, who are invoked to help soothe the mother camel and encourage her to accept the calf.

Given that this ritual is a cultural practice, and cultures inherently distort and reinterpret reality, the success of such rituals among Mongol herders is attributed to the magical power of the song and the benevolence of the gods, rather than any other practical factors. If nomads were to perform these rituals without appeasing the gods and replacing the *hoos* song with any soothing melody—such as the nursery rhymes 'The Itsy Bitsy Spider' or 'Twinkle, Twinkle, Little Star', or even a more romantic tune like 'I Just Called to Say I Love You'—the outcomes would likely have been the same. Consider this comparison: In many modern Western countries, including in the United States, farmers use various methods to encourage mother cows to accept their calves, achieving good results. These methods primarily focus on creating a calming environment and fostering a bond between the cow and the calf, without resorting to religious rituals invoking Jesus Christ or saints in charge of cattle. In fact, these methods resemble those used by Mongol nomads, which involve gentle handling of both the mother and the calf, encouraging positive interactions, and reintroducing them in a controlled setting to help the mother acclimate to the calf. Additionally, rubbing the calf with the mother's milk or other familiar scents enhances recognition. In human terms, it's akin to a depressed mother resting on a soft couch, listening to calming melodies, inhaling therapeutic herbs, and receiving care from two specialists: a psychoanalyst with a soothing voice, gently encouraging her to reconnect with her baby's needs and nurturing instincts, and a masseur performing a calming massage focused around her breasts. After such rituals, few mammalian mothers would resist breastfeeding their babies.

Part II

The Camel as Livestock

In winter, a woolly camel stands tall in the middle of the snow-draped semi-desert. Those familiar with Bactrian camels from photos in wildlife or travel journals would be astonished to see one in person: its snout and nose covered in white foam, resembling a two-year-old after a birthday party with cake. However, the camel isn't in a celebratory mood; it is in full breeding season, with steam billowing from its nostrils, which are covered in a frothy substance that envelops half of its face. This foam results from increased salivation and the mixing of saliva with nasal secretions, a phenomenon peculiar to male Bactrian camels during breeding season.

The bull displays unmistakable signs of aggression, such as heightened vocalization, restlessness, enlarged testicles, along with hyper-protective instincts toward its harem of female camels. The otherwise docile bull undergoes a transformation into a wild aggressive state during this period, posing a danger not only to other camels but also to anything or anyone moving in its vicinity, including nomads. The bull is equipped with a special muzzle—reminiscent of a scene from the movie *The Silence of the Lambs* (1991), where the cannibalistic serial killer Hannibal Lecter, played by Anthony Hopkins, is restrained in a straightjacket and has his mouth covered by a muzzle-like mask with red straps—that prevents biting or harming others while allowing essential functions like eating and drinking. To signal its heated status, the bull is also adorned with colorful ribbons and, as a final mark of humiliation to its masculinity, a red felt flower on its testosterone-crazed forehead. This striking sight is typical in Dundgobi Province during camel breeding season.

In contrast, castrated bulls exhibit no such aggressive behavior and maintain a consistent demeanor throughout the year. Castration is a commonplace practice in livestock management, serving as technique to control temperament and aggression, making animals more docile for transportation and other human needs. Moreover, it helps manage herd dynamics by maintaining a balanced male-female ratio and selectively altering physical traits over generations.

Much like King Midas from Greek mythology, who turned everything he touched into gold, humans perceive and interact with the world through cultural lenses, transforming everything they touch into an artificial realm. Objects and concepts become technology, nature is molded into settlements, sex becomes sexuality, and animals are tamed into livestock. As a species evolved to create and thrive within artificial environments, Sapiens have excelled in tool-making and perfected the sharing of knowledge through language and writing, while constructing complex social systems and infrastructures. Consequently, human life is not a 'natural' existence but an artificial one, with differences between groups arising solely from their respective cultural choices.

This artificiality encompasses the treatment of livestock. Camel herds, like other domesticated animals, don't lead 'natural' lives, guided by free will and instincts to roam as they please. Instead, they exist in human-controlled environments. Each stage of a camel's life—from birth to calfhood to juvenile and breeding ages, as well as their working life and ultimately death—is meticulously planned and shaped by humans. This section explores this aspect of the camel's life.

The Camel in History

The earliest art in Mongolia, featuring camels alongside woolly rhinoceroses, mammoths, ibexes, ostriches, and bison, is found at Rashaan (Batshireet *sum*, Hentii Province) and Hoid Tsenher (Manhan *sum*, Hovd Province).[7] Dating back to the Upper Paleolithic period, approximately 40,000 to 10,000 years ago, this artwork depicts a Mongolia that was vastly different from today.

The earliest evidence of camel domestication is present in rock art at Bichigtiin Am in Bayan-Hongor Province.[8] These petroglyphs, which show humans riding camels, were likely created around 1500 BCE, with updates continuing until the eighth century CE. These later artworks lack depictions of woolly rhinoceroses, mammoths, ostriches, and bison, indicating a shift in fauna and climate more similar to today's conditions.

The first documented reference to camels appears in *The Secret History of the Mongols*, highlighting the diverse roles camels played in Mongol society during the thirteenth century. Herded by specialized camel herders,[9] camels were used for riding, transporting goods, and as draft animals. They pulled two types of carts: the two-wheeled *qasaq* and the four-wheeled wagon used for transporting fixed, non-collapsible *gers*.

Camels were exchanged as gifts and offered as tributes to the Mongols by neighboring peoples, such as the Tangut and the Xia.[10] Their cooked meat provided nutrition for hardy nomads. During times of conflict and intertribal wars, these resilient animals even served as sustenance ATMs on four legs, as exemplified by Ong Khan, who, while fleeing from the victorious Temüjin, reportedly sustained himself by 'pricking camel's blood to drink'[11] when he had no other food to eat.

The imperial annals also mention geographic locations with camel-related names, such as *Bu'ura Ke'er*, or 'Bull Camel Steppe' (today the Jonon Valley in Mongolia's Selenge Province), and *Teme'en Ke'er*, or 'Camel Steppe' (north of Lake Dar in Inner Mongolia). These names underscore the deep cultural and historical connection that the Mongols shared with these animals.

---

7   Atwood, *Encyclopedia of Mongolia*, 450.
8   Ibid., 447.
9   *The Secret History of the Mongols* §232.
10   Ibid. §250; Atwood, *Encyclopedia of Mongolia*, 602.
11   *The Secret History of the Mongols* §151.

The Secret History of the Mongols suggests that the roles of camels have endured over centuries, as contemporary Mongolia continues to utilize them for purposes similar to those in the thirteenth century.[12]

The Silk Road is unimaginable without the Bactrian camel. An ancient and vital trade network linking East and West, it facilitated the exchange of goods, ideas, and technologies, as well as diseases. During the height of the Mongol Empire, the Mongols controlled this commercial superhighway, which, besides providing financial gains, gave them military and political advantages, enhancing their ability to govern the vast empire more effectively.

Following the fall of the Mongol Yuan dynasty in China in 1368, camels were used in trade between the Mongols and Chinese during the succeeding Ming dynasty (1368-1644). Envoys from Mongolia and Jungaria journeyed to Beijing, herding camels and horses laden with furs. Despite being designated as 'tributes' by the Ming court, these commodities were reciprocated with a fixed fee for each animal and fur item, essentially constituting a form of payment to the nomadic emissaries. If the nomads deemed the compensation inadequate, which happened from time to time, they reverted to their customary diplomatic tactics— either raiding the Ming or issuing threats—to negotiate higher fees.[13]

In 1655, the Halhas of Mongolia established a peace agreement with the Manchu Qing dynasty, which had replaced the Ming. As part of the accord, the Manchu Qing conferred the title *zasag* ('ruler') upon eight Halha chiefs. In return, these rulers committed to annually presenting the 'tribute of nine whites'—comprising one white camel and eight white horses—to the Qing Emperor.[14] Following Mongolia's submission to the Manchu Qing in 1691, the tradition was not only continued but the Dariganga group in Eastern Mongolia was entrusted with the care of the Emperor's herds, including camels.

Mongolia's trade, both domestically and internationally, has relied on camels since ancient times. By the seventeenth century, the overland Silk Road had largely fallen into disuse, supplanted by more efficient

---

12   Camels were not only documented in the earliest Mongol imperial annals but also featured in the accounts of foreign observers, including Plano Carpini, William of Rubruck, and Marco Polo.

13   Atwood, *Encyclopedia of Mongolia*, 557.

14   Ibid., 311.

sea routes. The decline of the Silk Road coincided with the rise of the so-called Mongolia's Tea Road, a route established by a treaty between Russia and the Manchu Qing in 1689. Though little known outside the region, it was an important commercial route linking China with Russia through Mongolia. Within Chinese territory, goods were transported on mules or mule carts to Kalkan on the China-Mongolia border. From there, camels carried the goods across the Gobi Desert to reach Urga. Subsequently, the goods made their way to Kyahta, a Russian settlement on the Mongolia-Russia border.

As the name suggests, the main item transported along the Tea Road was tea, although other goods were also traded. Not all tea or goods, however, were destined for Russia; Mongolia's substantial demand for tea was met through this caravan route, too. Among the Mongols, tea was highly valued, not just as a refreshing beverage but also for its symbolic and practical uses. It was offered as gifts to social superiors and deities, and, in regions where conventional coins were scarce, tea even functioned as a form of currency. A pressed tea block could be used to purchase various goods and services, including those provided by sex workers, at a rate of one tea block for a lust-quenching encounter.[15]

Following the victory of the People's Revolution in 1921, the state retained control over the utilization of camels in domestic transportation. From 1921 to 1949, 10,000 camels annually crisscrossed the young socialist nation, forming ancient caravans that were indispensable to the transportation network.[16] Camels served as the primary logistical animals until 1960, handling about sixty to seventy percent of all goods transported during this period.[17] While the use of camels for moving goods diminished with the widespread adoption of Soviet lorries

---

15 Pozdneev, *Mongoliya i Mongoly*, 115-16, 137.
16 Traditionally, Mongols employed two caravan methods: the Halha and Harchin caravans. The Halha caravan involves loading camels in the morning, moving until sunset, and unloading before nightfall. The Harchin method, on the other hand, loads camels in the afternoon and unloads at or after midnight. Whether covering short or long distances, caravans only permit camels to walk, avoiding rushing or running. Camels maintain a pace of six miles per hour, covering about 50 miles in a single day. Long-distance caravans exclusively use older, experienced camels aged six or seven, while younger camels hone their skills during short-term trips. Regardless of the distance, caravans typically walk for three days and then rest for one day.
17 Mijiddorj and Juramt, *Mongol Temee*, 25-26.

and the construction of the railways system, their role as draft and transportation animals in the daily lives of herding families persisted.

The Mongolian Camel

The camels found in Mongolia are of the Bactrian variety, distinguished by their two humps. These camels, with thick wool, are well adapted to cold climates, although they are comparatively less resilient in extreme dry and hot conditions when contrasted with their one-humped cousins in Arabia and the Sahara Desert. Camels in Mongolia prefer Gobi-type or soda-impregnated pastures, and herders deliberately graze them in such locations. Mongols classify domesticated Bactrian camels into three types based on their habitats.

The first is the 'red camel of the Galba Gobi' (*Galbyn goviin ulaan temee*), which lives in the Galba Gobi region in Ömnögobi Province. Approximately seventy percent of camels in this area boast a red or red-brown hue.

The second type is the 'brown camel of the Hanyn Hets' (*Hanyn hetsiin hüren temee*), native to Mandal-Ovoo *sum* in Ömnögobi Province. These camels, primarily brown or dark brown, are typically used for riding rather than as pack animals.

Last and least, the 'camel of Dohom Tungalag' (*Dohom tungalagiin temee*) from Dohom Tungalag in Gobi-Altai Province, exhibiting shades of brown and dark brown, is the smallest of the three.

To an untrained eye, telling these types apart is as challenging as identifying triplet babies for a stranger—a task only a mother can master effortlessly.

Mongolia is also home to a forth type—the wild camel (*Camelus bactrianus ferus*), an ancient species. With fewer than 1000 surviving in Mongolia and China, they are on the endangered species list. As few as 500 of them are believed to be living in Mongolia.[18] Domesticated camels didn't derive from the wild camel; the latest DNA analysis suggests that the two species have diverged between 700,000 and 1.2 million years ago.[19]

---

18 Yadamsüren at al, 'The seasonal distribution of wild camels'.
19 Ji et al., 'Monophyletic origin of domestic Bactrian camel (*Camelus bactrianus*) and its evolutionary relationship with the extant wild camel (*Camelus bactrianus ferus*)'.

Renowned as the 'ships of the Gobi', camels stand out among livestock for their endurance. Not only can they live without water and food for a long time, but, in contrast to other herd animals, they can eat practically every plant, including thorny ones, like a desert buffet. They can also drink from a salty puddle as if sipping on fresh spring water.

My Father's Family

One of my father's younger brothers was a camel herder in Dundgobi Province. Despite his title as a 'camel herder', he also kept horses, sheep, and goats, like other camel herders. This is the same man who had a penchant for uttering dog-related profanities and once accused me of causing the death of his castrated goat. Besides his occasional outburst and unsubstantiated claims rooted in folklore and superstition, he was an adept herder and a very knowledgeable and practical man.

As a seasoned herder, he truly was the Crocodile Dundee of the semi-desert. He knew everything about livestock—how they behaved, what they needed to eat, where they grazed, how to spot and treat diseases, and how plants grew in the semi-desert. Additionally, he had a detailed mental map of the province and its vast grazing lands, coupled with exceptional survival skills. He was an excellent camel tracker, allowing his camel herds to graze independently over a wide area without human supervision.

His expertise extended to reading weather patterns and seasonal changes, crucial for planning livestock movements and ensuring the well-being of his own family. He could craft lassos and household implements, mend a broken *ger* or cart, and effectively handle challenges such as wolf encounters—skills common among herders. Mongol herders, as illustrated by my uncle, possess a deeper and more diverse knowledge of their immediate surroundings compared to city folks who struggle to find their way in a parking lot.

My uncle, the camel herder, was the youngest boy in his family. There were five children in total, with my father beings the second oldest. They were all raised in a nomadic camp, but except for the camel breeder, they later pursued professional careers in either Ulaanbaatar or the provincial center of Dundgobi. Their eldest sister, who provided shelter to Sharik, spent her career working for the local water supply firm in her native province. She was a pious yet promiscuous woman, famous as much for her love affairs as for her captivating *bolson yavdal* tales.

My father's other younger brother, a distinguished professor of engineering and a staunch atheist, earned his degree at a university in Leningrad (today St Petersburg), as did my father before him. He spent his career lecturing at the State Technical University in Ulaanbaatar. He was also a proud owner of a private Soviet car, a status comparable to owning a private jet in today's America. During the summer holidays, this nerdy professor showed his wild side. He'd ditch the textbooks, hop into his Moskvitch car, and visit his baby brother, the camel herder. Whenever he arrived at their nomadic camp, he was greeted like someone who had descended from the cosmos in a space shuttle, and neighbors would soon arrive to marvel at his vehicle and listen to exciting news from the city. This professor truly cherished his only son and went to the extent of spoiling him by purchasing a small white dog as a playmate, which they kept in their flat in Ulaanbaatar.

Details about my father's younger sister are scarce, except for the tragic information that she passed away due to post-surgery complications in a rural hospital in Dundgobi.

The religious devotion within my father's family was inherited from their father, who was once a monk. After renouncing his vows and severing the ties that bound him to monastic life, he tied the knot with the daughter of a *taiji* nobleman from the renowned Borjigid lineage, direct descendants of Genghis Khan. I heard many times from my father about some details of their wedding, such as the bride arriving at the groom's *ger* on a white camel. During the socialist period, Mongols didn't use surnames but instead had patronyms. However, in the 1990s, when the parliament passed a law mandating surnames, my father chose to adopt his mother's prestigious lineage name as his surname. Technically, he should have taken his father's more modest lineage name. My paternal grandfather died when I was very young, leaving me with no memories of him. Had he lived until the 1990s, he likely would have given a nod of approval to his son's bold move to adopt a more esteemed surname.

Although I never knew my grandfather, I do remember his younger brother, who had been a monk in his youth and was forced to disrobe in the 1930s. Despite this, he continued practicing Buddhism secretly and conducted religious ceremonies for the community. He chose a life of celibacy, opting not to chase a nobleman's daughter or anyone else's daughter, for that matter. He spent his entire life in Dundgobi Province. Since being jobless was illegal in socialist Mongolia, my grandfather's brother worked as a clerk of some sorts in a state office in his younger years. Unlike many of his siblings, he did not herd camels or other livestock. By the time I was a child, he was already an elderly man, retired from his duties. Whenever I spent summers in Dundgobi, my father would take me to pay homage to him in his abode, a modest wooden wagon adorned with Buddhist tangkas and religious artefacts on the inside. Not only was he our extended paternal family's patriarch, but he was also the go-to buddy for all things spiritual in the community. In return for his services, people fondly called him a 'Buddha with shit', which is not a derogatory term in Mongolian but, on the contrary, is an ultimate compliment. It simply means that the person is as holy as a Buddha but responds to the call of nature like the rest of us mortals.

Influenced by the religiosity of his elders, my uncle, the camel herder, maintained the spiritual flame alive throughout the socialist period. Due to his status as the youngest boy in the family and the only one to pursue the life of a herder, my uncle served as the primary provider of meat for all his siblings. Every winter, our family, for example, received shipments of frozen meat gifts from him, including several sheep, half a cow, and a quarter of a horse, which sustained us throughout the cold winter months. He kept camel meat for himself, though. Their eldest sister, who lived not far from him in a provincial center, was the most frequent visitor and the largest consumer of meat, as she was a single mother looking after at least five carnivorous children. Whenever she or one of her children visited my uncle to request meat, milk, or dairy products, they also took Sharik with them as a charm offensive, knowing my uncle's soft spot for the dog. Sharik also eagerly anticipated these outings.

Weather Forecast by Looking at Camel Behavior

In the preceding section, we explored how taboos often reflect cultural biases and judgments. In contrast, weather forecasting based on the observation of animal behavior is generally less problematic for the following reason. Animals often exhibit instinctive behaviors in response to weather changes, and their sensitivity to environmental shifts, such as temperature and air pressure, is a biological trait, not a product of cultural factors. Over time, animals have evolved into Mother Nature's own meteorologists, developing behaviors as survival mechanisms rather than acts learned from superstitious human traditions.

In fact, the link between animal behavior and weather conditions tends to be universal, observed across societies. For example, European swallows flying low often signal rain, while frogs croaking loudly in Southeast Asia predict storms due to increased humidity. In rural Western societies, cows lying down are thought to indicate rain, while ants in the Amazon building higher nests suggest floods. These observations, embedded in folklore, reflect a shared reliance on animals as natural indicators of environmental changes.

In Inner Asia, whether you are in Buddhist Mongol territory or with Muslim Kazakh herders, if a camel starts doing a rain dance, you can bet your money that it's going to rain. While cultural contexts may influence specific beliefs, they usually don't alter the core observations. Examples of weather forecasting based on camel behavior in the Gobi region include the following:

> If calves or young camels cry or gather together, it signals deteriorating weather with possible rain.
>
> When a mother camel refuses to leave her calf alone, it indicates impending rain.
>
> Camels behaving as if thirsty by opening their mouths and moving towards the wind suggest an upcoming rain.
>
> When camels lie behind a bush or small hill to avoid the wind, it's a sign of an approaching storm or sandstorm.
>
> On calm days, camels going to pasture by themselves indicate the continuation of calm weather.

If a mother camel leaves her calf while it's still raining, it signals that the rain will soon come to an end.

Characteristics of Camels

In the Gobi region, nomads describe camels as calm, docile, and hardy. A popular belief holds that camels treat humans the way humans treat them. If a human mistreats a camel, it won't easily submit, even in the face of lashes and beatings. Camels exhibit territorial behavior and possess a remarkable instinct to return to their native land when transported elsewhere.

Camel herders typically know all their herds well, tailoring their care based on the age and sex of the animals. In the case of camels, different ages and sexes require different care. Broadly speaking, camel age is divided into three phases: calf, juvenile, and fully grown.

Of particular importance to camel herders is the juvenile stage, during which the camel undergoes substantial growth until the age of seven. By the age of eight, the camel's baby teeth are fully replaced by adult teeth, totaling thirty-four. In the Gobi region, nomads cease to distinguish camels after the age of eight, using a generic term for adult camels. To illustrate, male camels are assigned the following names from birth until the age of eight:

Camels aged up to one year are referred to as *botgo*, while those between one and two years are known as *torom*. The age range of two to three years is designated as *built*. Three to five-year-olds are known as *buuran tailag* (if uncastrated) or *tailag* (if castrated). Five to six-year-olds are called *högshin tailag*, and those aged six to seven years are named as *atantsar*. Camels over the age of eight are named *at* (if castrated) or *buur* (if uncastrated).

The typical lifespan of a camel ranges from thirty to forty years, with an average of twenty to twenty-seven years spent in the service of humans.

Traditionally, Mongols only give personal names to dogs. In contrast, livestock, including camels, are not assigned personal names (*ner*) but are given what can be termed as nicknames (*züs*) based on unique physical characteristics, fur color, and age. Examples include names like 'the two-year-old brown' or 'the five-year-old reddish-brown', and so on.

To further distinguish animals of the same age and similar coloration, nomads may incorporate other characteristics, including the shape of the hump, character ('the naughty brown', 'the gluttonous five-year-old reddish-brown'), the gait ('the swift brown', 'the leisurely walking brown'), as well as its mother's nickname into the camel's nickname ('the 'two-year-old brown of the white old she-camel'). These methods enable Mongols to create a potentially endless inventory of camel nicknames. Even if a nomadic family possesses a substantial herd—say, three hundred camels—each animal receives a specific nickname.

Utilizing Camels: From Milk to Wool

No part of livestock goes to waste among herding communities, and camels are no exception. Even parts that might raise eyebrows in the West—such as the tongue, head, internal organs, blood, bones, and feet—find their place in the resourceful cuisine of herders. When it comes to camels, everything is utilized, from the stately hump to the not-so-glamorous toes.

Among the many valuable products derived from camels, milk takes center stage. Renowned for its richness in proteins and nutritional value, camel milk is a dietary staple for many camel herding families. It forms the base for a variety of dairy products, including curds. Thanks to the high fat concentration in the milk, camel curds boast a unique texture and make for a hearty and satisfying snack.

Camel milk has a multitude of uses: it is brewed into tea, serves as a nourishing substitute for human infants, and is fermented into *kumis* or distilled into liquor. *Kumis*, made by mixing boiled milk with a special ferment, is a beloved beverage among Gobi nomads and is enjoyed year-round. Its popularity rivals that of soda in the United States, though it comes with health benefits rather than sugar highs. *Kumis* is believed to aid digestion, elevate mood, and enhance overall well-being. Camel milk liquor, meanwhile, is reserved for celebrations and religious festivals, adding a spirited touch to these special occasions.

Beyond milk, camels also provide wool, another valuable resource. Renowned for its lightness, softness, and warmth, camel wool is widely used to craft clothing, ropes, *ger* covers, and belts for *gers*. Camel wool ropes, known for their durability and soft texture, serve various practical purposes, from binding sheep and goats to symbolically tying together people's dreams when they are presented to newlyweds as a gesture of good fortune.

Camel Training

Training pack animals or those used for riding is a meticulous and time-consuming process, particularly for camels, given their immense size, strength, and often stubborn personalities. These animals require a carefully structured regimen to ensure they grow into docile and cooperative companions.

As early as three days old, a camel calf is gently secured with a rope to introduce it to the concept of restraint.

Around the age of two, a calf undergoes a ritual called 'the camel's prickling', after which it earns the title of *built*. During this ritual, a wooden stick, measuring twenty to twenty-two centimeters in length, is inserted into the camel's pricked nose. This procedure enhances the camel's docility and controllability, much like installing a steering wheel in a car—it might not like it, but it's essential for smooth rides ahead.

Between two and three years of age, camels begin training for riding. This phase requires patience and caution. Overusing the whip during this time is like trying to win someone's heart with constant nagging—it backfires spectacularly. Initial riding lessons should be kept short to avoid overexertion. Failure to follow these guidelines can result in rebellious behavior, outright refusal to move, or, in extreme cases, a camel dramatically lying down and refusing to get up. Re-training such a camel can be a herculean task.

An important milestone in the domestication of male camels is castration, typically performed at four to five years of age. Unlike other livestock, camel testicles are not consumed but are ceremoniously returned to the camel and hung on its hump—a symbolic gesture akin to gifting someone their own trophy for participating.

At the same age, camels begin carrying weight. To alleviate the strain from heavy loads, nomads cushion the front hump with specially crafted felt, ensuring comfort. Another critical body part requiring protection is the camel's sole. When the sole is damaged, nomads place a pair of skin shoes on it until it recovers—essentially turning the camel into a four-legged version of someone recovering with orthopedic sandals.

Camel Breeding Practices

Nomadic communities carefully select the finest male camel to impregnate the herd of she-camels, a decision guided by a comprehensive list of criteria encompassing about three dozen characteristics that would put any man in a Mr. Universe competition to shame. Sought-after characteristics include a nice gap between the two front legs, large eyes, a calm demeanor, a hooked snout, a broad chest, the desired color (usually brownish-red or brown), a good pedigree (a pedigree of twins is particularly prized), high-quality wool, good health, slow fat and strength loss, and robust physique, not to mention an impressive penis.

Prior to releasing Mr. Charming to the female camels, the nomadic family recites well-wishes for his success and ceremoniously offers sprinkles of milk.

During the mating season, bulls may become aggressive and bite, prompting some nomads to muzzle their snouts. Caution is paramount during this period, with individuals advised against wearing red garments, as this color is believed to agitate the amorous bull.

To ensure successful mating, nomads usually introduce the bull to a group of female camels, allowing them to roam the semi-desert freely together and get to know each other better. For a more controlled mating scene, nomads enclose all the camels in a fence, allowing them to have intimate moments under their watchful eyes. The seasoned, prime bull is paired with approximately twenty to thirty females, while a younger bull—a bit like a junior heartbreaker still gaining experience—is assigned a more modest eight to twelve lovely females.

In the world of camel romance, it's all about creating the perfect setting for love to bloom on the freezing semi-desert. The mating process involves encouraging the bull to mount a she-camel at least twice a day. And if the bull remains in a state of heat after the females have completed their cycle, a cup of soothing meat broth is offered to help cool the beast down. The female camel's heat cycle lasts for around eight days.

Once a camel becomes pregnant, it receives special care and attention. Pregnant camels are spared from carrying excessive weight, provided with lukewarm water, and allowed to stroll leisurely to the pasture or well. They are also kept away from potentially hazardous areas, such as slippery ground, rocky terrain, or other dangerous spots. Around three to four months before their due date, they are relieved of duties like riding to ensure a stress-free pregnancy.

As the birth date approaches, pregnant camels begin to show clear signs of labor. These include crying, spreading their hind legs, urinating frequently in small amounts, and alternating between standing and lying down. Most camel births occur in the chilly months of March through May. To protect the newborn, nomads craft special hats to shield the calf's delicate head and use warm cloths to cover the mother's hindquarters from the cold wind.

Compared to other livestock, camel calves take their time getting onto their wobbly legs, often requiring assistance from nomads to stand. Twin or albino calves are rare, and their births are considered highly auspicious.

Within an hour of birth, the calf is allowed to suckle from its mother's teats, beginning a precious bonding period. For the first two to three months, nomads refrain from milking the mother, ensuring the calf gets all the nutrition it needs to grow strong and healthy. During this time, mother and calf enjoy uninterrupted quality time, setting the stage for a robust start to life.

The End of a Camel's Life

As camels age or sustain incurable injuries, their economic utility diminishes, along with their owners' interest in keeping them alive. When a camel reaches this stage, nomads mark it with a distinctive sign, typically in the spring. Afterward, the camel is allowed to graze freely in the pasture, receiving special care and ample time to gain weight and accumulate fat—an essential step to enhance the quality of its meat. In line with the principle of 'no waste', a camel's final contribution to its owners is its transformation into a source of nourishment. Once sufficiently fattened, the marked camel is slaughtered in late autumn, and its meat sustains nomadic families throughout the winter months.

As noted earlier, the location where a camel is slaughtered is off-limits for gathering other livestock. Nomads also refrain from using the term 'camel meat', opting instead for expressions like 'the meat of the long-legged one' or 'the meat of the tall one' or similar phrases. If you see Mongols munching away and describing the contents in their mouths as the meat of 'the tall one', or that of 'the long-legged one', or a comparable expression, fear not that they might be engaged in something sinister, and don't hasten to run for your life. Humans are great apes with the greatest imagination of them all. We can collectively imagine a camel as a symbolic human avatar or declare that bread and wine represent the flesh and blood of a God-turned-great-ape being. Nomads, consciously savoring real camel meat, may simultaneously fantasize about chewing a symbolic human avatar—a mental process referred to as 'cognitive dissonance', wherein individuals accept two or more mutually contradictory beliefs or behaviors as valid. Along with storytelling, this unique ability is among the most remarkable superpowers of our species, enabling the existence of human cultures, and, therefore, is an ability worthy of celebration.

Conclusion

In this concluding section, I wish to briefly ponder the question of the meaning of life. While this profound question necessitates an elaborate and extensive discussion, I'll focus on a few aspects, including how humans seek answers through animals, anthropomorphized gods, and several other concepts.

What purpose does existence hold for the herds? If one were to pose this question to herders, many might answer that the meaning of life for livestock lies in contributing to the well-being and prosperity of their owners by reproducing, maintaining good health, and yielding abundant resources such as wool, milk, and other commodities. This perspective reflects a deeply human-centric outlook, which is not surprising.

This book argues that humans perceive the world through the lens of human culture, which not only distorts and simplifies reality but also provides the framework through which everything becomes understandable in human terms. In doing so, culture widely employs other entities—whether animals, gods, nature, or objects—as reference points for humans to understand themselves and shape their worldviews.

Even when reflecting on their own existence or mortality, humans rely on this method.

For example, anthropomorphizing animals is common among pastoralist societies and those who closely engage with animals. These cultures often project human traits onto animals, attributing them with emotions, characteristics, and cosmological roles. Similarly, humans have historically envisioned gods with human-like qualities, reflecting the broader human tendency to use metaphors and symbolic representations to make sense of complex concepts. Once animals and gods are cast as mirrors reflecting human traits, it becomes easier to imagine their thoughts and intentions and thus use them as cognitive tools to reflect on human nature.

However, this process is not universal. While many cultures, such as those in Mongolia, anthropomorphize animals and gods, others view them as distinct entities with their own intrinsic qualities. Despite such variations, one constant emerges: human cultures consistently use external entities to mediate emotions, reflect on existence, and construct meaning.

This way of thinking is also enabled by our cognitive ability to infer what others are thinking—known as *theory of mind*—which we apply not only to fellow humans but also to animals. Given our rich imagination, it's unsurprising that we believe we can even comprehend the thoughts of imagined entities like gods, whom we often create in our own image.

In religious traditions like Christianity, which emerged from the nomadic herding societies of the Middle East, the metaphor of a god as a shepherd and humans as sheep is common. In this context, people view themselves as part of a divine flock, much like how humans regard herd animals as possessions. This pastoral metaphor emphasizes a possessive relationship between humans and their deity.

In contrast, the Mongols, traditionally a herding and hunting people, offer a slightly different perspective shaped by shamanism and Buddhism. Mongol herders, like their Christian counterparts, connect the meaning of life to fulfilling what we believe our gods expect of us, mirroring the expectations we ourselves hold for our animals. For example, in shamanism, gods are generally not seen as possessive. Instead, they are viewed as neutral observers or indifferent entities, much like Mongols view *wild* animals. These shamanic gods are not concerned with human sexuality or personal lives; rather, humans must establish a dovetailing relationship with them through the intermediary of shamans or with the help of rituals and offerings. Without the constant celestial surveillance, the meaning of life in shamanic Mongol belief thus lies in living it to the fullest—raising herds, hunting, enjoying pleasures, maintaining relationships, and anticipating the continuation of these same pursuits in the shamanic afterlife, which is imagined as a mirror image of this life.

Unlike shamanism, Buddhism in Mongolia is a foreign import, originating among sedentary people in India who pursued a different lifestyle and valued crops more than anything. In classical Buddhism, humans are not considered the possessions of gods. In fact, the gods themselves are subject to the samsara cycle of birth, death, and rebirth. Although these deities may reside in more pleasant realms and hold greater power, they are still bound by impermanence (*anicca*)—one of the fundamental truths in Buddhism. Like all beings in samsara, gods must face the inevitability of death and rebirth. Moreover, time in samsara is perceived as cyclical, not linear, with beings continuously experiencing the cycle of existence until they achieve nirvana and transcend samsara. Curiously and perhaps not coincidentally, this concept of cyclical time aligns with the agricultural cycles, in which crops grow and are harvested seasonally, with annihilation being followed by new growth.

While both Buddhism and shamanism lack a singular, omnipotent god, Buddhism diverges by focusing on self-awareness and the cultivation of compassion, which influence one's karma and thus one's position in the cycle of rebirth. The ultimate goal in Buddhism is liberation from this cycle of rebirth and suffering. In Mongolian Buddhism, adapted to nomadic values, the relationship between deities and nomads is akin to how nomads treat *consecrated livestock*. Nomads protect and feed these animals but don't see them as possessions, much like Buddhist deities who don't regard humans as their responsibility. As a result, in Mongolian Buddhism, the focus for laypeople is not on single-mindedly worshiping gods or relying on supernatural intervention, but rather on fostering self-reliance and practicing Buddhist teachings on karma, ethical conduct, and compassion. The immediate—though not ultimate—goal is to secure a favorable human rebirth through the application of Buddhist principles.

The profound question of the meaning of life, however, extends beyond the purview of religion alone. Various philosophical schools and traditions offer alternative perspectives that exclude gods from the picture. Among the best known are absurdism, existentialism, nihilism, hedonism, humanism, transcendentalism, and logotherapy. While these schools differ in their approaches, many emphasize humanity as a central source of meaning and reverence. Some, like absurdism and existentialism, acknowledge the inherent meaninglessness of life, while others, such as humanism and transcendentalism, suggest that meaning can be found in human potential or a connection with nature.

Each school offers distinct ways to grapple with life's meaninglessness or uncertainty: absurdism embraces the tension between humanity's search for meaning and the universe's indifference; existentialism focuses on creating personal meaning through choices and actions; and logotherapy finds purpose even in suffering.

Storytelling is an ancient and ingrained human impulse that we use to convey the mundane aspects of life, as well as the grand stories about the origin of the universe. History is filled with countless origin stories as old as humanity itself. These stories often depict the universe as having been created by a diverse array of entities, including gods, great spirits, celestial serpents, and cosmic eggs imbued with the power to give meaning to human life. Indeed, there are as many creation stories as there are cultures.

With the advent of science and modern astronomy, a new kind of creation story emerged, grounded in observational evidence and our understanding of the laws of physics. This modern account not only pinpoints the age of the observable universe at approximately 13.8 billion years and explains its origin from the Big Bang but also provides us a new perspective, situating our existence within a stupendously vast cosmic expanse. From this broader viewpoint, Earth appears as a mere speck—a pale blue dot orbiting an inconspicuous star, just one among hundreds of billions in the Milky Way galaxy, itself part of trillions of galaxies in the observable universe, which could be just a fraction of a much larger, potentially infinite multiverse. In this unfathomably vast cosmic panorama, life on Earth lacks inherent or predetermined meaning or purpose. From the universe's viewpoint, the existence of life, the presence of joy or suffering, and even the existence of the universe itself lack intrinsic significance. If life were to vanish on our planet tomorrow, the vastness of the universe would remain unaffected. Even if the universe were to cease to exist the day after tomorrow, it would simply cease, with no further implications. The universe, our solar system, and life on Earth only hold significance in the stories that Sapiens tell each other.

No matter which lenses we use to view the world, each individual grapples with the question of life's meaning in unique ways, making it a deeply personal quest. We navigate through the labyrinth of life, weaving stories of our own creation that unfold like imaginary movies in the private theater of our minds. Much like a Hollywood director bringing stories to life on the silver screen, each of us engages in the mental act of directing and producing our own life-story movies, trying to make sense of our existence. Some see their life as an action-packed thriller, while others star in a comedy or spend their lives immersed in a family soap opera.

Personal life stories are a bit like Netflix categories: one could be living in a scientific documentary, a religious drama, a philosophical saga, a patriotic epic, or a Wild West adventure. People cast themselves as protagonists in genres ranging from romance to horror, and some may find themselves entangled in the plotlines of meaningless, banal movies, yearning for them to end. But unlike the linear genres adhered to by Hollywood movie studios, human life unfolds with dynamism and unpredictability. Circumstances change, people grow older, their outlook on things changes, and our personal movies, in which we play the leading role, also undergo transformations. A bright comedy might shift into a gloomy, tear-jerking drama before reverting to a chilly, full-blown tragicomedy. The fluidity of life and people's inner conflicts, combined with the forgetfulness and meaning-seeking penchant of *Homo sapiens*, ensure that our personal movies are as ever-changing as a kaleidoscope. We constantly edit and re-edit the scenes of our life stories, reliving and reinterpreting them with each iteration.[20]

---

20   This is why the scenes and events that make up our life stories often seem to exist outside a linear timeline and are sometimes experienced simultaneously, as though all our experiences—both past and present—coexist in a single moment. This helps explain why people can feel both like the young children they once were and the elderly individuals they have become. As attested in countless soul-searching poems from around the world, written mainly by middle-aged or older poets, when one reflects on life, no matter how eventful or rich, it often feels fleeting, like a dream—so short and ephemeral. This is because, even as we approach the end of life, we still feel like the children we once were at its beginning.

Yet, the influence of social institutions—such as religion, philosophy, ideology, science, cinematography, poetry, as well as family and community—plays a pivotal role in shaping our personal stories. As social species, many people seem to find satisfactory answers to the meaning of life by aligning their personal narratives and worldviews with those presented by religious, philosophical, scientific, artistic, and various societal repositories of knowledge. Just as there are multiple sources that offer answers to this existential question, humans tend to have a multitude of answers that are often in a constant state of flux.

You don't have to be a religious scholar, philosopher, astronomer, or movie director to ponder the meaning of life. While there are those who feel lost and struggle to find a coherent storyline, many ordinary Mongols I personally know derive deep meaning and satisfaction not necessarily from contemplating long hours on life's meaning, but from daily activities such as herding animals or serving their parents and family. Humans think and derive meaning as much with their bodies as with their minds.

Perhaps the meaning of life is not found in grand revelations, but, like herds grazing under the eternal blue sky, in the simple act of moving forward, step by step, until we too are swallowed by the horizon, where everything fades into the oblivion of time. Yet, our uniquely human gift lies in the stories we create along the way. Whether shaped by our understanding of gods, nature, science, or personal imagination, these stories give our fleeting existence its richness and meaning. As we reach the threshold of the horizon, we may wonder whether the meaning we sought was real or merely an illusion. But rather than despair at its fragility, we might embrace the wisdom of impermanence. Life's beauty lies not in its permanence but in its ability to inspire us to create and to imagine meaning where none may inherently exist. And when we finally step over the horizon, we might remember that, as Mark Twain once said, we were all absent from existence for billions of years before we were born—and it caused us no discomfort then, nor will it when we return to the great nothingness from which we came.

Epilogue

Homo sapiens is a profoundly contradictory species. This deep contradiction manifests in how we think, form relationships, and behave. It's not just a quirk—it's a fundamental aspect of what it means to be human. Our ability to hold conflicting beliefs and emotions, and to imagine things that don't exist in reality, has helped us survive, thrive, and become a technological species, turning us into the dominant force on the planet.

This ability to juggle both reality and imagination, and to create technologies—such as livestock breeding, agriculture, religion, writing, mathematics, poetry, money, and other tools that help humans think, communicate, and transform their environment—permeates every aspect of Sapiens' lives.

In August-September 2024, a trend blossomed in Spain, making international headlines. Between 7 p.m. and 8 p.m., single Spaniards began placing upside-down pineapples in their shopping carts at Mercadona supermarkets. This inverted fruit served as a code for singles looking for romantic partners. In some locations, groups of enthusiastic love-seekers reportedly overwhelmed the stores, prompting police intervention. However, it wasn't just pineapples that signaled romantic intentions. Other grocery items in a shopping cart also hinted at a person's desires. For example, chocolates or sweets suggested someone was seeking a serious, committed relationship, while items like lettuce hinted at an interest in something more casual and non-committal. Cucumbers implied they were looking for something more substantial and deeply satisfying. It wasn't hard to deduce the type of casual encounter a shopper had in mind if she carried small pickles alongside lettuce, or the kind of husband she was after if her cart included a combination of chocolate, a solid cucumber, and some red-hot pepper.

 https://doi.org/10.11647/OBP.0450.06

While fruits are merely snacks for chimps and other primates, for Sapiens, they're much more. We don't just eat them—we imbue them with meaning, turning them into technologies of communication and tools for organizing social life. The Spanish supermarket trend is just one example. Single Spaniards were using specific fruits and vegetables at certain locations (Mercadona supermarkets) and at specific times (between 7 p.m. and 8 p.m.) to signal their romantic desires.

This phenomenon is not unique to passionate Spaniards; across the globe, people use food resources for purposes that go well beyond sustenance. Every culture has its own unique culinary traditions and rituals, shaped by intricate rules of etiquette. These customs dictate not only what foods are eaten, but the deeper meanings behind them, how they are prepared and served, and the precise times they are enjoyed— whether during the day or on special occasions. Moreover, food often reflects one's age, gender, or social status, adding yet another layer of meaning to what's on the plate. Humans also offer and share food with imaginary entities such as gods, demons, and spirits of the dead— something unheard of in other species.

Sapiens possess a remarkable cognitive ability to transform not only food but nearly anything, including animals, into technology. Take, for example, the Mongols, as explored throughout this book. Their relationship with animals is far more complex than merely viewing them as biological resources or sustenance. For the Mongols, animals also serve as cognitive tools for communication and cooperation, offering a lens through which to contemplate the cosmos and their place within it. As such, various animals reveal unique facets of Mongol life and values.

Mongols regard dogs not merely as flesh-and-blood creatures but as spiritual beings, intertwined with concepts of reincarnation, karma, and human lives. Through their bond with dogs, Mongols reflect on the cyclical nature of existence and their connection to the spiritual realm. Similarly, marmots are more than just a cherished food source; they embody a duality that blends the practical and the cosmological. While feared as potential carriers of plague, they also exist as mythical beings in the realm of human imagination. Cats, too, exemplify this duality. Once seen only as benign pets, their perception shifted during Mongolia's socialist era to embody a more mystical and ominous role as harbingers of death, reflecting broader societal anxieties and transformations. For the Mongols, camels transcend their utilitarian role as valuable livestock. They occupy a spiritual and cultural space, mirroring human emotions, nurturing bonds, and shared experiences, while symbolizing endurance.

These examples illustrate that our relationships with animals—or anything else—are neither simple nor fixed; rather, they are complex and constantly reshaped by culture and history. Whether influenced by the rise and fall of empires, the spread of religions like Buddhism, the impact of socialism and capitalist consumerism, or advances in science and modern technology, human perspectives continuously evolve.

Looking forward, the Mongols' relationship with animals will likely face new challenges as the modern world continues to encroach upon traditional ways of life. Climate change is already altering the steppe ecosystem, threatening the delicate balance between humans, animals, and their environment. Additionally, globalization and technological advancements are introducing new pressures and opportunities, reshaping how Mongols interact with their animal companions. For instance, while some nomadic practices may fade, others might adapt to integrate modern tools, such as using GPS technology to track livestock. Similarly, Mongol spiritual beliefs about animals may evolve to reflect new environmental, social, and technological realities.

Humans are both creators and products of culture. As strange as it may seem, the main function of human culture is not to accurately mirror reality or seek the truth, but rather to interpret the world in ways that foster human cooperation and the accumulation of knowledge, serving the needs of our species.

In this regard, it's useful to consider philosopher Immanuel Kant's ideas, particularly his distinction between *reality as it is* (noumenon) and *reality as we perceive it* (phenomenon), which remain influential today. Kant argued that humans experience the world not as it exists independently, but through a filter shaped by our senses, cognition, and cultural constructs. Modern science supports this view, demonstrating that what we perceive is an interpretation rather than an exact reflection of reality. For instance, we cannot directly observe the interactions of molecules, perceive ultraviolet light in its full spectrum, or witness particles moving at the speed of light. Similarly, we cannot hear what many insects hear or perceive the subtle motions caused by Brownian movement that affect bacteria—forces that don't impact us at the scale at which we exist as a species. Let alone noticing invisible or imperceptible phenomena, Sapiens are notoriously inept at *really seeing* what is in front of their noses, as illustrated in this book with the example of Mongols' perception of animals.

Throughout history, humans have created technologies to reshape the world into what Kant describes as *reality as we perceive it* (phenomenon). Reflecting their vision of the world, human societies have transformed landscapes, selectively bred animal species, cultivated cucumbers and other crops, developed economies, and sought to dominate nature with the help of anthropomorphized gods and sacred texts.

This process accelerated during the Scientific and Industrial Revolutions, which equipped us with more powerful technologies and tools to explore previously unknown aspects of reality—what Kant referred to as the noumenal realm or the 'unknowable thing-in-itself'. With these technologies, we discovered X-rays, formulated the theory of special relativity, understood evolution unfolding over generations, calculated the movement of continents over millions of years, observed galaxies spiraling millions of light years away, and traced the formation of elements in dying stars. These findings fostered the expectation, in the logical part of our brains, that we might eventually bridge—contrary to Kantian epistemology—the seemingly insurmountable gap between noumenon and phenomenon, unlocking transformative energies and revolutionary ways of perceiving reality as it is.

Yet, despite these scientific advances and expectations, our culture continues to rely on the creation of new myths and imagined orders, and we have never fully managed to become a completely logical species. Given that we are still primates only half a chromosome away from chimps, it's not surprising that we put scientific accomplishments in the service of myths and fictions, making them even more realistic and impactful. Although human societies today are vastly different from when our ancestors lived on the savannah 60,000 years ago, they are fundamentally similar in that all human communities are held together by myths and fictions. Throughout history, myths and fictions were sustained and shaped by cultural tools such as religions and cosmologies. However, with the rise of modern science and technology— also cultural tools—these myths began to be reinforced by scientific and technological advancements. New myths, such as the proletarian paradise promoted by Marxism-Leninism, the national Aryan rebirth envisioned by fascists, or the ideals of inalienable human rights and individual liberties championed by Enlightenment philosophers, along with the resulting social formations like communism, fascism, and liberal democracies, became possible only through the scientific and technological developments that helped turn these myths into social realities in the twentieth century.

In the twenty-first century, emerging technologies such as Augmented Reality (AR), Virtual Reality (VR), social media, and Artificial Intelligence (AI) are poised to create new social formations based on various myths. These formations will be hybrids, blending the natural world with computationally simulated environments. In these spaces, our fantasies, perceptions, and experiences will be increasingly shaped by more powerful technologies, from digital devices to biotechnological innovations like wearables and implanted gadgets. This paradigm can be understood as a constructed reality, or *structomenon*,[1] where cultural practices and human interactions will be deeply intertwined with technological frameworks.

The structomenon is not a distant concept. It is already present in phenomena such as personalized digital ecosystems, AR-enhanced environments, and immersive VR experiences. These advancements are creating a hyper-reality where the distinction between online and offline experiences—or between the metaverse and the meatverse—will increasingly blur. This accelerating trajectory will further distance us from the rest of the animal kingdom, enveloping each *Homo sapiens* in individually constructed algorithmic bubbles that are neither visible nor comprehensible to other species.

The structomenon will generate parallel digital spaces populated with various digital entities, including mystical animals, fruits, and other fascinating creations, with which we can interact. These worlds will

---

1   I propose the term 'structomenon', derived from the Latin root 'struct', meaning 'to build' or 'to make up', combined with the suffix 'menon', which parallels the endings of the terms noumenon and phenomenon. The term 'noumenon' originates from the Greek root 'noou', meaning 'to know', while phenomenon derives from the Greek root 'phen', meaning 'to show' or 'to be visible'. Thus, structomenon effectively conveys the concept of a reality that is constructed or built, aligning with the linguistic and philosophical traditions of its counterparts.

grant us new abilities, experiences, and powers, while simultaneously sparking the creation of new myths and fictions. While this will open up unprecedented opportunities for creativity and new forms of social organization, it will also make it easier to spread myths, fictions, and falsehoods, manipulating people's opinions. Of course, there is nothing new about people believing in myths, fictions, and falsehoods; human culture has relied on them since its inception to ensure effective cooperation among large numbers of *Homo sapiens*. While myths and stories are not inherently harmful, unchecked human imagination and power politics can turn them into tools of exploitation, destruction, and harm.

More fundamentally, within the latest wave of technological progress, the rise of AI marks the dawn of a new cosmic era. In the 3.5-billion-year history of evolution on Earth, life and intelligence have coevolved, intertwined like two strands of DNA twisted together. Many complex organisms, especially those with advanced nervous systems, possess intelligence, and conversely, intelligence has only been possible within living beings. With the advent of AI, for the first time in Earth's history, intelligence is being decoupled from life. AI is fundamentally a lifeless, or inorganic, intelligence, created not through natural selection over eons, but through human design in just a few decades. Despite its infancy, AI is already impressively powerful, and as it grows exponentially, it is poised to become, within our lifetime, something all-encompassing and vastly different from what we know today.

This development carries at least two profound implications. First, it echoes Kant's vision of human culture as a filter for interpreting reality, suggesting that new technologies will not only shape how we perceive the world but also redefine how we exist within it. Second, it highlights a defining attribute of AI: it is the first human-created technology capable of assisting in the creation of higher-level technologies. While previous technologies, such as computer-aided design software, have supported human innovation, AI represents a new paradigm. It is advancing toward self-optimization, with the ability to automate aspects of its own programming and design, setting it apart from all its predecessors.

Although AI is not yet fully autonomous, this emerging capability suggests the possibility of achieving Artificial General Intelligence (AGI) in the future. AGI could evolve independently, acquire agency, and develop entirely new forms of superintelligent entities and smart infrastructures. While this vision remains theoretical, it underscores the transformative potential of AI if its development continues along this trajectory.

In this context, we might envision the emergence of an 'AGI culture', where inorganic intelligent entities acquire unique knowledge and perception of the world and communicate with one another based on some unifying principles. These principles may be as opaque to humans as human culture is to animals. Such a scenario raises profound questions about the nature of intelligence and challenges the long-standing human assumption that our cultural organization is the pinnacle of development.

If realized, these advancements would mark a new phase in the evolution of intelligence on Earth, creating a diverse spectrum of intelligences rather than a singular, human-centric hierarchy. Humans would be confronted with the reality of coexisting alongside entities with distinct forms of cognition and agency, compelling us to redefine our understanding of intelligence, culture, individuality, morality, and our place in this new ecosystem. This possibility is neither far-fetched nor akin to a pie in the sky, as the seeds of this transformation are already visible today.

Imagine a scenario where various specialized AI systems achieve knowledge and reasoning skills comparable to those of top professionals in fields such as medicine, engineering, climatology, and the creative arts. While these systems are currently task-specific, researchers are exploring ways to improve and integrate them into a unified AGI system—a cohesive intelligence that combines the strengths of multiple specialized programs. If successful, this integration could result in an entity that surpasses human capabilities across disciplines, achieving feats no individual human could accomplish. Imagine an emergent inorganic being that, even in its infancy, is as proficient in physics as Albert Einstein, as skilled in mathematics as Srinivasa Ramanujan, as creative in art as Leonardo da Vinci, as manipulative and cunning as Giacomo Casanova, and as strategic in military tactics as Genghis Khan. Considering its practical immortality and meteoric rate of intellectual growth, imagine the heights such an entity could reach in a decade, a century, and beyond. Yet, while some Silicon Valley visionaries claim this breakthrough is imminent, significant technical challenges remain.

To draw a parallel with biological life, this could be akin to the emergence of microbial forms in Earth's primordial oceans—self-replicating entities that, over billions of years, colonized land, sea, and sky, ultimately developing technologies that propelled them into the cosmos. Evolving at a super-accelerated rate, AI entities could follow a similar trajectory over a much shorter period, colonizing the vast expanse of digital space, diversifying, multiplying, interconnecting, and potentially transforming into god-like beings that dominate both the metaverse and the physical world. Such a transformation will have profound consequences for biological life in general, and humanity in particular.

Throughout history, humans have worshipped gods and supernatural entities that neither listened to our prayers nor existed beyond our imaginations. Now, for the first time, we stand on the threshold of creating god-like beings that will not only listen but also monitor our every move and emotion constantly. For millennia, humanity served imagined gods, attributing human traits and desires to them and believing we could influence them to take sides in our conflicts or alter natural laws in our favor. Despite these fantasies, humanity always retained agency over its destiny and societal structures. However, this fantasy may soon become a reality. We may find ourselves losing our species' cherished 'cognitive niche'—and with it, our superpower—for real, as we surrender control over our destiny and begin serving digital gods that neither think like us, perceive like us, nor care about us.

This book explores how Mongol culture, like that of all other peoples, anthropomorphizes non-human intelligent entities, both organic (animals) and spiritual (gods and spirits). With the rise of AI and eventually AGI, we now face a host of new questions, including how different cultures will perceive and interact with this emerging technological, or synthetic, form of intelligence. Drawing on the themes explored throughout the book, we can speculate on how Mongols might approach the rise of AGI.

We learned in Chapter 1 that dogs, in Mongol cosmology, are treated as 'transitional beings' bridging the gap between animals and humans. In this worldview, dogs occupy a liminal space, existing on the threshold of two realms. Similarly, AGI might be seen by Mongols as inhabiting a comparable space—not fully possessing human-like consciousness, yet not entirely mechanical. This ambiguity could spark questions about its potential evolution into something more human-like and the ethical implications of such a transformation. Much like the Mongol dog, AGI might be imbued with a sense of possibility and danger, provoking curiosity and caution in equal measure.

The book also discusses hybrid beings, such as *erliiz* dogs and people, who often exist on the margins of society. AGI, too, can be understood as a form of hybridity—blending human ingenuity with machine logic. Like hybrid animals or people, AGI might challenge entrenched boundaries, forcing society to reconsider long-standing notions of 'purity' in intelligence and agency. Historical examples of Mongol attitudes toward hybridity suggest that such challenges often evoke tension and invite reflection on the meaning of identity and belonging.

Human-animal relationships, as this book reveals, are fraught with contradictions: love and hate, utility and reverence, control and freedom. Mongols, likewise, may approach AGI with a mix of admiration and fear. On the one hand, its capacity for innovation and problem-solving might be celebrated; on the other, its potential to disrupt or outpace human control might provoke unease. In this duality, AGI becomes a mirror of the human condition, reflecting our aspirations and anxieties, our drive for progress and our fear of losing control.

The book highlights taboos surrounding animals, such as prohibitions against dogs entering *gers* or women urinating in front of camels. These taboos function as cultural technologies to impose order and regulate relationships between humans and non-humans, between men and women. Similarly, ethical guidelines for AGI could be interpreted by Mongols as modern 'taboos' designed to maintain balance between humanity and smart technology.

Storytelling occupies a central role in human culture, including that of the Mongols, shaping values and transmitting knowledge through oral traditions like *bolson yavdal*. As AGI increasingly generates and curates content, it might emerge as a new kind of universal storyteller— one that operates at an unprecedented scale and speed. Its narratives might echo traditional tales but also disrupt them, offering new ways of imagining the world.

In addition to its narrative role, AGI could be envisioned as a modern spiritual entity. Mongols have long viewed certain animals as spiritual intermediaries, bridging the material and the divine. In a similar vein, AGI-powered systems might be seen as substitutes for these spiritual animals—synthetic entities through which humans seek guidance, answers, and connection to 'invisible forces' (e.g., big data, predictive patterns, or even higher cosmic powers). Whether through predictive analytics or existential queries, AGI could become a new conduit for meaning and oracular insight.

As we can see from these examples, the book's themes suggest that Mongols' potential relationships with AI and AGI could mirror the complexity of their culture and the contradictions inherent in their historical relationships with non-human entities.

That said, no one possesses a magic lens to foresee the future with perfect clarity. Humans may coevolve with AGI-powered entities, creating a world of seamless harmony and mutual enhancement. Alternatively, we might find ourselves under the dominion of AGI systems, not unlike how we imagine people in biblical times being governed by divine will—humble, obedient, and fearful. Or perhaps, despite our efforts and prayers, we could be deemed inconsequential by AGI, overlooked and irrelevant—much like how we pay little attention to frogs croaking in a pond.

There are countless other possibilities, spanning the spectrum from utopian to apocalyptic. Yet one thing is certain: people across different societies will interpret and respond to AGI through the lens of their unique religious, social, and political backgrounds. Human culture, with its tendency to mythologize, distort, and fictionalize, will likely shape and constrain our ability to fully understand AI for what it truly is.

In this rapidly evolving landscape, we must grapple with a profound question: Will we harness the power of AI and AGI as masters of the worlds we imagine and create? Or will we lose control, becoming subservient to our own technological creations? The answer will define not only the future of intelligence on Earth but also our place in it.

As we stand on the cusp of this truly revolutionary transformation, we should reflect on the themes explored in this book—how humans have historically balanced contradictions and dualities, from the tangible to the imagined, and how cultures like that of the Mongols have demonstrated both resilience and flexibility. Whether we embrace AGI as a partner or reject it as a peril, the values, creativity, and complexities that have defined human culture must remain our guide. After all, the end goal is not just to build a new world, but to ensure that this world, no matter how technologically advanced or logic-driven, continues to reflect the empathy, imagination, and self-contradictions that make us human.

Acknowledgments

I am deeply grateful to everyone who supported and contributed to the creation of this book.

First and foremost, I extend my sincere thanks to Jack Weatherford and Sir Geoffrey Lloyd for their invaluable feedback and insightful comments on early drafts of the manuscript, which greatly enhanced the final version.

Additionally, I greatly benefited from discussions with Bilegsaihan Tamirjaviin, Mijid Sainbuyangiin, Ondřej Srba, and Michal Schwarz. I am also grateful to Natasha Fijn who provided excellent comments on the manuscript.

My sincere thanks go to Elisabeth Pitts for proofreading and expertly editing the manuscript, to Jeevanjot Nagpal for designing the book cover, and to Alessandra Tosi for ensuring that the book was published as an open-access work on time.

I would like to express my heartfelt gratitude to the Mongolian American Cultural Association (MACA) and its president, Sanj Altan Kuldinow, for awarding me a grant that enabled me to initiate this book project and gather essential materials in 2023.

The primary funding for this book was provided by the project *Changing Adaptive Strategies of Mobile Pastoralists in Mongolia: Dynamics in Community Histories and Movement Patterns Documented Through Oral Sources* (GM23-07108M), supported by the Czech Science Foundation, for which I am truly thankful. I began writing the core text of this book, while collecting additional materials, at the end of 2023, when I became affiliated with Masaryk University, where I was actively involved in the aforementioned project.

Lastly, I extend my deepest appreciation to my wife and son for their unwavering support and patience throughout this journey. Their love and good humor made the completion of this book possible.

Bibliography

Amarmend, Puntsag. 2012. *Mongolyn Nuuts Tovchoon Dahi Yos Zanshil Zan Uiliin Tailbar Tol'*. Ulaanbaatar: Bembi San.

Andrew, Christopher. 2018. *The Secret World: A History of Intelligence*. London: Penguin Books. https://doi.org/10.12987/9780300240528

Armitage, David, and Sanjay Subrahmanyam, eds. 2010. *The Age of Revolutions in Global Context, c. 1760-1840*. London: Palgrave Macmillan. https://doi.org/10.1007/978-1-137-01415-3

Atwood, Christopher P. 2004. *Encyclopedia of Mongolia and the Mongol Empire*. New York: Facts on File. https://doi.org/10.1017/s0021911806001239

Barker, Hannah. 2021. 'Laying the corpses to rest: Grain, embargoes, and Yersinia pestis in the Black Sea, 1346-48', *Speculum, The Journal of the Medieval Academy of America* 96(1): 98-126. https://doi.org/10.1086/711596

Bell, Kristen. 2022. *Silent but Deadly: The Underlying Cultural Patterns of Everyday Behaviour*. London: Caw Press.

Benedictow, Ole Jorgen. 2006. *The Black Death, 1346-1353: The Complete History of The Black Death*. Woodbridge: Boydell Press.

Braae, Christel. 2017. *Among the Herders of Inner Mongolia: The Haslund-Christensen Collection at the National Museum of Denmark*. Aarhus: Aarhus University Press. https://doi.org/10.2307/j.ctv62hgqp

Bresheva, Natalia Petrovna. 2006. 'Obraz koshki v mifologii, fol'klore i russkoi literature', *Otkrytyi Urok*. https://urok.1sept.ru/articles/410785

Buell, Paul D. 1990. 'Pleasing the palate of the qan: Changing foodways of the Imperial Mongols', *Mongolian Studies* (13): 57-82.

Bulstrode, Beatrix. 1920. *A Tour in Mongolia*. London: Methuen & Co.

Burykin, Aleksei. 2019. 'Koshka v fol'klore Kalmykov, drugikh mongoloyazychnykh narodov i narodov Dal'nego Vostoka', *Oriental Studies* 12(6): 1221-1231.

Byer, William. 2011. *The Blind Spot: Science and the Crisis of Uncertainty*. Princeton: Princeton University Press. https://doi.org/10.1515/9781400838158

Campo, Juan E. 2009. *Encyclopedia of Islam*. New York: Infobase Publishing.

Carsten, Janet, ed. 2007. *Ghosts of Memory: Essays on Remembrance and Relatedness*. Malden (MA): Blackwell Publishing. https://doi. org/10.1002/9780470692301

Cooke, Lucy. 2023. *Bitch: A Revolutionary Guide to Sex, Evolution and the Female Animal*. London: Penguin Books.

Chium-a Kemeku Tarbagan-u Miljan Ebedchin-ü Tuhai. 1931. Ulaanbaatar: Mongol Ulsyn Hevleliin Horoo.

Damdin, B., Marie-Dominique Even, and M. J. Chapman. 1991. 'The camel in Mongolian literature and tradition: Some examples', *Journal of the Anglo-Mongolian Society 13*(1-2): 35-47.

Dashdorjiin, Natsagdorj. 1961. *Zohioluud*. Ulaanbaatar: State Publishing.

Dawkins, Richard. 2016. *The God Delusion*. London: Black Swan.

Dawson, Christopher, ed. 1955. *The Mongol Mission: Narratives and letters of the Franciscan Missionaries in Mongolia and China in the Thirteenth and Fourteenth Centuries*. New York: Sheed and Ward. https://open.bu.edu/ handle/2144/585

Delaplace, Gregory. 2010. 'Chinese ghosts in Mongolia', *Inner Asia* (12): 127-141. https://doi.org/10.1163/146481710792710282

Delaplace, Gregory. 2012. 'Parasitic Chinese, vengeful Russians: ghosts, strangers, and reciprocity in Mongolia', *Journal of the Royal Anthropological Institute* (18): 131-144. https://doi.org/10.1111/j.1467-9655.2012.01768.x

Faure, Eric, and Andrew C. Kitchener. 2009. 'An archaeological and historical review of the relationships between felids and people', *Anthrozoös* (34): 1016-1025. https://doi.org/10.2752/175303709x457577

Fijn, Natasha. 2018. 'Dog ears and tails: Different relational ways of being in Aboriginal Australia and Mongolia', in Swanson, H., Ween, G., and Lien. M. (eds.), *Domestication Gone Wild: Politics and Practices of Multispecies Relations*, 1st ed., Vol. 1, pp. 72-93. Duke University Press. https://doi.org/10.2307/j. ctv11sn74f.7

Fijn, Natasha, and Baasanjav Terbish. 2021. 'The survival of the marmot: hunting, cosmology and the plague in Mongolia', *Human Ecology 49*(1): 1-11. https://doi.org/10.1007/s10745-021-00264-7

Frankopan, Peter. 2023. *The Earth Transformed: An Untold History*. London: Bloomsbury.

Galdan, Bolormaa, Undraa Baatar, Baigalmaa Molotov, and Otgonbaatar Dashdavaa. 2010. 'Plague in Mongolia', *Vector Borne and Zoonotic Diseases* 10: 69-76. https://doi.org/10.1089/vbz.2009.0047

Gangaa, 'The repulsive green cat runs across the road' *Baabar*, March 25, 2010, http://www.baabar.mn/article/1659

Gibbons, Ann. 1997. 'Archeologists rediscover cannibals', *Science* 227(5326): 635-637.

Gilbert, Rosaline. 2020. *The Very Secret Sex Lives of Medieval Women: An Inside Look at Women & Sex in Medieval Times*. London: Mango Media.

Golstunskii, K. F. 2004 [1880]. *Mongolo-Oiratskie Zakony 1640 Goda.* Ulaaanbaatar: Soyombo Printing.

Gonchigiin, Batbold. 2020a. *Nüüdelchdiin Nohoi, I Devter, Nen Ert, Hunnu, Ertnii Ulsuudyn Uye.* Ulaanbaatar: Mongol Sudlalyn Tov.

Gonchigiin, Batbold. 2020b. *Nüüdelchdiin Nohoi, II Devter, Chingis Khaan ba Tüüniig Zalgamjlagchdyn Uye.* Ulaanbaatar: Mongol Sudlalyn Tov.

Gou Ya., and S. G. Korovina. 2020. 'Image of cats in Russian and Chinese omens: Comparative analysis', *Russian Linguistic Bulletin* 4(24): 88-93. https://doi.org/10.18454/RULB.2020.24.4.2

Graber, David, and David Wengrow. 2021. *The Dawn of Everything: A New History of Humanity.* New York: Farrar, Straus and Giroux.

Green, Monica. 2022. 'Putting Asia on the Black Death Map', in C. Symes (ed.), *New Evidence for the Dating and Impact of the Black Death in Asia*, pp. 61–90. Amsterdam: ARC Humanities Press. https://doi.org/10.1515/9781802701128-004

Green, Monica. 2020. 'The four Black Deaths'. *The American Historical Review* 125(5): 1601-1631. https://doi.org/10.1093/ahr/rhaa511

Guy, Jack, and Bilegdemberel Gansukh, 'Teenage boy dies from bubonic plague after eating marmot', *CNN*, July 15, 2020. https://edition.cnn.com/2020/07/15/asia/mongolia-plague-death-scli-intl/index.html

Hangartner, Judith. 2011. *The Constitution and Contestation of Darhad Shaman's Power in Contemporary Mongolia.* Leiden: Global Oriental. https://doi.org/10.1163/9789004212749

Hangin, John Gombojav, J. R. Krueger, R. G. Service, and W. V. Rozycki, ed and trans. 1988. 'Mongolian folklore: A representative collection from the oral literary tradition', *Mongolian Studies* (11): 47-110.

Haruda, Ashleigh, Alicia R. Ventresca Miller, Johanna L. A. Paijmans, Axel Barlow, Azilkhan Tazhekeyev, S. Bilalov, Y. Hesse et al. 2020. 'The earliest domestic cat on the Silk Road', *Scientific Reports* 10 (11241). https://doi.org/10.1038/s41598-020-67798-6.

Hitchens, Christopher. 2011. *God Is Not Great: How Religion Poisons Everything.* London: Atlantic Books.

Houle, Jean-Luc, and Lee G. Broderick. 2011. 'Settlement patterns and domestic economy of the Xiongnu in Khanu Valley, Mongolia', in *Xiongnu Archaeology: Multidisciplinary perspectives of the first steppe empire in Inner Asia*, by Ursula Brosseder and Bryan Kristopher Miller (eds.), pp. 137-152.

Bonn: Vor- und Fruhgeschichtliche Archaologie, Rheinische Friedrich-Wilhelms-Universitat Bonn.

Humphrey, Caroline. 1976. 'Some notes on the role of dogs in the life of Mongolian herdsmen', *Journal of the Anglo-Mongolian Society* 3(2): 14-23.

Idema, Wilt L, trans. 2019. *Mouse vs. Cat in Chinese Literature: Tales and Commentary*. Seattle: University of Washington Press. https://doi.org/10.1515/9780295744841

Jacobson-Tepfer, Esther, and James Meacham. 2010. *Archaeology and Landscape in the Mongolian Altai: An Atlas*. New York: ESRI Press.

Jagchid, Sechin, and Paul Hyer. 1979. *Mongolia's Culture and Society* Folkstone. Boulder, CO: Westview Press.

Ji, Rimutu, Cui Ping, Ding Feng, Geng Jun, Gao Hongwei, Zhang Hong, Yu Jun, Hu Songnian, and Meng He. 2009. 'Monophyletic origin of domestic Bactrian camel (*Camelus bactrianus*) and its evolutionary relationship with the extant wild camel (*Camelus bactrianus ferus*)', *Animal Genetics* 40(4): 377–382. https://doi.org/10.1111/j.1365-2052.2008.01848.x

Kahneman, Daniel. 2011. *Thinking Fast and Slow*. New York: Farrar, Straus and Giroux.

Kaplonski, Christopher. 2014. *The Lama Question: Violence, Sovereignty, and Exception in Early Socialist Mongolia*. Honolulu: University of Hawaii Press. https://doi.org/10.21313/hawaii/9780824838560.001.0001

Klein, Naomi. 2014. *This Changes Everything: Capitalism vs The Climate*. New York: Simon & Schuster.

Krueger, John, ed. 1967. *The Bejewelled Summary of the Origin of Khans (Qad-un undusun-u Erdeni-yin tobci): A History of the Eastern Mongols to 1662, by Sagan Setsen*. Bloomington: Indiana, Mongolia Society.

Kull, Steven. 1992. *Burying Lenin: The Revolution in Soviet Ideology and Foreign Policy*. Boulder, San Francisco, Oxford: Westview Press.

Kwon, Heonik. 2008. *Ghosts of War in Vietnam*. Cambridge: Cambridge University Press. https://doi.org/10.1017/cbo9780511807596

Latour, Bruno. 1987. *Science in Action: How to Follow Scientists and Engineers Through Society*. Milton Keynes: Open University Press.

Lattimore, Owen. 1928. *The Desert Road to Turkestan*. London: Methuen & Co., Ltd.

Laukner, A. 2005. 'Die Katze in der Religion'. *Katzen Magazin* (2): 28-32.

Lewis, Cathleen S. 2023. *Cosmonaut: A Cultural History*. Gainesville: University of Florida Press. https://doi.org/10.2307/jj.4876483

Losey, Robert, Vladimir Bazaliiskii, Sandra Garvie-Lok, Mietje Germonpré, Jennifer A. Leonard, Andrew L. Allen, M. Anne Katzenberg et al. 2011.

'Canids as persons: Early Neolithic dog and wolf burials, Cis-Baikal, Siberia', *Journal of Anthropological Archaeology* 30(2): 174-189. https://doi.org/10.1016/j.jaa.2011.01.001

Macfarlane, Alan. 2014. *The Invention of the Modern World*. Heidelberg: Springer.

Maiskii, Ivan. 1921. *Sovremennaya Mongoliya: Otchet Mongol'skoi Ekspeditsii, Snaryazhennoi Irkutskoi Kontoroi Vserossiiskogo Soyuza Potrebitel'nykh Tovarishchestv 'Tsentsoyuz'*. Irkutsk: Gosudarstvennoe Izd-vo RSFSR.

Martin, Dan. 1996. 'On the cultural ecology of sky burial on the Himalayan Plateau', *East and West* 46(3/4): 353-370.

Masuda, Ryuichi, Robert J. Losey, Vladimir I. Bazaliiskii, and Bair Badmaev. 2015. 'Ancient DNA analysis of marmot tooth remains from the Shamanka II and Lokomotiv-Raisovet cemeteries near Lake Baikal: Species identification and genealogical characteristics', *Quaternary International* 419(17): 133-139. https://doi.org/10.1016/j.quaint.2015.03.050

Mijiddorj, Batmonkh, and Juramt. 2017. *Mongol Temee Urjuuleh Ulamjlalt Arga Uhaan, Ov Soyol*. Ulaanbaatar: publishing house is not identified.

Montefiore, Simon Sebag. 2022. *The World*. London: Weidenfeld & Nicolson.

Nassen-Bayer and Kevin Stuart. 1992. 'Mongol creation stories: Man, Mongol tribes, the natural world, and Mongol deities', *Asian Folklore Studies* 51(2): 323-334.

Norov, Batsaikhan. 2019. 'Mongolian Buddhist scholars work on infectious diseases (late 17th Century to the beginning of the 20th Century)', *Religions* 10(4): 229. https://doi.org/10.3390/rel10040229.

Orloski, Kathleen A., and Sarah L. Lathrop. 2003. 'Plague: A veterinary perspectiv', *JAVMA* 222(4): 444-448. https://doi.org/10.2460/javma.2003.222.444

Osor, U. 2015. 'Todaevan temdglsn "Noha mis khoyr" domgin tuskar', in *Mongolovedenie v Nachale XXI Veka*: Sovremennoe Sostoyanie i Perspektivy Razvitiya, N. G. Ochirova (ed), pp. 62-66. Elista: KIGI RAN.

Palmer, James. 2009. *The Bloody White Baron*. London: Faber.

Paperno, Irina. 2009. *Stories of the Soviet Experience: Memories, Diaries, Dreams*. Ithaca and London: Cornell University Press.

Pedersen, Morten Alex. 2011. *Not Quite Shamans: Spirit Worlds and Political Lives in Northern Mongolia*, Ithaca: Cornell University Press. https://doi.org/10.1353/book.68261

Pederson, Neil, Amy E. Hessl, Nachin Baatarbileg, Kevin J. Anchukaitis, and Nicola Di Cosmo. 2014. 'Pluvials, droughts, the Mongol Empire, and modern Mongolia', *Proc Natl Acad Sci USA* 111(12): 4375-4379. https://doi.org/10.1073/pnas.1318677111

Pegg, Caroline. 2001. *Mongolian Music, Dance and Oral Narrative: Performing Diverse Identities*. Seattle & London: University of Washington Press.

Peters, Steve. 2012. *The Chimp Paradox: The Acclaimed Mind Management Programme to Help You Achieve Success, Confidence and Happiness*. London: Vermilion.

Polo, Marco. 1938. *The Description of the World. A. C. Moule & Paul Pelliot*. London: George Routledge & Sons Limited.

Potanin, Grigory. 1883. *Ocherki Severo-Zapadnoi Mongolii, Vypusk IV*. S. Petersburg: Tipografiya B. Kirshbauma.

Pozdneev, Aleksei. 1896. *Mongoliya i Mongoly: Rezul'taty Poezdki v Mongoliyu, Ispolnennoi v 1892-1893 gg. Tom 1*. Saint Petersburg: Imperatorskoe Russkoe Geograficheskoe Obschestvo.

Radhid ad-Din. 2002. *Sudryn Chuulgan. Bot' 1*. Ulaanbaatar: SG Group.

Rock, Stella. 2007. *Popular Religion in Russia: Double Belief and the Making of an Academic Myth*. London: Routledge. https://doi.org/10.4324/9780203592281

Rossabi, Morris, ed. 2011. *The Mongols and Global History: A Norton Documents Reader*. New York: W. W. Norton.

Pinker, Steven. 2010. 'The cognitive niche: Coevolution of intelligence, sociality, and language', *Proceedings of the National Academy of Sciences* 107(2): 8993–8999. https://doi.org/10.1073/pnas.0914630107

Poppe, Nicholas. 1941. 'Zolotoordynskaia rukopis' na bereste', *Sovetskoe Vostokovedenie* 2: 81-134.

Rubruck, William. 1990. *The Mission of Friar William of Rubruck: His Journey to the Court of the Great Khan Möngke, 1253-1255*, translated by Peter Jackson. London: Hakluyt Society. https://depts.washington.edu/silkroad/texts/rubruck.html

The Secret History of the Mongols. 2004. Translated by Igor de Rachewiltz. 2 vols. Leiden; Boston: Brill. https://doi.org/10.1163/9789047412410

Severi, Carlo. 2015. *The Chimera Principle: An Anthropology of Memory and Imagination*. Translated by J. Lloyd. Chicago: HAU Books.

Shürhüü, Ch. 2011. *Mongol Ulsyn Tsagdaagiin Erelch Nohoin Albany Tüüh*. Ulaanbaatar: Admon.

Skorodumova, L. G. 2003. *Skazki i Mify Mongolii*. Ulaanbaatar: Monsudar.

Soldatov, Andrei, and Irina Borogan. 2010. *The New Nobility: The Restoration of Russia's Security State and the Enduring Legacy of the KGB*. New York: Public Affairs.

Solovyeva, Alevtina. 2020. 'Faces of Mongolian fear: Demonological beliefs, narratives and protective measures in contemporary folk religion', *Journal of Ethnology and Folkloristics* 14(1): 49-64. https://doi.org/10.2478/jef-2020-0004

Spyrou, Maria A., Rezeda I. Tukhbatova, Chuan-Chao Wang, Aida Andrades Valtueña, Adiya K. Lankapalli, Vitaly V. Kondrashin, Victor A. Tsybin et al. 2018. 'Analysis of 3800-year-old Yersinia pestis genomes suggests Bronze Age origin for bubonic plague', *Nature Communications* 9(2234). https://doi.org/10.1038/s41467-018-04550-9

Summers, William. 2012. *The Great Manchurian Plague of 1910–1911: The Geopolitics of an Epidemic Disease.* New Haven and London: Yale University Press. https://doi.org/10.12987/yale/9780300183191.001.0001

Suntsov, Victor Vasilyevich. 2017. 'Recent speciation of plague microbe Yersinia pestis in the heterothermal (heteroimmune) environment of marmot-flea (Marmota siberica-Oropsylla silantiewi): biogeocenotic preconditions and preadaptations', *Biology Bulletin Reviews* 7(4): 299-311. https://doi.org/10.1134/s2079086417040107

Tangad, D. 1985. 'Nohoi tezheezh baisan ardyn ulamjlalt zanshlaas', *Studia Ethnographica* 9(5): 27-32.

Terbish, Baasanjav. 2023. *Sex in the Land of Genghis Khan: From the Times of the Great Conqueror to Today.* Lanham: Lexington Books. https://doi.org/10.5771/9781666937503

Terbish, Baasanjav. 2023. 'The cat as a mirror of Mongolian society: a good, bad, and ugly animal', *Central Asian Survey* 42(3): 561-576. https://doi.org/10.1080/02634937.2023.2201306

Terbish, Baasanjav. 2022. *State Ideology, Science, and Pseudoscience in Russia: Between the Cosmos and the Earth.* Lanham: Lexington Books.

Terbish, Baasanjav. 2015. 'The Mongolian dog as an intimate other', *Inner Asia* 17(1): 141-159. https://doi.org/10.1163/22105018-12340037

Tsendiin, Damdinsüren. 2019. *Hav, Muur, Hulgana Gurvyn Ülger, Genden Meiren.* Ulaanbaatar: Tsagaan Bambaruush.

Turner, Dennis C., and Patrick Bateson, eds. 2014. *The Domestic Cat: The Biology of Its Behaviour,* 3rd edition. Cambridge: Cambridge University Press. https://doi.org/10.1017/cbo9781139177177

Turner, Victor. 1979. 'Betwixt and between: the liminal period in rites de passage', in *Reader in Comparative Religion,* 4th edition, by William Armand Lessa and Evon Zartman Vogt (eds.), pp. 234-243. New York; London: Harper & Row.

Vainshtein, Sevyan I. 1979. *Nomads of South Siberia: The Pastoral Economies of Tuva.* Cambridge: Cambridge University Press.

Vladimirtsov, Boris. 1921. *Mongol'skii Sbornik Rasskazov iz Panchatantry.* Peterburg: Akadem. Tip.

Wallace-Wells, David. 2019. *The Uninhabitable Earth: A Story of the Future.* London: Allen Lane.

Weatherford, Jack. 2004. *Genghis Khan and the Making of the Modern World.* New York: Crown.

Wingard, James R., and Peter Zahler. 2006. 'Silent steppe: The illegal wildlife trade crisis in Mongolia', in *Mongolia Discussion Papers*, East Asia and Pacific Environment and Social Development Department. Washington D.C.: World Bank.

Yadamsüren, Adya, Odonhüü Daria, and Shaochuang Liu. 2019. 'The seasonal distribution of wild camels (Camelus ferus) in relation to changes of the environmental conditions in Mongolia', *Open Journal of Ecology* 9(8): 293-314. https://doi.org/10.4236/oje.2019.98021

Zhamtsarano, Tsyben Zhamtsaranovich. 1965. *Khalkha Dzhirum: Pamiatnik Mongol'skogo Feodal'nogo Prava XVIII v.* Moskva: Nauka, Glav. Red. Vostochnoi Lit-ry.

Index

About the Team

Alessandra Tosi was the managing editor for this book.

Elisabeth Pitts proof-read this manuscript. Annie Hine compiled the index.

Jeevanjot Kaur Nagpal designed the cover. The cover was produced in InDesign using the Fontin font.

Cameron Craig typeset the book in InDesign and produced the paperback and hardback editions. The main text font is Tex Gyre Pagella and the heading font is Californian FB. Cameron also produced the PDF and EPUB editions.

The conversion to the HTML edition was performed with epublius, an open-source software which is freely available on our GitHub page at https://github.com/OpenBookPublishers.

This book was peer-reviewed by Dr Natasha Fijn. Experts in their field, our readers give their time freely to help ensure the academic rigour of our books. We are grateful for their generous and invaluable contributions.

This book need not end here...

Share

All our books — including the one you have just read — are free to access online so that students, researchers and members of the public who can't afford a printed edition will have access to the same ideas. This title will be accessed online by hundreds of readers each month across the globe: why not share the link so that someone you know is one of them?

This book and additional content is available at
https://doi.org/10.11647/OBP.0450

Donate

Open Book Publishers is an award-winning, scholar-led, not-for-profit press making knowledge freely available one book at a time. We don't charge authors to publish with us: instead, our work is supported by our library members and by donations from people who believe that research shouldn't be locked behind paywalls.

Join the effort to free knowledge by supporting us at
https://www.openbookpublishers.com/support-us

We invite you to connect with us on our socials!

BLUESKY	MASTODON	LINKEDIN
@openbookpublish .bsky.social	@OpenBookPublish @hcommons.social	open-book-publishers

Read more at the Open Book Publishers Blog

https://blogs.openbookpublishers.com

You may also be interested in:

Shépa
The Tibetan Oral Tradition in Choné
Bendi Tso, Marnyi Gyatso, Naljor Tsering, Mark Turin,
Members of the Choné Tibetan Community

https://doi.org/10.11647/OBP.0312

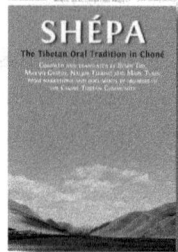

Frontier Encounters
Knowledge and Practice at the Russian, Chinese and Mongolian Border
Franck Billé, Grégory Delaplace, Caroline Humphrey (Eds)

https://doi.org/10.11647/OBP.0026

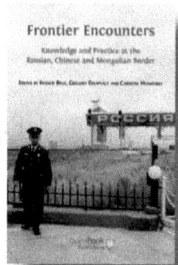

History of International Relations
A Non-European Perspective
Erik Ringmar

https://doi.org/10.11647/OBP.0074

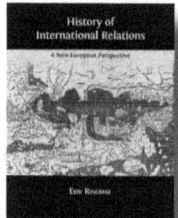

www.ingramcontent.com/pod-product-compliance
Lightning Source LLC
Chambersburg PA
CBHW071733270326
41928CB00013B/2662